STRUGGLE ON THEIR MINDS

STRUGGLE ON THEIR MINDS

THE POLITICAL THOUGHT

of

AFRICAN AMERICAN RESISTANCE

ALEX ZAMALIN

Columbia University Press
New York

Columbia University Press
Publishers Since 1893
New York   Chichester, West Sussex
cup.columbia.edu

Library of Congress Cataloging-in-Publication Data

A complete CIP record is available from the Library of Congress.
ISBN 978-0-231-18110-5 (cloth)
ISBN 978-0-231-54347-7 (e-book)

Columbia University Press books are printed on permanent
and durable acid-free paper.
Printed in the United States of America

Cover design: FaceOut Studio

FOR ALISON, SAM, AND ANITA

CONTENTS

ILLUSTRATIONS

ACKNOWLEDGMENTS

I have been fortunate to receive support from many people. I would like to thank my editor, Wendy Lochner at Columbia University Press, for her constant enthusiasm for the project, as well as three anonymous reviewers for their thoughtful feedback, which substantially improved the quality of the final manuscript. I would like to thank my colleagues at University of Detroit Mercy for providing support and encouragement throughout the process, especially Stephen Manning, Genevieve Meyers, Rosemary Weatherston, Amanda Hiber, Mary-Catherine Harrison, Megan Novell, Karl Ericson, and Sigrid Streit. I am particularly grateful to Michael Barry and Nick Rombes for taking time to offer incredibly helpful suggestions that informed the scope and some of the animating ideas in the book. My students at UDM provided the first testing ground for many of the book's arguments, and I am grateful for their enthusiasm. For research assistance, I would like particularly to thank Jewuel Boswell and Lydia Mikail.

Beyond UDM, I am also thankful for the encouragement and friendship of Dan Skinner, Jeff Broxmeyer, Mark Navin, and Hunter Vaughan. In addition to reading numerous drafts of the manuscript and providing generous and thoughtful feedback throughout the process, Jon Keller has enriched my understanding of the American political tradition and has helped me become a clearer writer. Max Burkey's influence on the manuscript cannot be overstated. Max always provided an ear to discuss many of the book's ideas in its earliest stages, helped refine its final arguments, and has consistently pushed me to be a more expressive and honest writer.

Special thanks also go to my extended family, Arnold Zamalin, Marina Zamalin, Raya Zamalin, Emil Zamalin, Ron Powell, Frona Powell, Aaron Powell, and Liz Powell. Above all, I would like to thank my wife, Alison Powell, who has dedicated endless hours of her life to enriching mine. Her poetry and scholarship continue to inspire me in profound ways, and her companionship and friendship know no bounds. Without her presence in my life, this book would not have been written. My son, Sam, helps me grow day in and day out. His wisdom and endless capacity for finding magic and beauty in the world is truly humbling. My daughter, Anita, reminds me to appreciate the wonder of the unknown. Her smiles brighten my day, and her strength is energizing. It is to Alison, Sam, and Anita that I dedicate this work.

STRUGGLE ON THEIR MINDS

INTRODUCTION

The Political Thought of African American Resistance

This book examines the political thought that emerges from the long history of African American political resistance to racial inequality in the United States. This is the story of abolitionists asserting in political manifestos that slavery must be abolished by any means necessary, slaves revolting against their masters, journalists chastising the American institutions that turn a blind eye toward the lynching of African Americans, and radicals policing the police and calling for the abolition of the American prison system. Examining the work of five of the most theoretically significant but still underappreciated African American political resisters and the movements of which they were a part—slavery abolitionists David Walker and Frederick Douglass; Ida B. Wells, who was the key figure of the antilynching movement; Huey Newton and the Black Panther Party for Self-Defense he helped organize; Angela Davis and the prison-abolition movement—*Struggle on Their Minds* argues that one central dimension of African American resistance has been to revise core values in the American political tradition.

This book challenges the view that the only democratically valuable kind of African American political resistance is one that conforms to the dominant values of American culture. Resistance is often depicted as politically threatening—captured by the current U.S. Department of

Defense's *Dictionary of Military and Associated Terms*, which defines a "resistance movement" as "an organized effort by some portion of the civil population of a country to resist the legally established government or an occupying power and to disrupt civil order and stability."[1] As a political activity that contests existing constellations of state power, resistance appears to undermine political stability and the rule of law. More often than not, however, the term is demonized, conjuring images of unbridled violent rebellion or militancy—for example, anarchists who called for abolishing the American government and communists who called for an overthrow of capitalism. Those few resistance movements redeemed in the American imagination—and this almost always happens retrospectively—are redeemed only because they call for gradual political reforms and because they frame their objectives in dominant American values like individualism, limited government, and private property: for instance, suffragettes advocating for women's political rights or labor activists struggling for better working conditions.

The rich history of African American resistance has been viewed in a similar way. Frederick Douglass and Martin Luther King Jr. have—through a selective interpretation of their most patriotic writings—been elevated to the status of American founding fathers, but many black radicals, such as Martin Delany, Marcus Garvey, Malcolm X, and Audre Lorde, have been dismissed, if not treated with contempt. To make matters worse, a long history of racist narratives about African Americans being angry and disorderly has helped link the idea of African American resistance with criminality. In a certain sense, this has continued today, when, for many white Americans, black resistance often signifies not political agitation but an unwillingness to accept cultural norms of upstanding citizenship and a rejection of the nuclear, male-led family.[2]

Not only has resistance been demonized; it has also justified state violence. Over the past few years, by far the most common colloquial invocation of the term "resistance to arrest," a refusal to obey police orders, has become a key justification for police brutality toward African American men—most notably, Michael Brown, the eighteen-year-old who was fatally shot by a white police officer, Darren Wilson, in Ferguson, Missouri, in August 2014, and Eric Garner, a forty-three-year-old who was strangled to death by another white police officer, Daniel Pantaleo, in July 2014.

Against this backdrop, *Struggle on Their Minds* recovers a tradition of African American political resistance across U.S. history that revises longstanding American political thinking about concepts such as power, language, community, judgment, action, and the role of emotion in politics. This revision can be made serviceable for building a more democratic society in the United States, where racial inequality is as entrenched as ever, where economic inequality is still waging war on working people, and where women's reproductive rights, queer people's freedoms, and undocumented immigrants' safety are being threatened.

RESISTANCE IN THOUGHT AND PRACTICE

In the broadest sense of the term, "resistance" simply names the act of contesting authority. In American literature, no phrase captures this more succinctly than what Herman Melville's Bartleby in the eponymous story says to his employer who wishes to fire him: "I'd prefer not to."[3] Resistance entails taking charge of one's life and refusing to accept the extant configurations of the way things are. Resistance can be public or private, collective or individual, directed internally or externally, enacted by those who are powerful or those who are weak. Resistance can also be intellectual. The Western political-theoretical tradition was born out of resistance: Plato's crafting of an ideal aristocratic state where philosopher-kings ruled in *The Republic* went against the orthodoxy of ancient Athens, which prided itself on democratic existence, and Thomas Hobbes's proto-social-scientific approach to state building in *Leviathan* challenged theories of divine right that legitimized English monarchic rule.[4]

Resistance can name many activities. But few terms are as commonly used, misused, and overused as they are poorly defined, are as elastic as they are omnipresent. Resistance talk often confounds more than it clarifies because academics have seemingly found resistance to exist anywhere and everywhere since the late 1960s.[5] This intellectual shift was animated by political struggles from below—when feminists resisted the patriarchy, peaceniks resisted war, hippies resisted American bourgeois culture, workers resisted the excesses of global capitalism, students resisted the censorship of speech on college campuses, and people in the Global South resisted colonialism.

These social movements only confirmed what had been expressed theoretically since at least the aftermath of the French Revolution of 1789, which witnessed the overthrow of the monarchy and the instantiation of French republicanism: Resistance has been the story of the downtrodden, the marginalized, those lacking political voice who seek emancipation. Wide-ranging examples include everything from G. W. F.'s Hegel's bondsman overcoming his lord to Karl Marx's workers rising up against their capitalist exploiters to Henry David Thoreau, Gandhi, and Martin Luther King arguing for nonviolent civil disobedience against state-sponsored racism.[6] The political anthropologist James Scott is right that everyday acts of resistance have always been "weapons of the weak," part of what he calls the "hidden transcript" that is not publicly invisible.[7]

If the past half century in the academy can be characterized as the "age of resistance," no thinker was more influential for inspiring it than the French intellectual historian Michel Foucault. He contended that power is not simply hierarchical—smoothly flowing from a concentrated entity such as the modern state toward the powerless citizens below it—but that it is dispersed throughout life in language (what we say and how we say it), laws (the political rules and regulations we live by), and various knowledge systems (what we know) and that it is often cultivated in unseen ways by those who are politically weak.[8] For Foucault, power and resistance were closely linked: "As soon as there is a power relation, there is a possibility of resistance. We can never be ensnared by power: we can always modify its grip in determinate conditions and according to a precise strategy."[9]

Few intellectual disciplines have so often embraced Foucault's framework or have been as concerned with locating historical episodes of resistance as African American studies. We are reminded that slaves resisted their masters not only through slave rebellions[10] but through various cultural expressions such as song, dance, and folklore, which were often defined by irony—what Ralph Ellison called "changing the joke and slipping the yoke."[11] During the Jim Crow era, African Americans in the South transformed the segregated bus into a theater (they told jokes and cursed) to challenge the hold white southerners had on public space.[12] African Americans today resist through everyday talk in barbershops and through hip-hop music and fashion.[13]

Critics such as Jeffrey Ferguson have thus tried to explain the implications of this academic turn to African American resistance over the past forty years. Rather than study whether, how, and in what ways black resistance has become manifest over time, Ferguson wonders whether scholars' quest for finding it in spaces where it seems either difficult to imagine (such as the slave plantation) or where it seems too obvious (such as in literature, whose value is often defined precisely when it is breaking from convention) has not ironically reproduced the same romantic understanding of black agency that they once aimed to critique. For Ferguson, the everyday triumphs some scholars have found among ordinary black people living amid pervasive structural constraints is as simplistic as earlier studies that assumed African Americans to be politically docile because of these constraints.[14]

In a similar vein, the political scientist Richard Iton, in his recent study of the politics of black popular culture in the post-civil-rights era, cautions against viewing resistance as inherently revolutionary, reminding us that "resistance, once it becomes routine and recognized, can be anticipated and welcomed by dominant authorities, and fetishized and folded into the broader process of institutionalizing dominant hegemonic understandings."[15] Resistance is not a static term. Despite its allure for an emancipatory politics, it is only as good or bad as its enactors. The anarchist can easily be a full-blown misogynist; the Black Power advocate, deeply homophobic; the socialist feminist, a latent racist.

This book's aim is not to examine sociologically why resistance has become such a fashionable framework or to confirm the argument that resistance *does* exist in unseen spaces, or is a part of all sorts of political projects,[16] or—committing the error Iton warns against—that it always requires uncritical valorization. Instead, it is to provide an intellectual history of when resistance to racial inequality was palpable in key African American political movements. If resistance is at once an activity and an experience that resists comprehensive analysis because it has no singular essence—if there is no way ever to develop fully a philosophical definition of the practice itself—we should study moments in which what occurs can clearly be called "resistance."

This book's focus is on figures associated with *political* resistance movements from below, by which I mean movements that have political concerns ranging from the organization of the state and the economy to the distribution of rights, freedom, and equality to the nature of political rule.[17] African American political resistance movements have existed throughout African American history. Slave revolts were commonplace—Nat Turner's slave rebellion in 1831 in Southampton County, Virginia, was not an exception. Nineteenth-century radical abolitionists crafted speeches, manifestos, and newspaper editorials in order to call upon white and black Americans to resist slavery. Early twentieth-century black communists called for seditious acts against American capitalist exploitation, black nationalists called for black relocation to Africa, and the 1960s Black Power movement called for everything from black self-determination to anti-imperialism.

Describing these ideologically diverse movements through the general term of "resistance" might give some skeptics pause: Why use "resistance movement" rather than "protest movement" or its associated strategies such as direct action, organizing, public demonstrations, strikes, boycotts, or marches? What distinguishes "resistance" from these related practices and terms, and what analytic clarity does "resistance" provide?

First, resistance generally captures the various moments of saying "no" and so encapsulates myriad tactics. Second, unlike "protest," which is usually associated with working from within and attempting to "fix" the system, resistance is not necessarily tethered to what appears politically acceptable. To appreciate this distinction better, recall Bayard Rustin's distinction between "politics," by which the African American civil rights activist meant official political institutions such as legislatures or political parties that could articulate clear demands that would materialize into real legislative reforms, and "protest," by which he meant social agitation divorced from electoral politics or legislative struggles. Using Rustin's distinction, we can go further. Resistance is distinct not only from protest but also from formal politics, and protest is, much more closely than resistance, situated within the field of formal politics.[18] Political reformers can engage in resistance, but protest is not equivalent to resistance, although it can be one of its many varieties.

A quick glance at the resistance figures of this book also illustrates that its aim is not to offer an exhaustive history of African American political resistance. On the one hand, my concern is with people who resisted racial inequality, which has been and still is catalyzed by the ideologies of white supremacy and racism. Despite its different manifestation across U.S. history, through what the sociologist Loïc Wacquant calls the four "peculiar institutions" (slavery, Jim Crow, the black ghetto, and mass incarceration) that have "confined" and "controlled" African Americans, structural racial inequality has served systematically to deprive black Americans of access to socioeconomic and political equality. Racial inequality has never been a matter of individual personal choices—where a relatively small minority of people harbor prejudice toward people of a different race—it is a structural problem created by political institutions, laws, and regulations that give greater freedom to white Americans and restrict it for black Americans.[19]

On the other hand, my focus on these figures has to do with the fact that they are some of the important African American political thinkers whose political-theoretical insights—with the exception of Douglass—have received surprisingly little attention from political theorists. What also unites them is that, like one of the most culturally prominent associations with resistance—as uncompromising, unruly, irreverent, and militant—some of their major ideas can fit under the broad umbrella of radicalism. Radicalism names a fundamental "to-the-root" critique and reconceptualization of the world as it exists; it also signifies something of an intensity of pitch and commitment that isn't easily associated with gradualism.[20]

Nonetheless, a question remains: Why not study Martin Luther King Jr. or the civil rights movement he helped organize, especially since it was without question the most successful, if not the most popular and widely discussed, American social movement? Apart from the fact that there seems little need to deepen an ever-increasing and already exhaustive literature,[21] it is also the case that King, before his conversion in the late 1960s from more mainstream liberal to disenchanted social democrat, generally partook in many of the key tropes of the American liberal political tradition—calling for African American social integration into mainstream white society, for legal nondiscrimination and political equality, and for all Americans to adopt a robust notion of civic love.[22]

Still, King was not the only theorist of the civil rights movement. Some of its most theoretically important though not fully appreciated ideas emerged from local democratic struggles. Most notable was the 1964 Freedom Summer, organized by Bob Moses, Ella Baker, Fannie Lou Hamer, and James Forman of the Student Nonviolent Coordinating Committee (SNCC). Student activists registered black Mississippians to vote and trained them in nonviolent civil disobedience through Freedom Schools and Freedom Houses. These figures (along with King) accomplished more for racial justice than any other American activists in the twentieth century, and they also exemplified the best of radical democratic practice. Yet if King's and the SNCC's tactics and activities radicalized in profoundly democratic ways certain strains of American political practice, Walker, Douglass, Wells, Newton, and Davis were especially significant because their ideas pushed the boundaries of American political thought and theories of citizenship.[23]

In examining this aspect of their thought, this book departs from the three dominant frameworks for studying political resistance. Sociological approaches ask: What kind of social conditions allowed resistance movements to succeed or fail?[24] Cultural approaches ask: What kind of symbols did they draw upon? What kind of narratives did they devise?[25] Structural-institutional approaches ask: How have resistance movements institutionalized themselves into political parties or created successful, concrete political victories?[26]

My interest, however, is in the unique political ideas that emerge from the precise existential moment of resistance.[27] This moment—when the resister is saying "no," engaging in direct action or a critique of the system—is a unique site of political theory for several reasons. The resister is trying to break free from conventional ways of being while trying to legitimize why it is happening. The resister challenges what is practical and illuminates what isn't, juxtaposing what encourages human flourishing with what disables it. The resister grapples with the question of means and ends—the question of the norms of action—while trying to create a new language for a future that doesn't yet exist. The resister, just like the act of resistance, is often in a precarious state, where risk is ever present, where limitation is abundant. To resist, one must be moved to resist. So the resister is in an existential state of flight and is often possessed by some feeling, whether joy and ecstasy or pessimism and anguish.

My aim is not to follow historians or political scientists who have productively studied the various tactics of African American resistance movements and painted a rich picture of the emergence of the various countercultural ideologies that have underpinned them, from black nationalism, feminism, and conservatism to black Marxism and Black Power.[28] The overarching purpose of this study is instead to situate African American political resistance in the context of the American political tradition and the historical-intellectual milieu from which it emerged. Abolitionism emerged when intellectual debates about centralized power and state sovereignty were raging, when slaveholders were developing sophisticated intellectual racist justifications for slavery, when transcendentalism was hotly contesting the meaning of freedom, and when revolutionary socialist movements were gripping the imagination of the entire world. The antilynching movement took shape at the tail end of the Gilded Age, the end of Reconstruction, and the birth of Jim Crow and advent of progressivism and populism, when debates about individualism, democracy, and government obligation were widespread. The Black Panthers emerged in the 1960s, when the liberal dream of the civil rights movement was becoming increasingly questionable and when the American counterculture of free speech, antiwar, feminist, and anti-imperialist activism was in full bloom. The prison-abolition movement has emerged over the past thirty years, paralleling the right-wing assault on the gains of the civil rights movement and the proliferation of law-and-order policies, which have led to an explosion of incarceration rates for people of color. It has also done this alongside broad intellectual shifts like the rise of poststructuralist, feminist, and queer critiques of power, identity, and freedom.[29]

Rather than being exegetical, my aim is twofold. First, it is to understand the meaning and orientation of the American political tradition and one of the most significant countercultural traditions within it—the African American one. Are liberalism and civic republicanism the only traditions of American political thought? Do African American thinkers cultivate political theories that cannot be encapsulated by these terms, and, if they do not, how exactly so? Second, it is to use African American resistance to complicate and deepen the tradition of thinking about practices of democratic citizenship: How should citizens live and act collectively? What practices, habits, or ways of being must they cultivate in everyday life or in collective political actions?[30]

RESISTANCE AND AFRICAN AMERICAN INTELLECTUAL LIFE

This book challenges the view that African American political thinkers simply embraced the standard ideas of American political culture, which revolves around the public philosophies of liberalism and civic republicanism. In the postwar period, writers such as Louis Hartz, Richard Hofstadter, and Daniel Boorstin famously argued that American political culture is primarily—if not singularly—defined by the liberal tradition.[31] By this, they meant that there has always been widespread consensus about John Locke's vision of a society in which there is a limited rather than expansive government, where representative government rather than direct popular rule is embraced, and where individual freedom rather than a commitment to socioeconomic equality is championed.[32]

Others, such as Rogers Smith, have rejected this view as far too simplistic and cheery, suggesting instead that the malignant ideologies of biological hierarchy and difference—of "racial ascriptivism"—espoused by the gamut of white supremacists, social Darwinists, misogynists, and xenophobes have never been absent from American culture and have often coexisted alongside liberal thinking.[33] But since there is widespread agreement that ascriptivism should be confronted and rejected from American culture, the most powerful normative alternative to liberalism has been seen as civic republicanism, which challenges liberalism's commitment to individualism and instead stresses the importance of active political participation and involvement in one's polity and in maintaining a critique of political corruption and rational self-interest.[34]

Walker, Douglass, Wells, Newton, and Davis, however, revised core values that both traditions embraced. First, in their writing power needed to be reimagined as dispersed beyond official political institutions—through everyday acts and through ordinary citizens.[35] It was an elastic concept whose contours depend upon those who wield it.[36] When wielded by those who support social domination, resisters insist, power undermines the agency of those over whom it is exercised. When deployed by the masses—(white) Americans—power can create political and socioeconomic oppression and violent, even deadly physical encounters. Power operates through the physical organization and segregation of communities, crumbling public housing, and prison walls. Compromised are not only people's political rights or individual freedom but also their bodily and psychological integrity. Power physically incapacitates and erodes the foundations upon which one can realize one's self-worth to act creatively.

At the same time, much more so than the most social-democratic thinkers in the American tradition, African American resisters embrace a performative notion of democratic power.[37] Here individuals name—and in so doing bring into existence, rather than simply describe—the normative legitimacy of the socioeconomic resources necessary to achieve the idea of positive freedom (the idea that freedom is about individual flourishing rather than protection from government), even if these resources are not sanctioned by existing political regimes.

This notion of power contains the second core revision that emerges from the political thought of African American resistance: the centrality of language and rhetoric for liberation. If the American tradition—which prides itself on a no-nonsense, realistic, and analytic approach to politics—either fails to appreciate or completely rejects the link between language and politics,[38] resisters embrace naming as a form of claim making. Words can condemn marginalized populations—when, for instance, those who transgress the law are named "criminals," a naming that, too often, harbors coded racial and class associations. But words also have emancipatory potential. They can redeem the humanity of those who are denied it and rhetorically dramatize a horizontal notion of rule, where all are preemptively endowed the authority to exercise judgment.

Third, African American resisters deepen American thinking about community.[39] Resisters draw attention to how the dominant community's norms—for instance, expectations about American moral exceptionalism, rigid gender hierarchies, and the unquestioned celebration of capitalism—can stifle critical dissent. In a deeper sense, resisters insist that no community is ever static or homogenous. A community is an ephemeral entity that emerges spontaneously through shared interests and feelings and in brief moments of everyday solidarity. Communities can therefore dissipate as quickly as they emerge.

Fourth, resisters embrace a robust notion of democratic judgment. Rejecting the allure of abstract, disembodied political thinking, such judgment is defined by empathetically accounting for a wide range of unexpected and oppositional perspectives. Against arguments that champion pragmatic judgment that evaluates competing outcomes to preserve national unity or the public good,[40] this mode of judgment begins with the question: What kind of physical effects might the outcomes have for human beings? Do they create suffering, and, if so, is that suffering acceptable? Acknowledging the complex humanity often hidden behind one's social status is at the heart of such judgment. Knowing, for instance, that slaves have dignity despite their subjection and lack of freedom, that prisoners still have commitments to justice despite the crimes of which they are convicted, that white police officers and prison guards, who have more in common economically with those whom they police, may themselves be blind to this commonality because of the institutions of which they are part.

Against the implicit assumption of invulnerability embedded in the American idea of the rational sovereign actor,[41] democratic judgment, for resisters, also means appreciating one's own vulnerability—that all are prone to making errors of judgment and behavior and that what they take to be true and accurate may be incorrect and require revision. And this means becoming vulnerable to others—where one no longer acts with the presumption of certitude and adopts a rich form of hospitality toward those who appear before them. This includes knowing that political thinking is informed by lived experience rather than abstract reason. And it is this experience and the identities through which it is orchestrated that frames the understanding of what people might want and need.

When viewed from this perspective, what becomes apparent is that African American intellectual life has not been characterized simply by a narrow debate over various political strategies and tactics concerning black politics—for example, racial integration against separatism, violence against nonviolence, or a politics based in shared identity or shared interest—but instead has centered on reinterpreting time-honored American political ideals in significant ways.[42] Furthermore, resisters have regularly gone beyond what the African American studies critic Jerry Watts has influentially identified as the widespread intellectual strategy—adopted by African American thinkers as diverse as James Baldwin, Ralph Ellison, and Amiri Baraka—to appropriate the status of victimhood to secure from whites cultural recognition and political demands. Watts writes: "Victim status hinges on the desire of the victimized to obtain from the victimizer recognition of his or her victimized status and the willingness of the victimizer both to accept the victimized as his or her creation and to grant to the victimized the desired recognition."[43] If anything, this book demonstrates that African American resistance actually reformulated the terms through which whites could understand black oppression and the meaning of an emancipatory politics in the United States.

RESISTANCE AND DEMOCRATIC CITIZENSHIP

The ideas that emerge from African American resistance can also enrich contemporary practices of democratic citizenship. At its core, resistance shares a fundamental concern with many of the ideas associated with small-"d" democracy—by which I mean the organization of life in which the people rule their polity in common. Democratic theory has arguably been the dominant paradigm of academic political thought over the past thirty years, ever since the collapse of the communist bloc in the late 1980s and the ensuing democratization movements throughout the globe. Democratic theorists have theorized everything from the politics and norms of democratic communication, judgment, and ethics to recognition and care ethics, popular legitimacy, and the ever-ephemeral meaning of "the people."[44]

Resistance, like democracy, is associated with the idea of agency—the notion that even within conditions of massive constraint, a yearning for something more humane cannot be fully squashed. Resistance, like democracy, is connected to emancipation, loosing the shackles of domination that stifle human imagination. Resistance is associated with subversion, just as the *demos*—the people—in democracy is given authority to subvert what counts as politics.[45]

Yet African American resisters offer especially fruitful tools for theorizing democratic citizenship because of the racialized conditions in which their ideas emerged and to which they responded.[46] First, they provide an important answer to a still underappreciated question concerning the requisite practice of citizenship for populations that are overlooked by many Americans: the most vulnerable among us. These are not only poor African Americans but also poor women, migrant workers who have no rights, and trans citizens whose rights are at best tenuous. They are citizens, in other words, whose rights are incredibly precarious, if ever practically enforced.[47]

But rather than simply address the normative requirements for full democratic citizenship—does it require full voting rights or socioeconomic resources, negative freedom, positive freedom, or nondomination, direct political participation in local settings, or good rule by elected political elites?—the question resisters answer is this: What understanding and practice of action must be adopted by those who are subjugated—especially those who are racially subjugated?[48]

Rather than assume that action can be finalized once it achieves particular goals—a certain public policy, piece of legislation, political victory—African American resisters insist that action needs to be reimagined as based in ongoing, unending contestation. Action needs to be seen as a practice not where one assumes either the inevitability of success or the necessity of failure but where one attends to the deep limitations that structure life while maintaining hope in the possibility of liberation. Everyday life also needs to be seen as a site of action where one comports oneself *as if* what one strives for is already possible in one's life and ordinary social interactions. Action needs to be seen as something that reveals or even alters one's commitments, rather than what realizes them. Deferring to its unknown possibilities can enable one to learn something new about one's identity and the untapped possibilities of other citizens.

Second, resisters answer another underappreciated question at the heart of democratic (and black) politics: What are the terms through which those who are dominated ought to make their appeals? Democratic theorists have been preoccupied with studying the sites and avenues of action—whether popular struggles for rights and freedom should be conducted through official political venues like the courts, Congress, the presidency, and through the voting booth or through unsanctioned settings such as the streets, boycotts, or sit-ins.[49] And theorists of black politics wonder whether it should be organized through pragmatic solidarity—shared interests—or shared identity.[50] But African American resisters ask something different: How should democratic (or black) citizens engage the dominant cultural narratives of social groups?

Walker, Douglass, and Wells were more patriotic than Newton and Davis, but all of them challenged conventional understandings of American patriotism. At times, this entailed turning patriotism into a grotesque inversion of what it claimed to stand for—how the American commitment to public welfare becomes the justification for underfunded ghettos that look like prisons or how the ideal of moral courage leads to horrific forms of punishment, disproportionately enacted on people of color, which erodes the moral conscience of those who directly authorize or silently condone it.[51] At other times, this challenging entailed changing key American terms. Exemplary democratic responsibility meant a commitment to acknowledging injustice truthfully, which entailed a rejection of self-interested economic materialism (and sometimes one's investment in property).

Third, African American resisters centralize the democratic importance of emotion. Given its rationalism, the American tradition has generally been skeptical of emotion or has tried to rid politics of it entirely.[52] When American thinkers *have* taken emotion seriously, however, they have generally fallen into two camps. On the one hand, although such a key text as Jefferson's Declaration of Independence renders the pursuit of an emotion—happiness—an inalienable right to be protected by government, emotion there is seen less as an energizing dimension of democracy and more as a personal experience that simply shouldn't be denied citizens. On the other hand, American thinkers such as Madison, Hamilton, and Calhoun were focused on theorizing a government capable of addressing popular fear of perceived political instability.

Departing from these two approaches and illuminating how emotions have a powerful role in democratic struggle, Walker, Douglass, Wells, Newton, and Davis did not simply endorse an influential argument of contemporary critical race studies, which has emphasized the importance of mourning.[53] Mourning opposes the trinity of American culture—blind rationalism, willful amnesia, and cheery optimism. The interrelated feelings of melancholy and grief associated with mourning, by contrast, allow for working through past and current racial traumas.

African American resisters, however, emphasize how emotions can do much more than help citizens acknowledge or work through historical trauma. Emotions can provide citizens a sense of their self-worth, help disclose unseen motivations behind a given reality, politicize a reality that seems apolitical, and dramatize the moral urgency of action. Cynicism exposes society's abdication of its democratic commitments. Anguish makes one fearless to begin anew. Hope keeps alive the wish for a more democratic future to come. Shame illuminates the tension between inclusionary ideals and corrupt exclusionary practices, and rage foregrounds one's dissatisfaction in ways that cannot be easily ignored.

RESISTANCE AND RACIAL JUSTICE

Despite overwhelming evidence that American racial inequality is not only real and as pervasive as ever in virtually every realm of life, many Americans still believe—especially after the legislative victories of the civil rights movement and the election of the first black president, Barack Obama, in 2008 and again in 2012—that we live in a so-called postracial moment.[54] To develop a practice of citizenship capable of addressing this reality, we might draw from the tradition of African American democratic individualism, which includes arguments about the importance self-examination and attentiveness to the tragic essence of democratic commitment and the value of unconditional generosity.[55] Furthermore, considering the various strategies for black politics might lead us to arguments about political coalition building and nonviolent civil disobedience as well as to the significance of not overlooking the fruitful dimensions of difference in collective action.[56]

But unlike these positions—or others advanced by African American thinkers on a wide range of issues including white supremacy, gender, political struggle, self-rule, capitalism, and colonialism[57]—Walker, Douglass, Wells, Newton, and Davis offer acute insight into a practice of citizenship capable of responding to three central impediments to contemporary racial equality: a system of massive incarceration that unequally punishes black men and women, a system of police brutality in which black citizens live in a state of insecurity in their neighborhoods, and a system of de facto segregation that separates black and white citizens physically, emotionally, and politically.

First, their ideas can help citizens confront the problem of American punishment, which affects everything from black voting rights to economic opportunities, from death by the death penalty to the organization of the family and the black community.[58] They counsel citizens to be suspicious of moralism. Moralism creates binaries between those who transgress the law and those who do not and helps obscure political discussion about systemic problems of injustice. Crucial to this is struggling against injustice with—rather than without or independent of—those who experience it. This means refusing the comforts and certainties of paternalism, which requires little existential risk and, paradoxically, only cements within interpersonal relationships the very external social inequalities against which one struggles. One must take seriously an idea of democratic self-determination; sometimes this involves socioeconomic resources for the needy, and sometimes it involves programs of reconciliation, which center on repairing trust in communities riven by moral wrongs.

Second, in the wake of recent public attention to events in communities across the United States—Ferguson, Staten Island, Cleveland, Cincinnati, Chicago, Baltimore, North Charleston, Baton Rouge—where unarmed black men were killed by police officers, African American resisters provide resources to address the problem of police brutality toward black communities, which centers upon an excessive and unchecked deployment of state power, often infused with racialized assumptions. Direct political protests can transform public space into something that emphasizes people's interests and aspirations rather than something that is defined by the necessities of public safety or order; symbolic gestures (like citizens' policing the police or hunger striking) can draw attention to the state's failure to deliver on its claim to protect its citizens. Such action can also help force those who enact violence—whether on behalf of safety, moral necessity, or democratic popular sovereignty—to ask whether it squares with a robust commitment to justice.[59]

Third, their ideas can help us respond to the problem of African American physical and spatial de facto segregation from white Americans, which reflects and exacerbates white Americans' willful blindness toward injustice—their unwillingness to dispense with the comforts of their social status and white skin privilege, their fear of collective interracial living, and their apathy toward black suffering.[60] Unflinching truthful acknowledgment of white racial innocence should be supplemented by rejecting the fantasy of racial separatism—whether black or white. The notion of pure, organic identity and communities espoused by both political nationalists and racial supremacists should be renounced and replaced with race treachery—an action where those who are socially constructed into a certain race reject its benefits and allures for the sake of democracy. What is equally necessary is a form of interracial agonistic communication that is ongoing and consists of seriously engaging all pluralistic claims, interests, and experiences.[61]

CHAPTER OUTLINE

Chapter 1, "David Walker, Frederick Douglass, and the Abolitionist Democratic Vision," argues that one core theoretical contribution of the African American abolitionists David Walker and Frederick Douglass was a response to the problem of action in the face of immeasurable constraint. In his *Appeal* (1829), Walker provoked disenfranchised citizens to take seriously their own capacity for judgment, to appreciate oppositional perspectives and their own human finitude in ways that challenged the Federalist, Anti-Federalist, and slaveholding political thought of his time. Walkers also modeled how cynicism could be something that engendered a scrutiny of individual goodwill, human nature, political power, community, and collective responsibility in emancipatory ways.

Douglass, writing twenty-five years later in *My Bondage and My Freedom* (1855) about his experience of physically confronting his slave master, Edward Covey, made vivid that emancipatory action required acknowledging how feelings of anguish engender democratic faith and how human dignity is not simply a given but is made vivid through public contestation. Unlike Walker, Douglass also highlighted the experiential dimension of theorizing freedom and the ways shame could be subverted for democratic ends.

Chapter 2, "Ida B. Wells, the Antilynching Movement, and the Politics of Seeing," argues that the antilynching writings and political activities of the African American journalist Ida B. Wells sought to articulate a political theory to respond to the problem of extralegal violence directed toward the socially marginalized in liberal regimes. Wells urged citizens to acknowledge the devastating ramifications of the Gilded Age defense of instrumental thinking and its uncritical understanding of popular sovereignty. Her narratives about lynching showed how narrative could be repurposed for democratic ends. Human complexity and plurality needed to be embraced, and punishment needed to be seen as affecting American political culture. Following the American Progressives who tried to repurpose the genre of horror for democratic ends, Wells tried to instill disbelief in white Americans so they would question their complicity in injustice while warning how their feelings of shame could preempt critical political reflection. Not only did Wells also reveal a counterimage of interracial human intimacy that opposed Jim Crow antimiscegenation laws, but she showed how hope was about straddling the line between constraint and utopian dreaming rather than assuming the inevitability of progress.

Chapter 3, "Huey Newton, the Black Panthers, and the Decolonization of America," maintains that the writings of Huey P. Newton and the political practices of the Black Panther Party for Self-Defense sought to answer a question that was not fully addressed by Martin Luther King Jr. and the civil rights movement: how to articulate a political theory serviceable for citizens who not only have few economic resources but are also subject to debilitating living conditions.

In addition to undermining arguments about American exceptionalism, arguments that were all the rage in American postwar culture, Newton articulated a vision of action based in the idea of existential intellectual rebirth, that involved collective responsibility, and that was geared toward the radically new. Through the tactics of armed self-defense and policing the police, Newton and the Panthers together illuminated an idea of popular power that required state power to justify its existence. Through his embrace of empathetic perspectivalism, Newton made ethics a central component of radical democratic politics. Through their politicized use of rage, Newton and the Panthers dramatized how emotion is a powerful resource for political communication.

Chapter 4, "Angela Davis, Prison Abolition, and the End of the American Carceral State," argues that Angela Davis's call for abolishing the prison-industrial complex reflects a normative vision of the impossible. By describing punishment as race conscious and centered on social control, Davis challenged the view of some prominent criminologists and the American public at large that punishment was colorblind. Abolishing the American prison system, she suggested, required citizens to engage in rigorous self-examination, strengthen socioeconomic networks, and cultivate community-based practices of reconciliation. Critical Resistance, the political organization of which Davis was a founding member, as well as various forms of prisoner protest, have deepened her ideas.

The conclusion, "The Future of Resistance," explains what African American resistance can tell us about American culture and democracy in general. It also offers an explanation for why resistance has taken the form it has. It then contextualizes the contemporary racial-justice movement Black Lives Matter and its struggle against racial inequality within the history of African American resistance.

1

DAVID WALKER, FREDERICK DOUGLASS, AND THE ABOLITIONIST DEMOCRATIC VISION

O n August 22, 1831, a slave rebellion sent a shockwave through the American republic. Nat Turner, a precocious and charismatic slave who saw himself as a prophet driven by a divine vision, mobilized a group of slaves in Southampton County, Virginia, who unleashed a deadly assault on at least fifty-five white Americans. Nothing scared white slaveholders more than slave rebellions. Turner's and, several decades later, the white abolitionist John Brown's failed attempt to inspire a slave uprising in Harper's Ferry, Virginia, in 1859 were probably the two most famous of the nineteenth century, but—starting with Gabriel's Rebellion in 1800, a failed plot in which literate and privileged slaves sought to capture Richmond, Virginia, during the fraught presidential election between the Federalists and the Republicans—they were far from exceptional: Slave conspiracies, runaway plots, attempts at poisoning their masters, and insurgencies were widespread, even if not always memorialized.[1]

Turner's revolt was squashed two days later, and, although he was in hiding for several months, Turner would be hanged and eventually skinned—according to some accounts, parts of his body became heirlooms.[2] The decision of the Virginian state to deny Turner a funeral recalled Sophocles's tragedy *Antigone*, in which the authoritarian political-realist ruler Creon punished his rebellious nephew Polynices by denying him a proper burial, to prevent public grieving, which might foment even more resistance in Thebes.[3] The play's eponymous heroine, Antigone, refused her uncle Creon's decree through nonviolent civil disobedience—by burying Polynices, her brother.

After she was caught by the authorities, Antigone's final protest was an inwardly directed act of suicide—a statement that said she, not the state, would have ultimate say over her death—but, in contrast, those slaves like Turner who died while protesting slavery did so while trying to confront those who enslaved them. For enslaved Americans—who had no political rights, no freedom of mobility, little hope for personal flourishing, and who lived with the constant threat of humiliation, if not violence—a life of complete bondage was much worse than the price of death, which was the cost of failed resistance. How, then, could black people fashion a practice of agency under these brutal circumstances? What kind of insights does slave rebellion offer about democratic citizenship?

Arguably no word other than "slavery" so formed the discursive backdrop of many American revolutionary arguments against British imperialism. Yet it was invoked more as an abstract idea than as an empirical reality—an idea completely devoid of its most obvious manifestation in the Southern colonies: the enslavement of black Americans. For many early Americans, slavery was positioned as the antithesis of political liberty.[4] But if slaves had been given a voice in the Constitutional Convention in the summer of 1787, they would have said that the domination at the heart of African American slavery was much more than the deprivation of certain public freedoms like freely speaking and assembling and electing political representatives. Slavery was instead the deprivation of a minimally decent existence. Slaves were barred from education and were made to be illiterate; they had no recourse to the law; they were restricted to the plantation and forced to labor without any sort of compensation; and they were beaten, whipped, raped, and murdered at will.[5]

The intellectual flight from this experience was impossible for the African American abolitionists David Walker and Frederick Douglass.[6] Walker was born legally free in 1785 in North Carolina to a free mother and slave father; Douglass was born into slavery in Maryland in 1818. Before dying at the young age of forty-four—rumors circulated that he was poisoned, but the official cause was tuberculosis—Walker would become one of the leading abolitionists in Boston through his involvement in various civic and religious organizations and through writings in the short-lived *Freedom's Journal*. Douglass's life was much longer and more public. His deeply affecting speeches—he was arguably the greatest orator in the American tradition—drew upon his own experience of escaping slavery as a teenager and made vivid the brutality of slavery in ways that had profound effects on the American public.

If one were asked to distill the primary similarity between Walker's and Douglass's abolitionist political thought, it would be that each invoked a nationalist argument about natural rights—usually drawn from the Declaration of Independence—to identify the tension between the moral American ideal of democracy and the immoral scourge of slavery.[7] But there were significant differences between the two thinkers. Walker, who advocated slave resistance by all means necessary (including violence) in his most famous text, *Appeal, in Four Articles; Together with a Preamble, to the Colored Citizens of the World, but in Particular and Very Expressly to Those of the United States of America* (1829), was much more militant than Douglass, who, especially in his earliest speeches, used the rhetorical tactic of moral suasion popularized by William Lloyd Garrison's newspaper *The Liberator* to persuade white Americans to abolish slavery through political compromises and electoral avenues.[8] Although Walker criticized the fantasy of black emigration to Africa, he is nevertheless correctly viewed as one of the first black nationalists, given his defense of black solidarity.[9] Douglass, however, was always an integrationist who sought to fold his political thought into the larger project of American exceptionalism.[10]

Exclusively focusing on these differences, however, can make us overlook an unappreciated project in which both were involved: an alternative practice of democratic citizenship that would seriously and directly address the problem of action under paralyzing and totalizing constraints. The rhetoric of Walker's *Appeal*—replete with declarative statements, provocative exclamations, and searching questions—cast disenfranchised citizens as agents capable of political judgment in ways radical for the time. The text's cynical tone articulated the democratic significance of deciphering the hidden interests behind declarations of moral benevolence. Furthermore, Walker insisted that a critical form of direct resistance could be energized through appreciating human finitude. He exposed in vivid ways how social division could intensify elite political power and how ideas such as human nature, responsibility, and patriotism needed to be reimagined.

More vividly than Walker, Douglass, in his second autobiography, *My Bondage and My Freedom* (1855), recounting his own direct resistance to his slaveholder Edward Covey, uniquely described slavery as a tool of psychological colonization. Yet Douglass, unlike Walker, used this analysis to remind readers that human dignity could never be fully divorced from action. Finally, Douglass centered attention on the way that anguish and shame could do powerful political work for resistance and argued that such emotional experience was central for theorizing the meaning of freedom.

THE LANGUAGE AND RHETORIC OF THE *APPEAL*

What understanding of slave agency was necessary to justify resistance? The 1830 edition of the frontispiece of Walker's *Appeal*—originally published on September 28, 1829, in Boston, where he was both a key contributor to *Freedom's Journal* and a salesman of used clothing—answered this question in a way few black Americans and no slaveholders would have accepted. At the center of the painting, the African American's outstretched arms, reaching toward a cloud while standing upon a mountain, reiterated Walker's prophetic argument that a just God would eventually smite the white perpetrators of slavery and redeem its black victims.[11] Walker must have heard this argument repeatedly at the antislavery AME (African Methodist Episcopal) Church in Charleston, South Carolina, where he moved in 1822, which was at the center of the failed Vesey conspiracy plot, which involved the former slave Denmark

Vesey's plot to kill the governor of South Carolina and leave Charleston in flames.[12]

Vesey's apocalyptic vision was expressed through his desire to turn Charleston into a dystopian hell, but no black American in the early nineteenth century so effectively used the pen to inflame slaveholders like Walker. If Vesey's concern was strategizing rebellion, Walker was not only supplying its political theory but also sketching the new black political subject who could enact it. This explains why after the *Appeal* was circulated by hand and through a loose underground network throughout the American South, Southern planters offered a three-thousand-dollar bounty for Walker's head and ten thousand dollars for his capture.

What the *Appeal*'s frontispiece told black readers did not sit well with slaveholder political thought. First, the absence of shackles, which symbolically and physically characterized slave life, suggested that black people could still become free, even if they had no political liberty under slavery. By shifting perspective away from liberty, which slaveholders believed needed to be regulated by government and could only be found through life in an organic society with well-defined social roles, and toward freedom, Walker defined self-determination as an internal condition of freedom. This internal condition of freedom could be the foundation for collective political struggle for liberty.

Second, the African American's looking upward into the realm of ideals told readers that transcendent principles were essential for animating one's freedom struggle. The radicalism of these ideals was found in the way they functioned like a fleeting horizon that could never be reached, but only approximated, in the world. Struggling to achieve these ideals with no end in sight, rather than stopping after some limited victories, the *Appeal*'s frontispiece suggested, needed to define black politics. Third, the person's ambiguous positioning of their hands—at once summoning and receiving a deity decidedly absent from view, hidden above the heavens—suggested that emancipation required direct action in the world.

At the center of the *Appeal*'s rhetoric was indignation toward the twin viruses of American slavery and American racism, which entered a new phase by the 1820s, when the 1819 Missouri Compromise limited

FIGURE 1.1 Frontispiece to David Walker's *Appeal*, 1830.

Source: Library of Congress, https://www.loc.gov/pictures/resource/cph.3c05530/.

the spread of slavery in the new Western territories but nonetheless kept it in place below the Mason-Dixon Line.[13] To communicate the gravity of this unbearable condition of racial domination, the *Appeal* deployed exclamations, sometimes as many as six after a sentence, repeated in dizzying fashion throughout the text. Walker announced: "But I tell you Americans! that unless you speedily alter your course, *you* and your *Country are gone!!!!!!*"[14] Slavery destroyed white moral conscience and precluded the possibility of living in the light of truth, creating a condition instead where sin and greed ruled the day: "Their hearts have become almost seared, as with an hot iron, and God has nearly given them up to believe a lie in preference to the truth!!! And I am awfully afraid that pride, prejudice, avarice and blood, will, before long prove the final ruin of this happy republic, or land of *liberty!!!!*[15]

Compare Walker's words to the tone and substance of two of the most famous American political manifestos up until that point: Thomas Jefferson's Declaration of Independence (1776) and Thomas Paine's *Common Sense* (1776). Not only does the Declaration fail to mention American slavery by name—and *Common Sense* barely mentions it—but both texts wanted to outrage white Americans who could not partake in the joys of representative citizenship but who still had basic freedoms of mobility and social dominance over both women and slaves. For Jefferson, the real problem was arbitrary and unelected political power. For Walker, the real problem was brutal social and economic exploitation. "Governments," Jefferson said, "long established should not be changed for light and transient causes. . . . But when a long train of abuses and usurpations, pursuing invariably the same Object evinces a design to reduce them under absolute Despotism, it is their right . . . [to] provide new Guards for their future security."[16] Likewise, if for Paine tyranny was defined by an abnegation of the rule of law—"for as in absolute governments the King is law, so in free countries the law ought to be King; and there ought to be no other"[17]—then, for Walker, tyranny was the undemocratic, even if popularly sanctioned, rule of an immoral majority.

Similarly, although its preamble and four Articles— "Article I: Our Wretchedness in Consequence of Slavery," "Article II: Our Wretchedness in Consequence of Our Ignorance," Article III: Our Wretchedness in Consequence of the Preachers of the Religion of Jesus Christ," and "Article IV: Our Wretchedness in Consequence of the Colonizing Plan"—mirrored the rhetorical structure of the U.S. Constitution to re-found a polity serviceable for black Americans,[18] the *Appeal*'s rhetoric also had a much more ambitious purpose than either it or the Declaration. The *Appeal*'s aim was not to lay the foundation for a certain kind of government but actually to transform the self-perception of the marginalized. Addressed as it was "to the Colored Citizens of the World," there was something truly stunning about the *Appeal*'s assumption of the unquestioned status of African American citizenship when it was overtly denied through slavery or highly constrained through discriminatory practices in the North.[19] Walker couldn't have put it clearer: The *Appeal*'s purpose was to awaken in what he saw as his "wretched" black brothers "a spirit of inquiry and investigation respecting our miseries and wretchedness in this *Republican Land of Liberty!!!!!!*"[20]

Strikingly, throughout the text, Walker's assertion of black citizenship was accomplished rhetorically: through the question mark. After the exclamation point, which appeared over four hundred times in a text of roughly thirty thousand words, no rhetorical device in the *Appeal* received as much play as the question mark, which appeared over two hundred times, doing the treasonous work of placing black people into a position to see themselves as agents capable of critical reflection at a moment when this position was denied them by slaveholders.[21] Not all questions in the *Appeal* were constructed with the same objective. Many that Walker raised merely aimed to foment indignation about a reality that he believed was indisputable, rather than inspire independent reflection from his readers. He was convinced in his religious conviction that God would punish the white enslavers: "Will he let the oppressors rest comfortably and happy always? Will he not cause the very children of the oppressors to rise up against them, and oftimes put them to death?"[22]

Other questions, however, did much more politically. Take the following example, where Walker asked readers to consider that, if they were of Moses's "excellent disposition,"

Would we not long before this time, have been respectable men, instead of such wretched victims of oppression as we are? Would they be able to drag our mothers, our fathers, our wives, our children and ourselves, around the world in chains and hand-cuffs as they do, to dig up gold and silver for them and theirs? This question, my brethren, I leave for you to digest; and may God Almighty force it home to your hearts.[23]

Asking readers to explore what freedom would look like expressed Walker's recognition that different experiences and imaginations could lead to different answers, within which would be different views of the good life. Placing readers in a position to answer freely "yes" or "no" to his questions also expressed Walker's defense of a mode of reflective judgment in which the potential of error was not simply rejected but seen to be intrinsic.

In Walker's own view, however, freedom could never be viewed abstractly. One could only evaluate it by considering social context. Addressing emancipated black people, he wrote:

Do any of you say that you and your family are free and happy, and what have you to do with the wretched slaves and other people? . . . Look into our freedom and happiness, and see of what kind they are composed!! They are of the very lowest kind—they are the very *dregs!*— they are the most servile and abject kind, that ever a people was in possession of! If any of you wish to know how FREE you are, let one of you start and go through the southern and western States of this country, and unless you travel as a slave to a white man . . . or have your free papers . . . if they do not take you up and put you in jail, and if you cannot give good evidence of your freedom, sell you into eternal slavery, I am not a living man.[24]

Astute observation of the world, Walker insisted, revealed that freedom was not simply about mobility or lack of violent domination; it was instead black autonomy from the sovereign white gaze and racist institutions—especially in the South and West—that could exercise their power in arbitrary ways. Freedom could not be dependent upon a faith in fellow citizens not to deny a person his or her citizenship or political rights; it was about not worrying that this could become a possibility at any moment.

Walker's rhetoric may have reframed black Americans' self-perceptions of racial inferiority, but his assumption that black people had equal capacity for reason would have been denied by the slaveholding class, which did everything in its power to repress the public visibility of black reason by precluding them from civic discourse. To make his claim about equality resonate, sometimes he described how racism created a cycle of violence, which left all vulnerable to its brutal effects. Warning white Americans to stop this cycle before it unleashed a racial civil war, he wrote: "But remember, Americans, that as miserable, wretched, degraded and abject as you have made us . . . some of you, (whites) on the continent of America, will yet curse the day that you ever were born. You want slaves, and want us for your slaves!!! My colour will yet, root some of you out of the very face of the earth!!!!!!"[25]

At other times, Walker emphasized the God-given undeniable dignity of all human beings: "For you must remember that we are men as well as they. God has been pleased to give us two eyes, two hands, two feet, and some sense in our heads as well as they. They have no more right to hold us in slavery than we have to hold them."[26] At times, however, Walker characterized equality as bodily vulnerability. Note in the above passage the emphasis on God giving human beings two eyes, hands, and feet. In another passage, he cast the body as a source of suffering that neither blacks nor whites can escape. Drawing a parallel between the "social death"[27] that defined slavery and what would also be easily recognizable in whites' own lives (the inescapability of weakness, fragility, and death), he wrote, "Are we MEN!!—I ask you, O my brethren! . . . Are they not dying worms as well as we?"[28] White supremacy was a political truth, and white slaveholders were responsible for unequal rates of premature death for black people, but talk of fundamental racial inequality made little sense when one recognized that no one could be completely invulnerable from an uncontrollable force like death.

Walker also understood that morality could help equalize those who were unequal. The *Appeal* embodied how religion could be a revolutionary force put in the service of ending oppression.[29] Slaves had no political power, but, Walker insisted, they could wield moral power and be judged equally to whites on moral terms:

> Have they not to make their appearance before the tribunal of Heaven, to answer for the deeds done in the body, as well as we? Have we any other Master but Jesus Christ alone? . . . What right then, have we to obey and call any other Master, but Himself? How we could be so *submissive* to a gang of men, whom we cannot tell whether they are *as good* as ourselves or not, I never could conceive. However, this is shut up with the Lord, and we cannot precisely tell—but I declare, we judge men by their works.[30]

Although primarily addressed to black Christians, the radical potential of this statement was not constrained by religious conviction. Morality was a great equalizer whose existence depended on deeds, not words. On the one hand, just like acknowledging the slave's mortality—their death—could inspire in them a sense of fearlessness to act, so could acknowledging their morality lead them to refuse unjust laws. Fidelity to moral principle could encourage vigorous black dissent.[31] On the other hand, Walker's understanding of morality also highlighted something powerful about human vulnerability. If truth was found in God's will (and so the absolute moral truth would never be fully known until one experienced divine judgment), then one needed always to resist hubris in believing in their moral righteousness. As he wrote elsewhere: "The Americans may be as vigilant as they please, but they cannot be vigilant enough for the Lord, neither can they hide themselves, where he will not find and bring them out."[32] Translated into an idiom for citizenship, one needed to work against their wishes to demonize others.

AMERICAN CYNICISM

Taking seriously a critical mode of judgment would have helped black Americans shift internal perceptions about being inferior, but what kind of disposition did they need to adopt toward those who dominated them? Walker's answer was cynicism.[33] Soon after the *Appeal*'s publication, the only thing that matched whites' cynicism toward Walker's authorship (they couldn't fathom that a black person could compose such a well-researched, critically engaged, theoretically sophisticated, and deftly written text) was Walker's cynicism toward white Americans actually believing his claims:

> I say, I do not only expect to be held up to the public as an ignorant, impudent and restless disturber of the public peace, by such avaricious creatures, as well as a mover of insubordination—and perhaps put in prison or to death, for giving a superficial exposition of our miseries, and exposing tyrants.[34]

Walker's words remind us that cynicism can erode the possibility of honest communication—the last thing one would want to embrace in organizing a national liberation organization such as Walker's short-lived Massachusetts General Colored Association (MGCA), created in 1828, or the African Lodge of freemasons, of which he was a member.

But more than simply *guarding* against the vulnerability that may come with being outsmarted or duped, Walker's use of the word "exposition" captured how cynicism's emancipatory value comes from the way it actually *exposes* the world in which one lives, piercing the official discourse of public justification, drawing attention to what is lurking in the shadows, unsaid, implied. Before the *Appeal*'s publication, the most famous cynics in American political thought were the Anti-Federalists, who excoriated and described as too naïve the authors of *The Federalist*—Madison, Hamilton, and Jay—for failing to recognize that the self-interest foundational to human nature could always corrupt the most civic republican of political institutions, where political elites ruled with patriotism and a sense of the public good. As the Anti-Federalists famously put it in "Brutus no. 2": "Rulers have the same propensities as other men; they are as likely to use the power with which they are vested for private purposes, and to the injury and oppression of those over whom they are placed, as individuals in a state of nature are to injure and oppress one another."[35]

Walker's cynicism, however, was not directed toward virtuous political rule but toward moral benevolence. Take Walker's reflections on former secretary of state Henry Clay's proposal to send free black Americans to Africa, so that they could create a colony that might encourage slaveholders to emancipate their slaves. Walker first cited a speech of Clay's that said free black Americans

> neither enjoyed the immunities of freemen, nor were they subjected to the incapacities of slaves, but partook, in some degree, of the qualities of both. From their condition, and the unconquerable prejudices resulting from their colour, they never could amalgamate with the free whites of this country. It was desirable, therefore, as it respected them, and the residue of the population of the country, to drain them off.

Walker then asked:

> Is [he] a friend to the blacks, further, than his personal interest extends? Is it not his greatest object and glory upon earth, to sink us into miseries and wretchedness by making slaves of us, to work his plantation to enrich him and his family? Does he care a pinch of snuff about Africa—whether it remains a land of Pagans and of blood, or of Christians, so long as he gets enough of her sons and daughters to dig up gold and silver for him?[36]

At another moment in the text, Walker would unleash his ire at Elias Caldwell, clerk of the U.S. Supreme Court, who claimed that the African colonization plan actually represented white Americans' love of liberty—specifically, their desire to extend it to black Americans. Quoting Caldwell, Walker wrote:

> He says, "surely, Americans ought to be the last people on earth, to advocate such slavish doctrines, to cry peace and contentment to those who are deprived of the privileges of civil liberty, they who have so largely partaken of its blessings, who know so well how to estimate its value, ought to be among the foremost to extend it to others." The real

sense and meaning of the last part of Mr. Caldwell's speech is, get the free people of colour away to Africa, from among the slaves, where they may at once be blessed and happy, and those who we hold in slavery, will be contented to rest in ignorance and wretchedness, to dig up gold and silver for us and our children. Men have indeed got to be so cunning, these days, that it would take the eye of a Solomon to penetrate and find them out.[37]

For Walker, relocating freed black Americans to Africa would only intensify slavery. Stifled would be the potential for black solidarity and resistance; alleviated would be the feeling of white guilt. Although Walker's critique of Clay and Caldwell expressed his implicit agreement with the Federalists and Anti-Federalists that self-interest had been one guiding motivation of human behavior, it also conveyed that the skepticism cynicism unleashes—compared, for instance, to dispositions like pragmatism, which tries to approach problems with how they can best be solved, or irony, which teases out the humorous contradiction between what is expected and what occurs—is especially valuable when it is centered on an ideological system of white supremacy that dominates through doubletalk.

Many slaveholders and ostensible moderates like Clay and Caldwell invoked decidedly liberal, Enlightenment arguments about the importance of private property, freedom, and popular sovereignty to keep enslavement intact.[38] If this was the ideological armor through which slavery functioned, then cynicism—which could pierce and dismantle the view that freedom can only be achieved through emigration to Africa and that black cultural progress and emotional health required white stewardship—was as powerful as the pistols and knives used in slave rebellions.

If no abolitionist could doubt the importance of exposing the lies through which white supremacy operated, then few went so far as Walker to call for the importance of confronting rather than dismissing white racist views. At the heart of Walker's ire was Thomas Jefferson's famous "Query XIV," in *Notes on the State of Virginia* (1785), which described black people as naturally incapable of philosophical genius and that asserted—without any moral qualms or indignation—the ease with which slaves could be murdered: "When a master was murdered, all his slaves in the same house, or within hearing, were condemned to death."[39] Walker wanted readers to feel his own indignation at Jefferson's words:

> Do you believe that the assertions of such a man, will pass away into oblivion unobserved by this people and the world? If you do you are much mistaken—See how the American people treat us—have we souls in our bodies? . . . I am after those who know and feel, that we are MEN, as well as other people; to them, I say, that unless we try to refute Mr. Jefferson's arguments respecting us, we will only establish them.[40]

Walker's very decision to engage with Jefferson's antidemocratic racism, which itself stood in an uneasy relationship with Jefferson's defense of natural rights,[41] performed a hallmark of democratic citizenship that was undeveloped in Jefferson's own radically democratic defense of a local ward system in which citizens locally and directly controlled their political fates in a town-hall setting. Jefferson proposed that this would allow "the voice of the people" to be "fairly, fully, and peaceably expressed, discussed, and decided by the common reason of society."[42] Jefferson saw democracy as a matter of direct popular rule, but Walker thought—and the *Appeal* embodied how—it meant nothing without fully understanding opposing political-theoretical positions and required embracing a mode of political communication animated by disagreement rather than consensus.[43] For Walker, it was not enough to agree or learn how to disagree respectfully about issues pertaining to collective political life; one needed to learn and respond directly to the very positions that actually threatened one's existence. This was not a cordial discussion about policy but a matter of life and death.

Walker urged black Americans to practice autonomous critical reflection: "We, and the world wish to see the charges of Mr. Jefferson refuted by the blacks *themselves* . . . for we must remember that what the whites have written respecting this subject, is other men's labours, and did not emanate from the blacks."[44] On the one hand, understanding

Jefferson's position could enable black Americans to test it against their own knowledge (as well as the sense that they themselves are capable of knowledge without white paternalism) that they "know and feel." On the other hand, engaging Jefferson's position could allow black Americans to see that white racism was incredibly dangerous. Seeing in full force Jefferson's position regarding the dispensability of black life would bring into relief racism's lethal intensity (white racism is not innocuous and is always on some level the first step toward unleashing violence and death) and the conceptual fragility of the racist argument. This would show that racism not only legitimizes racial violence and domination but that both are necessary to secure the intellectually weak arguments upon which it subsists.

ABOLISHING SLAVERY

At the heart of Walker's resistance to slavery was the articulation of an effective argument for abolishing slavery. This was no easy task given the way slavery was debated in American culture. Indeed, many moderate, even nonslaveholding, white Americans appreciated Abraham Lincoln's views in his 1858 debate with Stephen Douglas. At the outset of his speech, Lincoln described slavery as a political problem in which the salient criteria for abolition centered on whether it would create more or less national disunity or whether it was economically feasible or politically practical. As he put it:

> My first impulse would be to free all the slaves, and send them to Liberia. . . . But a moment's reflection would convince me, that . . . in the long run, its sudden execution is impossible. . . . What then? Free them all, and keep them among us as underlings? Is it quite certain that this betters their condition? . . . What next? Free them, and make them politically and socially our equals? My own feelings will not admit of this; and if mine would, we well know that those of the great mass of white people will not.[45]

Understanding that decisions about slavery based on cost-benefit analyses or the maintenance of political order would likely keep the racially unequal status quo in place, Walker refused Lincoln's approach and instead evaluated slavery in moral terms: "The sources from which our miseries are derived, and on which I shall comment, I shall not combine in one, but shall put them under distinct heads and expose them in their turn; in doing which, keeping truth on my side, and not departing from the strictest rules of morality."[46]

But Walker's shift away from political to moral necessity also coexisted alongside an attempt to redescribe the barometer for abolishing slavery. The barometer, for him, was whether it inflicted physical and emotional suffering, not whether it deprived people of political liberties or rights—the right to free speech, to assembly, equal protection under the law—or whether it would create political backlash from the white electorate. He wrote:

> If he is not a tyrant, but has the feelings of a human being, who can feel for a fellow creature, he may see enough to make his very heart bleed! He may see there, a son take his mother, who bore almost the pains of death to give him birth, and by the command of a tyrant, strip her as naked as she came into the world, and apply the cow-hide to her, until she falls a victim to death in the road! He may see a husband take his dear wife, not infrequently in a pregnant state, and perhaps far advanced, and beat her for an unmerciful wretch, until his infant falls a lifeless lump at her feet![47]

Walker knew that thinking about the physical effects of slavery on those who endured it would more likely force one to engage slavery as it was lived rather than as a rational calculation about whether emancipation was or was not politically viable. The above passage also tells us about Walker's implicit embrace of the argument that morality is at once affected by emotion and, in an important sense, is itself an emotional sentiment.[48] Sentimentalism here is meant to inspire in readers a feeling of moral outrage and to see slavery as a moral wrong that consists of depriving human beings of everyday experiences. Enslavement was defined by a life where the constant threat of violence replaced love and where humiliation replaced dignity.

Perhaps because appeals to reason had rarely worked on slaveholders, Walker thought appealing to emotions would be more effective for moving all Americans from a condition of passivity to action. Witnessing these "cries and groans in consequence of oppression [that] are continually pouring into the ears of the God of justice,"[49] he believed, could encourage white Americans to ask whether such a life would ever be acceptable for anyone and facilitate greater soul-searching for the reasons why many simply stood by idly. "If you will allow that we are MEN, who feel for each other," Walker asked, "does not the blood of our fathers and of us their children, cry aloud to the Lord of Sabbath against you, for the cruelties and murders with which you have, and do continue to afflict us?"[50]

Another of Walker's resistance strategies for abolition, however, was to describe black suffering as historically exceptional:[51]

I promised in a preceding page to demonstrate to the satisfaction of the most incredulous, that we, (coloured people of these United States of America) are the *most wretched, degraded* and *abject* set of beings that *ever lived* since the world began, and that the white Americans having reduced us to the wretched state of *slavery*, treat us in that condition *more cruel* (they being an enlightened and Christian people), than any heathen nation did any people whom it had reduced to our condition. These affirmations are so well confirmed in the minds of all unprejudiced men, who have taken the trouble to read histories, that they need no elucidation from me.[52]

Notwithstanding their historical accuracy, these assertions make the notion of American exceptionalism much more difficult to sustain.[53] American exceptionalism—replete with an ostensible commitment to equality, rights, progress, and justice—becomes retold as a story of unparalleled violence and human degradation.[54] The *Appeal's* embodiment of a Manichean Christian moralism—the strict dichotomy between good and evil—never stopped Walker from warning his black readers to see that the white American conviction that they were "enlightened" and that they were a "Christian people" was contradicted by and actually helped perpetuate "wretchedness and endless miseries . . . to be poured out upon [black] fathers, ourselves and [black] children."[55] American exceptionalism could no longer be used to inspire hope of just political change. Walker's political plea to black Americans was clear. They were to anticipate always the unseen and creative forms future white domination might take. They were to assume that the answer to this question would always be a resounding *yes*: "I will ask one question here—Can our condition be any worse?—Can it be more mean and abject?"[56]

But exposing how slavery inflicted exceptional suffering or that America was unexceptional was not entirely adequate for addressing one of the major intellectual defenses of slavery, which centered on arguing that it was comparatively better than freedom under capitalism. Slaveholder intellectuals were appalled by the elitist snobbery and heartlessness of Northern abolitionists. "Compare his condition [the American slave's] with the tenants of the poor houses in the more civilized portions of Europe," John Calhoun declared. "Look at the sick, and the old and infirm slave, on the one hand, in the midst of his family and his friends, under the kind superintending care of his master and mistress, and compare it with the forlorn and wretched condition of the pauper in the poor house."[57] George Fitzhugh went even further, arguing for poor whites to be enslaved. After all, "had [free white workers] been vassals or serfs, they would have been beloved, cherished and taken care of by those same landlords and employers. Slaves never die of hunger, scarcely ever feel want."[58]

Aware of these distorted arguments, Walker proposed a different way to judge the ethics of slavery. Expanding the notion of family from the nuclear household to humanity, Walker saw the insult to one's dignity to be as serious a crime as that of economic exploitation. Quoting Jefferson's view in the *Notes* that "I advance it therefore as a suspicion only, that the blacks, whether originally a distinct race, or made distinct by time and circumstances, are *inferior* to the whites in the endowments both of body and mind," Walker declared: "This very verse, brethren, having emanated from Mr. Jefferson . . . has in truth injured us more, and has been as great a barrier to our emancipation as any thing that has ever been advanced against us. I hope you will not let it pass unnoticed."[59] Furthermore, he asked: "Have [they] not, Americans, having subjected us under you, added to these miseries, by insulting us in telling us to our face, because we are helpless, that we are not of the human family?"[60] and "Have they not, after having reduced us to the deplorable condition of slaves under their feet, held us up as descending originally from the tribes of *Monkeys* or *Orang-Outangs?*"[61]

Dignity for Walker meant something other than what it did for slaveholders: It was a basic status of equal human worth, rather than an esteemed social status where one comported oneself with measured pride and unbridled honor.[62] But embedded in Walker's rhetorical questions was something powerful: an attempt to make indignation the measure for abolition. Adequate redress of moral wrongs places into positions of power those who have been wronged. It is their judgment that determines whether dignity has been violated or properly been upheld. Furthermore, moral injury is irreducible to and more difficult to measure (and thus redress) than economic or political deprivation. Because it is not easily quantifiable, indignation can become a potent source for resistance and create spaces where those who experience it can make more and more demands upon those who violate it.

POWER AND DEPENDENCE

Walker's time in slaveholding cities such as Wilmington and Charleston must have led him to appreciate how power was protean because its manifestations depended on the specific practices through which it was enacted and authorized. No one in the American tradition before Walker had so thoughtfully disentangled the complex yet interwoven relationship between those who ruled and those they ruled over. On the one hand, the classic American statement on power, Alexander Hamilton's "Federalist no. 70," described the importance of the executive branch (the president) having power that was unitary and indivisible, characterized by qualities like "decision, activity, secrecy, and dispatch."[63] But for Hamilton, it was precisely the closely linked relationship between the people and elites that diminished his concern of absolutism. In his view, "the restraints of public opinion" would curtail the excessive power of political elites.[64] Yet what Hamilton failed to grasp with much depth—or intentionally wanted to ignore, for he was a statesman as much as a philosopher—was something Walker understood: the creative way elites could deepen their own power through creating a condition of self-inflicted subjugation in those they dominated.

In Walker's view, this occurred through elites producing a condition of ignorance in the oppressed. The second article of the *Appeal*, entitled "Our Wretchedness in Consequence of Ignorance," said that "Ignorance, my brethren, is a mist, low down into the very dark and almost impenetrable abyss in which, our fathers for many centuries have been plunged"[65] and that "ignorance, the mother of treachery and deceit, gnaws into our very vitals."[66] For Walker, ignorance had the effect of destroying the black solidarity crucial for resistance. Every time a son beat his mother, a father killed his infant, or slaves spread "news and lies, making mischief one upon another,"[67] focus would be displaced away from the source of their suffering—slavery. Meanwhile, slaveholder power would remain unquestioned, if not become strengthened—"the reason our *natural enemies* are enabled to keep their feet on our throats."[68] So too was this displacement accomplished through slaveholders creating competition between slaves and free blacks, who were so desperate to earn a living that they often helped recover fugitive slaves or enslave those who were free. No group did Walker despise more: They were "in league with tyrants, and who receive a great portion of their daily bread, of the moneys which they acquire from the blood and tears of their more miserable brethren, whom they scandalously delivered into the hands of our *natural enemies!!!!!!*"[69]

In another example of a woman slave who brought to safety a white slaveholder after he survived the rebellion of sixty slaves he was leading to dig for gold and silver, Walker lamented the horrifying effects of mixing ignorance with empathy. Here, slaveholder power worked through the slave's self-policing. Empathy was something of a moralizing discourse of power where the oppressed subject participated in his or her own oppression.[70] Walker wondered:

> Was it the natural *fine feelings* of this woman, to save such a wretch alive? I know that the blacks, take them half enlightened and ignorant, are more humane and merciful than the most enlightened and refined European that can be found in all the earth . . . there is a solemn awe in the hearts of the blacks, as it respects *murdering* men: * (* Which is the reason the whites take the advantage of us).[71]

These lines capture Walker's critique of Madison's solution to the problem of human plurality and freedom. In "Federalist no. 10," Madison thought the solution for keeping both alive was to create more factions, which would compete against one another so that no single one would become too powerful, giving all a voice. As he explained: "Extend the sphere, and you take in a greater variety of parties and interests; you make it less probable that a majority of the whole will have a common motive to invade the rights of other citizens."[72] But neither the problem of unequal voice nor unequal resources especially bothered Madison. If Madison truly considered this, perhaps he would have seen what Walker understood well: how competition between those who are voiceless and powerless keeps those who have both voice and power in good shape. Subjugated people fighting over limited goods keep racial inequality intact.

Yet we should express skepticism about Walker's questionable view that slave-on-slave violence, manipulation, and empathy were somehow productive merely of ignorance or lack of willpower rather than physical compulsion or necessity. And we should rebuke Walker's ideas, which surface throughout the *Appeal*, of nineteenth-century racial naturalism—the long since rejected view that races have biological and heritable characteristics that define human behavior.[73] We should also notice that Walker's example of black treachery centered on a black slave woman raises the question of whether the *Appeal* is narrowly concerned with liberating black men and whether his notion of virtue was deeply masculine.[74] He declared at one point, "Oh! my coloured brethren, all over the world, when shall we arise from this death-like apathy?—And be men!! You will notice, if ever we become men, (I mean *respectable* men, such as other people are,) we must exert ourselves to the full."[75]

Finally, we should worry about Walker's own inability to straddle the delicate line between warning citizens about the subjugating power of empathy and rejecting empathy at all costs. Rejecting empathy entirely in favor of no-nonsense political realism allows violence to enter the picture. The paragraph after the anecdote about what he perceived as the traitorous enslaved black woman not only expressed Walker's problematic conviction in the virtue of manhood but was one of the few places in the *Appeal* where he explicitly endorsed violence as a form of self-defense—"that it is no more harm for you to kill a man, who is trying to kill you, than it is for you to take a drink of water when thirsty; in fact, the man who will stand still and let another murder him, is worse than an infidel, and, if he has common sense, ought not to be pitied."[76]

HUMAN NATURE, RESPONSIBILITY, AND PATRIOTISM

Another of Walker's ambitions in the *Appeal* was to recast the meaning of human nature to make it serviceable for resistance. This was understandable given that arguments about human nature were central to many nineteenth-century American defenses of slavery. Usually, this entailed adopting some version of Aristotle's argument in the *Politics*—that slaves completely lacked the "deliberative faculty" and were unsuited for citizenship.[77] The *Appeal*'s entire argument and rhetorical ambition was about rejecting this view, but Walker's own thinking about human nature did not simply reiterate Locke's argument about individuals being generally peaceful[78] or echo Rousseau's argument that human beings naturally felt pity.[79]

For Walker, human nature—or what might be more appropriately called the behavior of those who find themselves in the human condition—was socially constructed and always evolving:

> The whites have always been an unjust, jealous, unmerciful, avaricious and blood-thirsty set of beings, always seeking after power and authority . . . [In ancient Greece and Rome and later in Gaul, Spain, and in Britain] cutting each other's throats . . . they used all kinds of deceitful, unfair, and unmerciful means . . . we see them acting more like devils than accountable men.[80]

One can dispute Walker's view that white Americans had always been historically violent but nonetheless notice how his words suggest that this was by no means necessary. Walker's emphasis on deeds reveals his view that action creates human identity, while his emphasis on immoral activities illuminates the difference between some essential and impermanent human behavior. This becomes even clearer in the following passage, where he expresses his "suspicion of [white people], whether they are *as good by nature* as we are or not. Their actions, since they were known as a people, have been the reverse."[81]

Walker's oft-repeated notion of "natural enemies" is therefore both misleading and can be explained through his understanding of human action. Racial hostility is not natural but is instead productive of a social relationship. For evidence, consider the following statement: "I have several times called the white Americans our *natural enemies*—I shall here define my meaning of the phrase. . . . I say, if we *are* men, and see them treating us in the manner they do, that there can be nothing in our hearts but death alone, for them, notwithstanding we may appear cheerful, when we see them murdering our dear mothers and wives, because we cannot help ourselves."[82] Note Walker's juxtaposition of blacks' death wish for whites—something that runs counter to any feeling of empathy—with the claim that this feeling emerges in one's "heart," which conjures the very sentimentalism with which he wants all citizens to register suffering. This emotional ambivalence is produced through a relationship of power. Indeed, Walker's own ambivalence engendered in him a feeling of hope that white Americans could change their wayward ways: "But Oh Americans! Americans!! I warn you in the name of the Lord, (whether you will hear, or forbear,) to repent and reform, or you are ruined!!!"[83]

The *Appeal* was no less remarkable for the intensity with which it chastised white Americans for defaulting on their moral responsibility as it was for its uncompromising plea to black Americans to rethink responsibility as something driven by the pursuit of collective freedom.[84] Invoking an antimaterialistic argument, Walker asserted that the pursuit of more wealth was of a lower order than struggling to liberate those who were enslaved: "Be looking forward with thankful hearts to higher attainments than *wielding the razor* and *cleaning boots and shoes*."[85] Walker revised the vaunted pursuit of happiness that the Declaration of Independence championed as one of the inalienable rights of democratic citizenship. Happiness, for Walker, was not based in personal edification but could only be realized through struggling to end the collective oppression of all people of color worldwide.[86] "Your full glory and happiness, as well as all other coloured people under Heaven, shall never be fully consummated," Walker declared, "but with the *entire emancipation of your enslaved brethren all over the world*."[87] Slaveholders would have been aghast—as many of them truly believed that the occasional slave song, laugh, or dance on the plantation (which was nothing but a coping mechanism) signified satisfaction with one's standard of living.[88] And Walker's call for actively participating for the common good in a way ("entire" rather than limited) and for a purpose (social rather than political liberation) would have been odd—if not worrisome and potentially dangerous—for some American civic republicans who believed that uncompromised social liberation was entirely outside the purview of political life.[89]

Marx and Engels, writing twenty years after Walker in *The Communist Manifesto* (1848), would have rejected Walker's revolutionary defense of racial solidarity at the expense of class solidarity, but they would have appreciated Walker's internationalist notion of struggle, which moved past the narrow confines of the U.S. nation-state and also found historical expression in actual uprisings in Antigua, the Bahamas, and Jamaica in 1830 and 1831.[90] Walker counseled a practice of revolutionary leadership that entailed acting with those who were not yet enlightened, even though his words may have sounded problematically paternalistic to some: "I conjure you in the name of the Lord, and of all that is good, to impute their actions to ignorance, and wink at their follies, and do your very best to get around them some way or other, for remember they are your brethren."[91]

Walker's internationalism militated against uncritical nationalism, but his *Appeal* was nonetheless couched in the language of national attachment—or something approximating civic love—that exceeded narrow racial identification.[92] In addition to refusing to renounce black birthright citizenship, saying, "this country is as much ours as it is the whites, whether they will admit it now or not, they will see and believe it by and by,"[93] citing the Declaration of Independence became Walker's own patriotic attempt to emphasize the American democratic hypocrisy at the heart of racial domination. "Compare your own language," Walker wrote, "from your Declaration of Independence, with your cruelties and murders inflicted by your cruel and unmerciful fathers and yourselves on our fathers and on us—men who have never given your fathers or you the least provocation!!!!!!"[94]

On some level, patriotism—even in its most benign forms—often seems to encourage uncritical deference to national institutions in ways that might allow inequality to remain intact.[95] Walker's brand of patriotism, however, had more democratic potential, which was expressed by the way he made public usefulness the measure of whether his ideas were politically successful.[96] At the outset of the *Appeal*, he declared: "I shall endeavor to penetrate, search out, and lay [the facts of slavery] open for your inspection. If you cannot or will not profit by them, I shall have done *my* duty to you, my country and my God."[97]

Patriotism here was measured not by uncritical love of country but directly by the kind of emancipatory value it had for oppressed citizens, who themselves were endowed with the authority to scrutinize patriotic claims. Even if this practice of patriotism didn't entirely solve the problem of unfettered national love, it nonetheless served as an important check on what kind of patriotic assertions were or weren't acceptable. For Walker, patriotism was not simply an embodiment of unconditional love toward national identity but was conditional upon a certain political achievement: collective liberation. Love required complete emancipation. One couldn't and shouldn't love one's country unless it liberated the most oppressed: "We ask them for nothing but the rights of man, viz. for them to set us free, and treat us like men, and there will be no danger, for we will love and respect them, and protect our country—but cannot conscientiously do these things until they treat us like men."[98]

DOMINATION AND HUMANITY

As one of the greatest egalitarian humanists of the nineteenth century whose thinking centered on the idea of freedom, Frederick Douglass was, like Walker, the man Douglass eulogized in 1883 as one of the first great antislavery pioneers,[99] one of the most perceptive American theorists of its opposite: bondage.[100] In painting the most intimate portrait of the experience of enslavement any American had ever read, *My Bondage and My Freedom* (1855), the second of his three autobiographies, interpreted slavery as a psychological experience of domination in ways that would have even surprised Walker. The *Appeal* can be read as an unwavering defense of the possibility of black people to exercise the exemplary virtues of citizenship despite domination. Some of *My Bondage*'s most despairing passages, however, suggested the exact opposite. "Under the whole heavens there is no relation more unfavorable to the development of honorable character [than slavery]," Douglass wrote, because the way it rigidly organized one's life produced an inner psychic chaos. "Reason is imprisoned here, and passions run wild."[101]

The slave's psychological colonization, for Walker, occurred primarily through ignorance, but Douglass believed that it occurred through making reflective human beings into automatons. The enslaved person became a bundle of nerves. Existential fear, dread, and unease were abundant. The outcome was devastating. The slave could not think of himself as having individuality:

"Tumble up! Tumble up, and to *work, work,"* is the cry; and, now, from twelve o'clock (mid-day) till dark, the human cattle are in motion, wielding their clumsy hoes; hurried on by no hope of reward, no sense of gratitude, no love of children, no prospect of bettering their condition; nothing, save the dread and terror of the slave-driver's lash. So goes one day, and so comes and goes another.[102]

Slavery created subjects who—after continued physical, emotional, and intellectual deprivation—learned to deny their own humanity. Here and elsewhere Douglass conveyed how slave resistance was incredibly difficult because there was no firm ground from which to resist.[103] Taking the definition given to us by physics, we could say that resistance entails a countervailing action against some force. But the slave was, for Douglass, something of "a fixture; he has no choice, no goal, no destination; but is pegged down to a single spot, and must take root here, or nowhere."[104]

Historians have marshaled copious evidence of slave resilience in the face of domination in a way that renders dubious Douglass's view of the traumatized, docile slave—an inflammatory narrative that would also resurface in the 1960s.[105] But judged less for its accuracy of depicting slave life and more as a narrative that theorized the relationship between social power and agency, Douglass implied a startling idea: that achieving freedom required shifting individual self-perception. In the aftermath of the Civil War, Douglass asserted that self-reliance greatly depended upon the government's ability to secure material goods for all citizens.[106] But never did he believe that gaining full political, social, or economic rights could simply overturn psychological colonization. A kind of Copernican transformation of one's mindset was necessary. But what did this entail, and how did one achieve it?

ACTION AND DIGNITY

Six years prior to the publication of *My Bondage*, Thoreau thought he had the answer, in what would eventually become one of the most famous nineteenth-century meditations on political dissent, "Resistance to Civil

Government" (1849). For Thoreau, the first step toward freedom was moral conscience, which would transform citizens from what he saw as passive, unthinking machines into active political subjects. Thoreau wrote: "The only obligation which I have a right to assume is to do at any time what I think is right . . . a corporation has not conscience; but a corporation of conscientious men is a corporation with a conscience."[107] If Douglass's appeals to white conscience to abolish slavery before the 1850s embodied Thoreau's argument, his view on racial domination throughout his autobiographies dramatized the limitations of Thoreau's view. How could slaves begin to appreciate their moral conscience if they had trouble seeing themselves as having dignity in the first place?

For Douglass, the ability to recognize one's dignity thus turned on direct action in the world. He would trace this idea in *My Bondage*'s most critically discussed chapter, "The Last Flogging," which detailed his transformative experience of resistance at the youthful age of sixteen. Douglass didn't read the *Appeal* as a youth, but several years after it was published his confrontation with his then-slaveholder, Edward Covey, a violent and impulsive "Negro breaker" who treated slaves as brutally as he treated his oxen, suggested that he didn't have to. We shouldn't simply overlook an important difference between Walker's and Douglass's acts of resistance: Walker's, enacted through a manifesto, was centered on fomenting collective black revolt against slavery; Douglass's was deeply personal. But Douglass's brief recollection of the event was as much a story of Douglass's life as it was a work of consciousness raising and political theory. One of its central points was this: Publicly resisting power allowed one to recognize one's own dignity.[108]

Here is how Douglass told it: Bloody and dejected after being beaten by Covey, he refused to acquiesce to the "tyrant's" will and instead "*was resolved to fight* . . . The fighting madness had come upon me, and I found my strong fingers firmly attached to the throat of my cowardly tormentor; as heedless of consequences, at the moment, as though we stood as equals before the law. The very color of the man was forgotten."[109]

Douglass echoed Hegel's view that the fearlessness emerging from violent struggle—between the lord and the bondsman—could be emancipatory, a view Hegel himself may have developed through carefully following the revolt of real black slaves against their white masters in the Haitian Revolution against French colonialism from 1791 to 1804.[110] As Hegel wrote: "For this consciousness . . . its whole being has been seized with dread; for it has experienced the fear of death, the absolute lord."[111] With nothing to lose—and with only his freedom to gain—Douglass, like the bondsman, struggles against Covey, the lord, and in so doing recognizes himself as an agent capable of killing him, of negating Covey's existence.[112]

Hegel thought the bondsman's experience of existential dread was crucial for self-recognition, but for Douglass, perceiving oneself as an actor in the world gave rise to the recognition of human dignity. An astute reader might wonder whether Douglass's own act of resistance did not challenge his earlier depiction of domination as compromising slave agency. But what if the incident with Covey not only signaled a turning point in Douglass's thought, where he now recognized that resistance was possible—Douglass's analysis of domination was, after all, described earlier in the narrative of *My Bondage*—but also his understanding that, as Hegel understood, domination created the very contours of resistance? If slavery transforms slaves into bundles of emotion, then it is precisely, according to Douglass, two emotions—anguish and what he calls a "fighting madness" (rather than reason)—that inspire resistance.

Anguish was an especially powerful emotion Douglass experienced during his stay at Covey's: "I was completely wrecked, changed and bewildered; goaded almost to madness at one time, and at another reconciling myself to my wretched condition . . . all my former hopes and aspirations for usefulness in the world . . . contrasted with my then present lot, but increased my anguish."[113] But Douglass would not be consumed by it. After the first beating at the hands of Covey, which forced him into hiding and eventually to seek help from the slaveholder that had initially lent him to Covey for a short time, Thomas Auld, Douglass described how

after lying there about three quarters of an hour, brooding over the singular and mournful lot to which I was doomed, my mind passing over the whole scale or circle of belief and unbelief, from faith in the overruling providence of God, to the blackest atheism, I again took up my journey toward St. Michael's, more weary and sad than in the morning when I left Thomas Auld's for the home of Mr. Covey.[114]

Douglass's Hegelianism went deeper than is generally appreciated (anguish, or despair for Hegel, was not simply a source of resignation but of engagement): As heavy as it is, anguish is not only debilitating but allows one to reflect upon one's commitment to survival and partake in serious existential reflection upon the meaning of commitment itself.[115]

But let us briefly return to the final sentence in the quotation cited earlier—"we stood as equals before the law. The very color of the man was forgotten"—which illustrates Douglass's view that resistance also deepens, rather than emerges from, one's sense of equality and undermines narratives of racial inferiority. Douglass's words capture how the very experience of volitional action creates the psychological reality that one possesses inviolable self-worth.

Douglass's argument makes sense once one realizes that human dignity is never an empirical fact. More so than anything else, it is an abstract normative theory of human worth—a theory that tells us the kind of value that *should* be placed on human life. We can debate whether dignity should be substantially conceptualized as a virtue—a cultivated act that speaks to something redemptive in one's character—or whether it is nothing more than a status afforded to all people, something they have irrespective of what they do.[116] But we can say with greater certainty that human dignity is nothing without some kind of acknowledgment. To put it differently, its existence depends on the person within whom it exists to acknowledge its existence.[117]

In Douglass's case, acting in the name of self-defense brought forth the recognition of his dignity. "My resistance was entirely unexpected," he told readers, "and Covey was taken all aback by it, for he trembled in every limb. '*Are you going to resist*, you scoundrel?' said he. To which, I returned a polite '*Yes sir*;' steadily gazing my interrogator in the eye, to meet the first approach or dawning of the blow, which I expected my answer would call forth."[118] Douglass continued, "the cowardly tyrant asked if I 'meant to persist in my resistance.' I told him '*I did mean to resist, come what might;*' that I had been by him treated like a *brute*, during the last six months; and that I should stand it *no longer*."[119] Analyzing this moment for what it tells us about Douglass's views on the redemptive power of physical violence misses the centrality of the performance that animates it. Self-defense creates the recognition that one's life is important enough to struggle to the death for. A verbal utterance—his declaration of "yes sir"—alongside his steady gaze and the cool awareness of his tone conveyed Douglass's understanding that he could neither be conquered nor was willing to relinquish his life. Volition gave rise to action, which gives rise to the recognition of volition, which, in turn, solidifies his recognition of dignity.

To appreciate this point further, notice the tension Douglass clearly elucidated between undignified action and what he described as the force necessary for dignity. In his concluding reflections in "The Last Flogging," he wrote, "this battle with Mr. Covey—undignified as it was, and as I fear my narration of it is—was the turning point in my '*life as a slave*' . . . A man, without force, is without the essential dignity of humanity. Human nature is so constituted, that it cannot *honor* a helpless man, although it can *pity* him; and even this it cannot do long, if the signs of power do not arise."[120] One way to read this is as evidence of Douglass partaking in a defense of manhood. His equation of force with dignity makes resistance the barometer for one's manhood.[121]

But another equally significant argument is at work here. Consider the striking tension between Douglass's characterization of his battle with Covey as "undignified" and his statement that force is necessary for dignity. One way to resolve this tension is to understand Douglass's appreciation of the political-theoretical difference between violence and force. Violence refers to a specific means used to inflict direct harm, while force refers to something—again to borrow the language of physics—that literally changes the motion of an object.[122] Douglass's use of violence—his attempt to suffocate Covey—is thus undignified because it cannot engender the recognition of dignity. This recognition can, however, be created through the direct action that Douglass is a force to be reckoned with—that he can affect the trajectory of the world and the lives of those around him.

EXPERIENCE AND COMMUNITY

Douglass's revolt against Covey was something of a transcendent experience that animated his sense of hope that a better future was within reach. But at the heart of his retelling was also a challenge to the view that political thinking could fully be divorced from, or was not in any strong way related to, embodied experience. Experience told Walker that freedom rarely existed for black Americans (free and enslaved), given the totalizing force of white supremacy, but Douglass more forcefully argued that the very meaning of what freedom was is determined by those denied it. He wrote:

> [My resistance to Covey] rekindled in my breast the smoldering embers of liberty; it brought up my Baltimore dreams, and revived a sense of my own manhood. I was a changed being after that fight. I was *nothing* before; I WAS A MAN NOW. It recalled to life my crushed self-respect and my self-confidence, and inspired me with a renewed determination to be A FREEMAN.
>
> He can only understand the effect of this combat on my spirit, who has himself incurred something, hazarded something, in repelling the unjust and cruel aggressions of a tyrant. Covey was a tyrant, and a cowardly one, withal. After resisting him, I felt as I had never felt before. It was a resurrection from the dark and pestiferous tomb of slavery, to the heaven of comparative freedom. I was no longer a servile coward, trembling under the frown of a brother worm of the dust, but, my long-cowed spirit was roused to an attitude of manly independence. I had reached the point, at which I was *not afraid to die.* This spirit made me a freeman in *fact,* while I remained a slave in *form.* When a slave cannot be flogged he is more than half free. He has a domain as broad as his own manly heart to defend, and he is really *"a power on earth."*[123]

Suggesting that Douglass had achieved "comparative freedom"—or that external bondage did not preclude him from being internally free—aligned with Emerson's claim that individual self-reliance could make one free.[124] Emerson argued that "nothing is at last sacred but the integrity of your own mind. Absolve you to yourself, and you shall have the suffrage of the world."[125] For both, personal freedom and political freedom were never as divorced in practice as they might have been in theory. A stronger view of personal freedom does not provide the promissory note for political withdrawal.[126] Yet if Emerson subscribed to thinking about freedom in ways divorced from real social conditions and experiences (conscience was conscience, freedom was freedom, irrespective of who was thinking about it), Douglass believed that his experience in the world gave rise to political-theoretical reflection.[127]

Resistance, for Douglass, engendered thinking about three temporal moments: the present (the kind of activity in which one is engaged), the future (what might otherwise be but is not yet), and the past (who one was and what they will not be).[128] Paradoxically, thinking about a reality that one had never experienced could only occur through experience—whether this entailed remembering the experience of deprivation or the joys or fears associated with one's present condition of agency. The meaning of freedom is therefore as much an existential experience as it is a product of experience.[129]

No less than rethinking freedom, Douglass reimagined community. Walker drew attention to the way human identity was dependent upon deeds; Douglass centered attention upon the way community not only appeared in unlikely everyday places but also emerged spontaneously. His argument challenged what was implied in Calhoun's *A Disquisition on Government* (1848), which asserted that community was fixed, an organic entity founded in history and tradition, which had a definable set of interests: "Man is so constituted as a social being. His inclinations and wants, physical and moral, irresistibly impel him to associate with his kind."[130] If Calhoun depicted community in this way to justify why slaveholders constituted an intractable social class who needed to be given veto power over any political decision, Douglass depicted community as ephemeral in order to create hope for the possibility of resisting power. "We were all in open rebellion, that morning," Douglass explained, in giving a synoptic view of what was happening as he fought with Covey, because one of Covey's slaves, Caroline, "was in no humor to take a hand in any such sport [of helping Covey subdue Douglass]," and one of Covey's hired slaves, Bill, "affected ignorance" when he "pretended he did not know what to do" and subversively played upon his status as laboring human chattel rather than a rational actor, claiming, "My master hired me here, to work, and *not* to help you whip Frederick."[131] Caroline's and Bill's micropolitical acts of black solidarity were as ephemeral and contingent as Douglass's resistance to Covey.[132]

Shifting attention away from the smaller black community of enslaved people to the larger white American one, Douglass reminded readers that black resistance could emerge because of American racist culture. Not only did black Americans often subversively play on racist myths about black passivity and stupidity—as did Bill with his feigned ignorance—but these racist myths also exercised a powerful hold on whites in ways that could keep black resistance alive. The very shame Covey experienced at being beaten by Douglass, an African American youth of sixteen, precluded him from acknowledging the encounter—he never spoke about it again. Covey's fear of collective white backlash allowed Douglass to continue plotting his escape. "Covey was, probably, ashamed to have it known and confessed that he had been mastered by a boy of sixteen," Douglass wrote, because he "enjoyed the unbounded and very valuable reputation, of being a first rate overseer and *Negro breaker.*"[133] In 1838, Douglass was finally successful, consummating in his own life the transition his second autobiography retold: from bondage to freedom, Douglass's two lifelong theoretical concerns.

SLAVERY AND CONTEMPORARY DEMOCRACY

Any sober observer of contemporary life will see that slavery is not a relic of the past. Slavery remains a serious international problem with real effects for many people—ranging from the lucrative global business of sex-trafficking young women to the continuing problem of unpaid labor for undocumented citizens. This reality is striking given that in our current moment many countries have—at least in theory, if not in practice—adopted democracy as the normative standard for governance. How could democracy and slavery coexist?

Taking seriously Walker's call for cynicism might help us answer this question. Rather than be fundamentally at odds with the modern democratic promises of progress, freedom, and equality, slavery coexists with or is actually essential for the achievement of these aspirations.[134] This is not a logical connection but rather a case in which democratic ideas can easily be deployed in deeply antidemocratic ways. Progress can become the justification for bringing populations into the capitalist workforce, even if these workers have no rights in the workplace; the aspiration for freedom (for some) can be the reason why some wish to exploit others; and equality may create anxiety (if all are equal, then some might fail to achieve what they want) about one's social status, which could lead the more anxious ones to authorize a system in which some people are marginalized and placed in a fixed social position (slaves).

Although the link between slavery and democracy may be more troubling than many acknowledge, few would disagree with the argument that achieving democracy requires citizens, and the governments that they legitimate, to take an active role in abolishing slavery. Walker and Douglass understood this well. Yet their own resistance to slavery reflected an exemplary practice of democratic citizenship that reimagined many core American ideals to make American democracy into something that was not restricted to the few but existed for the many.

Their practice and ideas can also be made useful for those who are currently struggling with a sense of political hopelessness or are living under intense constraints, especially those whose rights are tenuous. Walker and Douglass show how to cultivate a language of political critique that identifies and exposes the inner workings of oppression, how to make and remake communities, and how to establish decolonized identities and articulate emancipatory demands in spaces that neither legitimize nor sanction them.

They remind vulnerable citizens that negative emotions like anguish and fear can be important resources for political struggle, that democratic authority is never sanctioned but always seized, and that struggling for individual and collective freedom with a sense of moral responsibility may also require either strategically adapting to, or drawing unexpected sustenance from, the constantly evolving communities and social relationships in which this struggle takes place. Above all else, Walker and Douglass express an idea that is as simple as it is powerful: Struggle can be made possible even in the most impossible places and moments and is an indispensable instrument for democracy.

2

IDA B. WELLS, THE ANTILYNCHING MOVEMENT, AND THE POLITICS OF SEEING

On June 15, 1920, in Duluth, Minnesota, a photograph, which eventually became a widely circulated postcard, captured a crowd of white men smiling for a camera, beside the lifeless and shirtless bodies of two black men hanged from a lamppost; a third lay face down on the ground. Though this lynching was one of the most infamous and gruesome, it was just one of over three thousand, from 1890 through 1930, enacted by white citizens and directed toward black men. Lynching was a horrifying practice that seemed beyond the pale of human imagination. But it had a real social function: to solidify the rule of white supremacy and instill fear in black Americans like Elias Clayton, Elmer Jackson, and Isaac McGhie, who arrived in Duluth as part of a traveling circus. Nat Turner would be executed for a direct act of public resistance to slavery almost ninety years earlier. These workers had done no such thing.[1]

The justification for their lynching was also the culturally dominant one: that black men were raping white women behind closed doors. Time and time again—and in the Duluth case—this justification was revealed to be baseless, a product of white, male, racist fantasies. Yet lynchers also used other justifications, ranging from major allegations like murder to minor ones like burglary, so-called race prejudice,

FIGURE 2.1   Postcard photograph of June 15, 1920, Duluth lynchings.

Source: Image from Minnesota Public Radio, http://news.minnesota.publicradio.org
/projects/2001/06/lynching/olli.shtml.

making threats, rioting, and being irreverent to authority. Most per-
plexing of all, lynching was sometimes committed with no overt reason
in mind, as if to suggest that the murder of black people did not even
require justification.[2]

The Duluth photograph conveys that lynching was a national moral
and political problem, one that exceeded the geographic area of the
American South, where it happened most frequently.[3] The smiles of
the onlookers—as they surround the three dead black bodies—facing
the camera not only revealed the unimaginable darkness of the human
condition but also brazenly posed two questions to many whites across
the nation. Will you *really* punish us for protecting the honor of our
women and our way of life on behalf of our community, even if this is
done in such a gruesome way? If push came to shove, wouldn't *you* do
the same? The federal government's failure to pass antilynching legislation proved that the answer to the first question was a resounding *no*.
And the public support of many newspapers in defense of lynching
throughout the country—which itself reflected the tacit support of this

ritual in many segments of the American population—testified that the answer to the second was a resounding *yes*.

Not all Americans felt similarly. This chapter will discuss someone who devoted her lifework to raising consciousness about lynching and in doing so became one of the most important activist-intellectuals in American history: the African American journalist Ida B. Wells-Barnett. Born to enslaved parents in Holly Springs, Mississippi, in 1862, Wells came to public prominence when, in 1884, she directly resisted the "separate but equal" segregationist logic behind *Plessy v. Ferguson* (1896) a decade before it was decided by the U.S. Supreme Court, by refusing to give up her seat in the "ladies car" of a railroad in Tennessee after she was told by the train's conductor to go to the rear car, designated for "smokers." Then, after one of her black friends, Thomas Moss, was lynched in Memphis in 1892, Wells become a militant antilynching activist, fusing investigative reporting with the burgeoning field of social science to argue that lynching was a form of vigilante justice that desecrated American cultural commitments to the rule of law. Wrong were those who thought lynching was nothing more than a misguided attempt to enforce antiquated, if not frivolous, codes of Southern chivalry enacted by uneducated masses who foolishly believed the machinery of justice was just too slow and procedural to mete out swift punishments.

Wells theorized lynching as a form of racial terrorism aimed against the black community. Her analysis gave way to a progressive political agenda in which Wells attempted to persuade American lawmakers that lynching was a national crime that required national legislation. Wells's words and deeds made it clear that no American, especially no African American intellectual, could stand by idly as black people were murdered in cold blood.

Historians rightly characterize Wells as an exemplary black woman activist who rendered dubious American gender norms and spoke truth to white supremacy and whose words unsettled apathetic American citizens and the political leaders they elected.[4] Others take her to be unique for pushing the boundaries of the black intellectual.[5] Substituting the call for racial accommodation and personal uplift with one of direct political engagement made her the anti–Booker T. Washington.

Doing this in an impassioned manner made her an uncompromising version of W. E. B. Du Bois, who—despite his later conversion to the radical ideologies of pan-Africanism and communism—at the beginning of his career was still very much a race-conscious reformer who cared more about detached sociological work than about direct action.

But resisting American blindness toward lynching—as well as the culture of white supremacy upon which it depended—led her to revise key understandings of American citizenship. If devising a notion of citizenship capable of addressing the problem of action under immense constraint was at the heart of Douglass's and Walker's political thought, then nothing concerned Wells more than developing an emancipatory conception of citizenship capable of countering the problem of extralegal violence in liberal-democratic regimes.

Lynching reflects three acute problems especially common to democracy, a system where "the people" are endowed authority to popular rule.[6] First, there is the problem of vigilantism, where a group of people—irrespective of how much of a numerical minority they are—claim to speak for the entire people of which they are part and act on the basis of some unwritten law of popular sovereignty that threatens collective life. Second, there is the problem of passivity, where individuals and the government that they legitimize either maintain tacit consent or simply turn an apathetic eye toward injustice. Third, in democratic societies the idea of "the people" is always up for negotiation, and visual public spectacles are incredibly powerful for policing the boundaries of community by playing on citizens' emotions such as fear or love.[7] If we consider these problems as telling us something about the risks and unexpected implications of living a life in common with others, then we should also study the specific practices of citizenship—including the mode of action, that is, judgment and deliberation—that can help address them. Nothing preoccupied Wells more than outlining these practices, and the task of this chapter is to highlight them.

In Wells's view, conceptions of democracy that didn't account for the antidemocratic dimensions of instrumental thinking and popular sovereignty were to be rejected. A mode of political judgment that took seriously human complexity was to be embraced. Individuality needed to be reimagined as inviolable human dignity, and punishment needed to be seen from the perspective of its devastating moral effects, its impact on those who experienced it, and its cultural implications for democracy. Citizens needed to appreciate how public shame foreclosed democratic deliberation while recognizing that desire could remake one's commitments and identities in emancipatory ways. Hope needed to be seen as persisting between realistic constraints and continuing to agitate for justice. Adopting these ideas and practices would not guarantee an end to violence or the achievement of democracy. But Wells insisted that they would be an important first step toward this goal.

BLACK WOMAN JOURNALIST

Walker and Douglass were often blind to gender, even if they were not so enamored with black masculinity in ways that led them to endorse black patriarchy. Wells cared deeply about gender equality. But the intensity of her support for expanding the political franchise across gender lines, like the suffragettes of her generation,[8] was only matched by the regularity with which she invoked an essentialist definition of womanhood defined by bourgeois standards—of dutiful mother, meticulous homemaker, and loyal wife—endorsed by many nineteenth-century first-wave feminists. In "Woman's Mission" (1885), she wrote, "no earthly name is so potent to move men's hearts, is sweeter or dearer than that of mother."[9] She continued:

> What is, or should be, woman? Not merely a bundle of flesh and bones, nor a fashion plate, a frivolous inanity, a soulless doll, a heartless coquette—but a strong, bright presence, thoroughly imbued with a sense of her mission on earth and a desire to fill it; an earnest, soulful being, laboring to fit herself for life's duties and burdens, and bearing them faithfully when they do come; but a womanly woman for all that, upholding the banner and striving for the goal of a pure, bright womanhood through all vicissitudes and temptations.[10]

Wells grappled with the question posed by earlier white American feminists: how to construct an image of womanhood that rejects the tyranny of social convention when, paradoxically, social convention—however unjust—is precisely what endows many women with a sense of self and orientation in a male-dominated world.[11] Her answer to this question was as troubling as it was a reflection of her culture. The religiously infused ideals of moral virtue, manifest destiny, and commitment to Western civilization she believed women needed to embody were used as justifications not only for lynching but also for the American imperial excursions of the early twentieth century led by Theodore Roosevelt; for the social work of the temperance advocate Frances Willard; and by the social democrat Jane Addams, who sought to make life livable for the other half—the working poor who were casualties of the massive economic inequality of the Gilded Age. At times, unreconstructed views about normative civilization, which infused Wells's public shaming of white lynchers, themselves expressed overt racism. In the course of highlighting the brutality of lynching, she wrote that

> the red Indian of the Western plains tied his prisoner to the stake, tortured him, and danced in fiendish glee while his victim writhed in the flames. His savage, untutored mind suggested no better way than that of wreaking vengeance upon those who had wronged him. These people knew nothing about Christianity and did not profess to follow its teachings; but such primary laws as they had they lived up to.[12]

But if misogynistic and racist views were not entirely undermined by Wells's arguments, then they were extinguished through her political work as a political journalist, educator, activist, and public speaker at home and abroad in England. Fictitious was the patriarchic myth that a woman properly belonged to the realm of the household, under the supervision of her husband, because, to borrow a misogynistic argument of Aristotle's in *Politics*, she did not have "authority" over the "deliberative faculty," which was crucial for public life.[13] Equally dubious, Wells's activities demonstrated, was the view, to put it in words that Abraham Lincoln once used and that white supremacists would have endorsed, that people of color were "not equal" in "moral or intellectual endowment" to their white counterparts, who understood the virtues of citizenship in an exemplary way.[14]

Immersion in the black bourgeois circles of Memphis—where black culture and business were flourishing—led Wells to develop an ambivalent understanding of political leadership. At times, she echoed much of late nineteenth-century African American thought—ranging from the black nationalist Martin Delany and the pan-Africanist Alexander Crummell to the conservative Booker T. Washington—about the importance of black economic self-sufficiency, which required rugged individualism.[15] The African American citizen, she wrote, "must be taught his power as an industrial and financial factor. He must be shown that the turning of his money into his own coffers strengthens himself."[16]

Later in her career, Wells reversed course, beginning to emphasize citizenship over industrial education. Vocational education in some trade could not replace and was insufficient for acquiring civic virtue. Black freedom could not be bought by better skills; it required agitating politically. Directing her ire toward Washington, she wrote that "industrial education will not stand [the black American] in place of political, civil and intellectual liberty, and he objects to being deprived of fundamental rights of American citizenship to the end that one school for industrial training shall flourish."[17]

Wealth did not necessarily engender good leadership, nor was good leadership a passive activity where one simply modeled the kind of good economic behavior one wished others to adopt. As she asked rhetorically in "Functions of Leadership" (1885), "tell me what material benefit is a 'leader' if he does not, to some extent, devote his time, talent and wealth to the alleviation of the poverty and misery, and elevation of his people."[18] Leaders needed to fight for the common good irrespective of the economic costs and maintain truthfulness in the face of injustice. For Wells, what was needed was more

> men and women who are willing to sacrifice time, pleasure and property to a realization of it; who are above bribes and demagoguery; who seek not political preferment nor personal aggrandizement; whose

natural courage is strong enough to tell the race plainly yet kindly of its failings and maintain a stand for truth, honor and virtue.[19]

Wells's view of political responsibility also was deeply iconoclastic for its time. A rallying cry for Progressives was that without deeds, political change would only be a nascent idea. Few could deny something even deeper: Without words, ideas were impossible. In the cutthroat, highly lucrative market of the newspaper industry in the 1890s, words of "yellow journalism" were tools of incitement and sensation. No scruples existed when propagating the right falsehood—however egregious—to make an extra buck. Suffering was plentiful, easily exploitable, and emotionally resonating. Wells disagreed:

> If indeed "the pen is mightier than the sword," the time has come as never before that the wielders of the pen belonging to the race which is so tortured and outraged, should take serious thought and purposeful action. The blood, tears and groans of hundreds of the murdered cry to you for redress; the lamentations, distress and want, of numberless widows and orphans appeal to you to do the only thing which can be done—and which is the first step toward revolution of every kind—the creation of a healthy public sentiment.[20]

Responsible journalism meant not preying upon but amplifying and attending to the complex suffering of those who were the most vulnerable—children, who couldn't freely exercise their rights without parental authority, or those, such as orphans and widows, whose rights were deeply compromised, if ever guaranteed, for example, the New York City tenement slum populations that were the subject of Danish-American Jacob Riis's widely influential book of photojournalism *How the Other Half Lives* (1890).

Riis's photographs helped outrage the public, but his own disdain for and sometimes racist view of the immigrants he photographed raises two important interrelated questions: Might registering the suffering of vulnerable populations keep intact ideologies of racial or class hierarchy? Cannot one overlook the complex nuances of oppression or speak problematically on behalf of those whose voices can't be heard?[21] Wells understood these problems without any formal philosophical training years before they received their most influential articulation by one of the most esteemed American philosophers of her generation, William James.

In an 1899 talk, "On a Certain Blindness in Human Beings," James recalled how visiting the North Carolina countryside made him appreciate the fact of human finitude, the limitation of fully knowing people's experiences and motivations. After speaking to a mountaineer in the region, what James initially believed was nothing more than an ugly open field expressive of squalor was revealed to be a manifestation of resilience, "a symbol redolent with moral memories and [that] sang a very pæan of duty, struggle, and success."[22]

Technologies meant to improve our understanding of the world—the motion picture, photojournalism, and newspaper circulation—gave rise to the collective myth in the 1890s that everything could be fully known. Knowledge was less in a state of crisis than it was considered an antidote to suffering. Much like James transformed his own intellectual blindness about human plurality into an argument for greater humility about human knowledge, Wells turned the limitations of journalism (the creation of the public sentiment was the "only thing which can be done") into an argument for activism. Sometimes she put this point more directly to the reader: "You can help disseminate the facts . . . by bringing them to the knowledge of every one with whom you come in contact, to the end that public sentiment may be revolutionized. Let the facts speak for themselves, with you as a medium."[23]

Activism, for Wells, was a condition through which to minimize suffering rather than to speak for those who experienced it. The only thing the activist could do was to mobilize the public sentiments of outrage and shame to address the national disease of injustice—and this was possible because emotions were incredibly powerful. "Public sentiment," Wells wrote, "is stronger than the law."[24] The best thing the activist could do was to appreciate his or her own epistemological limitations.

Both positions stemmed from Wells's deeply held commitment to democratic individualism. Moving from passivity to action was both a

possibility for all—whites and blacks, leaders and ordinary citizens—
and it had to emerge from within rather than be imposed from without.
"Do you ask the remedy?" for lynching, she wondered. Her answer: "A
public sentiment strong against lawlessness must be aroused. Every individual can contribute to this awakening."[25]

THE BRUTAL CONTRADICTIONS OF DEMOCRACY

Few Americans were as concerned as Wells with the fate of democracy,
even at a time in U.S. history when the term was being hotly contested.
In the late nineteenth century, reformers tried to bring to American
shores the social-egalitarian democratic vision implicit in the French
Revolution's declaration of liberty, equality, and fraternity.[26] For some,
nothing mattered more than regulating the excesses of monopoly capitalism and big business of the Gilded Age, which many believed were
responsible for social ills.[27]

Yet Progressive reformers would be met with vociferous intellectual
resistance. For William Graham Sumner, social democracy's redistri-
bution of wealth encouraged political mediocrity that only led to bad
decisions. Reformers, Sumner lamented, ignored the "faults" of poor
people, while the person "who raises himself above poverty appears" to
them of "no account."[28] Sumner cared little for the plight of African
Americans and even less for those lynched in the Deep South. But had
he paid attention to Wells he would have learned that the virtues he ex-
tolled in capitalism did not simply unleash equal opportunity and pros-
perity for all but led to excruciating violence for some. A smaller-scale
version of those "captains of industry" Sumner championed in "The
Absurd Effort to Make the World Over" (1894) for their "power to command, courage and fortitude" were, as Wells described, the very leaders
of the bloodthirsty lynch mob.[29] "On Wednesday afternoon a meeting
of citizens was held," Wells explained in a speech in Boston, "Lynch
Law in All Its Phases" (1893), delivered one year before Sumner's article
was published: "It was not an assemblage of hoodlums or irresponsible

fire-eaters, but solid, substantial business men who knew exactly what they were doing and who were far more indignant at the villainous insult to the women of the south than they would have been at any injury done themselves."[30]

Less a critique of the economic inequality capitalism produced, Wells's observation disclosed the instrumental logic at the heart of lynching: that people could simply be manipulated for one's benefit rather than be considered as possessing inherent, inviolable human value, that is, be seen as ends in themselves. The young Marx believed this phenomenon was actually a chief function of capitalism, which treated workers as objects to be profited from and which made them see one another as exchangeable commodities. As he put it famously: "In estranging from man . . . his own active functions, his life-activity, estranged labor [under capitalism] estranges the species from man."[31] The black body, for Wells, was rendered into an inanimate object that had little moral status—much like the commodities workers were producing. Wells wrote: "The finding of the dead body of a Negro, suspended between heaven and earth to the limb of a tree, is of so slight importance that neither the civil authorities nor press agencies consider the matter worth investigating."[32] The deliberate, amoral, methodical mutilation of a black body—part by part—without any qualms represented a perversion of hyperrationalism and detachment. Lynching, Wells wrote, "is not the creature of an hour, the sudden outburst of uncontrolled fury, or the unspeakable brutality of an insane mob. It represents the cool, calculating deliberation of intelligent people."[33]

The rational violence of lynching, its ordered chaos, rendered dubious Jane Addams's explanation that lynching represented a moment of unhinged emotion. Addams was wrong, Wells explained, when she said that "human nature gives way under such awful provocation and that the mob, insane for the moment, must be pitied as well as condemned."[34] A tragic view of democracy—in which individuals were seen as vulnerable to passion and lapses of judgment—was the subtext of Addams's explanation, but Wells saw that the tragic denial of democratic freedom and psychological security to African Americans stemmed from the same logic that denied it to the poor people Addams wished to save. "It is strange," Wells continued, "that an intelligent, law-abiding, and fair minded people should so persistently shut their eyes to the facts in the discussion of what the civilized world now concedes to be America's national crime."[35]

Few moments in American history saw such an increase in philosophical defenses of unbridled individualism, but the late nineteenth century was also the age of the crowd. Seeing firsthand the spectacular crowds of the late nineteenth century—the lynch mob, newly arrived Irish immigrants living in close quarters, angry laborers, starving children—must have heightened Wells's appreciation about the way that the abstract idea of "the people" is distinct from the institutions it claims to legitimize and can be seized by whoever speaks on its behalf.[36] The crowd, which crystallized the problem of popular rule, frightened one of Wells's contemporaries, the French sociologist Gustave Le Bon, who argued in his classic study *The Crowd* (1895) that it captured how individuals deferred their personal responsibility to an unthinking collective, a condition in which reason was entirely absent and impulsiveness reigned supreme. "In the collective mind the intellectual aptitudes of the individuals, and in consequence their individuality," Le Bon wrote, "are weakened. The heterogeneous is swamped by the homogenous and the unconscious qualities retain the upper hand."[37] But for Wells the problem was the exact opposite: the ability of democratic popular sovereignty to encourage a troubling perception of individual judgment.

Wells asked rhetorically: "Who sits in judgment on the 'supposed' character of the lynched. . . . Who 'supposes' the victims of lynch law are bad characters? Those who suppose they are justified in murdering them, and must have some excuse for their crimes."[38] Democracy is usually associated with good judgments: citizens giving reasons for who they elect, how they rule directly, or—in a more legalistic sense—juries and judges giving rationales for their verdicts. However, if we take seriously the notion that all citizens—for better or worse—should have the authority of judgment, regardless of the way it is exercised, then calls to justify citizens' judgments can be treated with contempt.

The lynchers' judgment is distorted because one can insist that democracy is as much defined by the authority to make judgments about one's polity as it is through a respect of the rule of law—the latter being what lynchers reject. But the lynch mob's insistence on sovereign judgment may follow, even if not logically, from the idea of popular rule and the populist individualist culture in which it emerged.[39] Late nineteenth-century critiques of tyrannical elite rule morphed into the widespread view that ordinary citizens had all the right answers, as if this was uncontested.[40] Note Wells's word choice when referring to five black men lynched in 1893: "They were simply lynched by parties of men who had it in their power to kill them, and who chose to avenge some fancied wrong by murder, rather than submit their grievances to court."[41] Lynchers "simply" lynch and "chose" to avenge "some fancied" murder, with no second thoughts about the validity of their judgment to do so. The lynch mob, in Wells's depiction, provided the dark counterexample to Walker: Sovereign judgment does not aid in racial emancipation but rather justifies racially based murder and the perpetuation of white supremacy.

Central to lynching was also the democratic problem of collective inaction. If lynchers were a minority faction who enacted the will of the silent white majority, or what the sociologist Emile Durkheim called the "collective consciousness,"[42] then that tacit consent undermined a liberal, pluralistic society. Wells believed tacit consent could undermine, rather than enable, individual freedom.[43] Nowhere was this clearer than in the lynching of Eph. Gizzard. She recalled how "they took him from jail without resistance, dragged him through the streets, plunged knives deep into his body, and rained blows and kicks on him at every step; the militia and police, State and civil authorities looked on unmoved and inert."[44] If the mob's passivity arises from the seduction of anonymity that Alexis de Tocqueville brilliantly argued characterized democratic societies—where "all the citizens are independent and feeble; they can do hardly anything by themselves, and none of them can oblige his fellow men to lend him their assistance"[45]—then, for Wells, this desire for anonymity is what accounts for democracy's unequal dispensation of violence and unimaginable cruelty. For Wells, passive bystanders were as guilty as the murderers:

The men and women in the South who disapprove of lynching and remain silent on the perpetuation of such outrages, are particeps criminis, accomplices, accessories before and after the fact, equally guilty with the actual law-breakers who would not persist if they did not know that neither the law nor the militia would be employed against them.[46]

Racial tyranny was perpetuated through a radical kind of passivity where neither the state nor citizens interfered in the face of injustice. As Wells put it, when comparing lynching to slavery, "the same tyrant is at work under a new name and guise. The lawlessness which has been here described is like unto that which prevailed under slavery. *The very same forces are at work now as then.*"[47] For this reason, Wells believed a renewed commitment to the rule of law was necessary: "It is a well-established principle of law that every wrong has a remedy. Herein rests our respect for law. . . . In lynching, opportunity is not given the Negro to defend himself against the unsupported accusations of white men and women."[48]

ENVISIONING DEMOCRACY

Wells's attempts to reframe citizens' understandings of democracy were deepened by an alternative view of democratic judgment. Before W. E. B. Du Bois's first scholarly work, *The Philadelphia Negro* (1899), so richly deployed social-scientific data to account for the complexity and struggles of African American life in Philadelphia, there were Wells's essays, which signaled the unprecedented potential of social science to become a vehicle for political change.[49] Dispassionate empirical thinking, Wells and the early Du Bois believed, obviously had the advantage of rhetorically countering the passion of the lynch mob. The preface to Wells's *A Red Record* asserted that the text was "a contribution to truth, an array of facts, the perusal of which it is hoped will stimulate this great American Republic to demand that justice be done though the heavens fall."[50] Making good on this claim, throughout the text, a bold headline for the cause of lynching—"rape," "murder," "incendiarism," "burglary," "race prejudice," "quarreling with white men," "making threats," "riot-ing," "miscegenation," and "no reasons given," among many others—would be followed by nothing more than the date when it occurred and the name and location of the person who was lynched.[51]

Fiery indignation was at the heart of Walker's call to the black masses, and moral suasion defined Douglass's early writings to appeal to white people's sympathy, but a no-nonsense, cerebral appeal to people's natu-ral reason, which assumed them capable of personally enacting critical interpretation, defined Wells's approach: "To those who are not willfully blind and unjustly critical, the record of more than a thousand lynch-ings in ten years is enough to justify any peaceable movement tending to ameliorate the conditions which led to this unprecedented slaughter of human beings."[52] Disinterest could enable one carefully to assess competing perspectives and validity claims to arrive at a reliable under-standing.[53] So too could it animate civic love toward those who one had never met but who mattered as members of a collective polity.

But Wells did not simply stop with outlining the facts—as Du Bois had in *The Philadelphia Negro*. This was because lynching was as much a problem of knowledge (of inadequate facts) as it was of spectacle. On the one hand, there was the sensational and complex range of emotional responses that lynching produced—sadness, despair, laughter, shame, or joy—for those who participated in or simply looked at photographs of the rite. On the other hand, there was the spectacularly lifeless, tor-mented black body that had nothing to say, which perpetuated the cul-tural image of blacks as abject and voiceless and created space for white Americans to advance their own narratives about black identity. But what kind of optics of seeing could encourage a more democratic future, one in which freedom could be expanded across racial lines?

Wells's answer entailed transforming William James's philosophical project of radical empiricism into a political tool. James proposed that all philosophical reasoning—its questions, propositions, and arguments—must be determined by experience. In his famous definition of what he called "radical empiricism," he described how "the only things that shall be debatable among philosophers shall be things definable in terms drawn from experience."[54] Experience is not only the source of knowledge, but it creates the limits of what kind of knowledge is even possible.[55]

Wells went further. First, she highlighted the plurality of unseen experiences to disclose black complexity, of which vulnerability was central. In Henry Smith's lynching in Paris, Texas, for instance, she brought into relief not only the cruelty of the lynch mob but the cruelty of Smith's mental illness, making vivid that beneath his unimaginable deed of murdering a four-year-old girl was someone who was emotionally unstable—himself in need of compassion rather than punishment. "This man was charged with outraging and murdering a four-year-old white child, covering her body with brush, sleeping beside her through the night, then making his escape."[56]

Sometimes psychological vulnerability was a product of structural circumstances. Hamp Biscoe, a "hard working, thrifty" black farmer from Arkansas who lost his property after a dispute over an unpaid debt to a realtor who claimed to sell him the land, became increasingly anxious and agitated. After he and his wife were lynched after he had shot a white constable, John Ford, who attempted to enter his land to arrest him after repeated warnings not to, Wells described Biscoe's psychological state as follows: "The suit, judgment and subsequent legal proceedings appear to have driven Biscoe almost crazy and brooding over his wrongs he grew to be a confirmed imbecile. He would allow but a few men, white or colored, to come upon his place, as he suspected every stranger to planning to steal his farm."[57] Beneath the act of resisting arrest was a complex person. The threat of serious economic deprivation, if not homelessness, combined with the ensuing sense of despair destroyed Biscoe's sense of self-worth. The feeling that his perspective was being denied by the courts—"Biscoe denied the service and refused to pay the demand"—reflected Biscoe's sense of dignity.

Second, rather than view political thought as something emanating from reasonable speculation, urging one to think abstractly about hypothetical people living out hypothetical scenarios, Wells followed Douglass in arguing for embodied experience to drive political thinking. Douglass's belief was that doing this would pluralize monolithic definitions of freedom, but Wells wanted experience to be *the* test for the existence of justice. The sad state of the American legal system, epitomized by the U.S. Supreme Court's embarrassing support of Jim Crow in *Plessy*, made futile any appeal to equal legal protection supposedly guaranteed by the Fourteenth Amendment. The measure of justice, Wells insisted, needed to be how it affected (or was undermined through) living, breathing, and suffering bodies: "Repeated [physical] attacks on life, liberty and happiness of any citizen or class of citizens," Wells declared, "are attacks on distinctive American institutions; such attacks imperiling as they do the foundation of government, law and order, merit thoughtful consideration of far-sighted Americans."[58]

Third, Wells sought to shift people's vision away from the brutal immediacy of lynching and toward its larger but unseen cultural implications. Viewing the dangling lifeless black body could have led some to feel outrage or enjoyment. These emotional responses could stifle an examination of what lynching reflected about the human condition. Wells wanted to encourage the opposite, showing how the lynched body was a test case for American democracy. Eph. Gizzard was

> dragged through the streets in broad daylight, knives plunged into him at every step, and with every fiendish cruelty a frenzied mob could devise, he was at last swung out on the bridge with hands cut to pieces as he tried to climb up the stanchians. A naked, bloody example of the blood-thirstiness of the nineteenth century civilization of the Athens of the South.[59]

Wells's account of the lynching places one in the position to see not what the lynch victim does to deserve punishment but what deservingness means culturally. The frenzied stabbing and puncturing of a human being's delicate flesh and the dismembering of his hands describes the relative ease with which a fragile body that houses a person could be denigrated in a nation where liberal, democratic self-congratulation about American exceptionalism was widespread. "A large portion of the American people," she wrote elsewhere, "avow anarchy, condone murder and defy the contempt of civilization."[60] Gizzard's brutalized body testified to the way the liberal idea of bodily security was violated rather than preserved through warm shelter and nutritious food; how apathy, rather than compassion, was supreme; how unrestraint, rather than temperance, defined American public behavior.

Something similar was at work in Wells's skillful depiction of a lynch mob's attempt to capture Robert Charles, who became a fugitive after he refused to be arrested on his front porch for suspicious behavior by New Orleans police:

> The mob held the city in its hands and went about holding up street cars and searching them, taking from them colored men upon the public square, through alleys and into houses of anybody who would take them in, breaking into the homes of defenseless colored men and women and beating aged and decrepit men and women to death.[61]

The narrative highlights the mob's assault on the following vaunted American ideals: the city as a public, pluralistic space that allows for freedom of mobility; the protection from illegal search and seizure; the notion of private property; the idea of habeas corpus.

After reading Wells, few could deny that lynching was not only a highly stylized performance, a ritualized rite with defined rules and symbols—a culture unto itself within American culture—repeated over and over again, but that the thrill and pleasure this rite induced reflected the link between violence and self-expression (it was a creative act), personal identity (one had a sense of who they were by knowing they were not the person lynched), and membership in a community. This was reflected in the death of Lee Walker, who was lynched in Memphis after two women claimed that he had assaulted them after they refused to give him something to eat: "The crowd hurled expletives at him, swung the body so that it was dashed against the pole, and, so far from the ghastly sight proving trying to the nerves, the crowd looked on with complaisance, if not really pleasure."[62] And in that of Ed Coy in Arkansas: "The men and boys amused themselves for some time sticking knives into Coy's body and slicing off pieces of flesh. When they had amused themselves sufficiently, they poured coal oil over him and the woman in the case set fire to him."[63] Punctured flesh and shattered bones become a reflection of one's imagination: The more unique the violence, the greater feeling of identity. Recognition in public—from those who were moved in pleasurable ways—creates a community.

HORROR, DISBELIEF, AND SHAME

Describing lynching through the genre of horror was the way Wells sought to inspire citizens to act to achieve racial justice. Horror, according to the contemporary American philosopher Stanley Cavell, is a perception that relates to the "precariousness of human identity," that this identity can be "lost or invaded," that "we may be, or may become, something other than what we are, or take ourselves for; that our origins as human beings need accounting for, and are unaccountable."[64] Horror does not immediately appear to be valuable for expanding the polity democratically. The feeling of precariousness horror encourages seems to counter the thoughtful and reasoned reflection necessary for collective rule, while visceral disgust may or may not lead one to struggle for social justice.

Upton Sinclair never expressed ambivalence about horror's democratic potential. Groundbreaking less for its narrative style, metaphor, and plot and more for its influence on American politics, Sinclair's pseudojournalistic novel *The Jungle* (1906), which portrayed in fiction working-class people working under brutal conditions in the meat industry—where unsanitized factories mixed animal feces and other vectors of disease into food—helped inspire the U.S. Congress to pass both the Meat Inspection Act and the Pure Food and Drug Act. Sinclair juxtaposed the way factory workers were "part of the machine . . . and every faculty that was not needed for the machine was doomed to be crushed out of existence" with the "thousands of rats [that] would race about" the "meat stored in great piles in rooms."[65] Horror, for Sinclair, became a genre through which to blur a sacred boundary between human and animal.

Less concerned with adopting Sinclair's attempt to create a parallel between human and animal, Wells was interested in developing what was implied in his novel: the ways that horrifying human identities were constituted through a process over which they had no choice or control. An example of this was captured in her description of the Sam Hose lynching in Atlanta, Georgia—an African American worker who killed his white employer, Alfred Cranford, after a tense dispute about his wages:

> First he was made to remove his clothing, and when the flames began to eat into his body it was almost nude. Before the fire was lighted his left ear was severed from his body. Then his right ear was cut away. . . . The scene that followed is one that never will be forgotten by those who saw it, and while Sam Hose writhed and performed contortions in his agony, many of those present turned away from the sickening sight, and others could hardly look at it. Not a sound but the crackling of the flames broke the stillness of the place, and the situation grew more sickening as it proceeded. . . . He writhed in agony and his sufferings can be imagined when it is said that several blood vessels burst during the contortions of his body. When he fell from the stake he was kicked back and the flames renewed. Then it was that the flames consumed his body and in a few minutes only a few bones and a small part of the body was all that was left of Sam Hose.
>
> One of the most sickening sights of the day was the eagerness with which the people grabbed after souvenirs, and they almost fought over the ashes of the dead criminal. Large pieces of his flesh were carried away, and persons were seen walking through the streets carrying bones in their hands.
>
> When all the larger bones, together with the flesh, had been carried away by the early comers, others scraped in the ashes, and for a great length of time a crowd was about the place scraping in the ashes. Not even the stake to which the Negro was tied when burned was left, but it was promptly chopped down and carried away as the largest souvenir of the burning.[66]

Hearing news of the Hose lynching, Du Bois rushed to deliver a well-ordered, legalistic statement about the facts of the case to the white journalist and children's book author Joel Chandler Harris, to be published in the *Atlanta Constitution*. A gruesome sight made him stop dead in his tracks. Just up the road, Hose's knuckles were being displayed in a grocery-store window. Turning back immediately, Du Bois became convinced that the detached social-scientific work that had informed *The Philadelphia Negro* was unconscionable.[67] *The Souls of Black Folk* (1903), the collection of essays published four years later, expressed Du Bois's conversion from naïve social scientist to political activist. In that text, critical analysis mixed with experimental prose to create a stream-of-consciousness account of the lived experience of race as a kind of double consciousness: of being both black and American.[68]

Rather than simply humanize black Americans as did Du Bois, Wells described how black dehumanization was less an a priori truth and more a meticulous white supremacist social construction. Highlighting the intensity and methodical accuracy with which they dismembered Hose's body piecemeal also reflected the *wish* to excise black people from humanity. Publicly destroying black bodies communicated white anxiety about black equality. If black inferiority were truly a biological phenomenon that could not be changed (according to social Darwinist theories of scientific racism that were taken seriously, black men were hypersexual, intellectually feeble, lazy, immature, duplicitous, and criminal), then the symbolic act of lynching seemed unnecessary.[69] Dehumanization thus had to be achieved. Wells's language illuminated this clearly when she told how six black men in Memphis "were made the target of murderous shotguns, which fired into the writhing, struggling, dying mass of humanity, until every spark of life was gone."[70] Strategically using the passive voice—black men were "made the target of" as opposed to them "being targeted"—emphasizes the process of how human beings were made lifeless despite their protests. Giving agency to an inanimate instrument of violence—it was the shotgun, not the person that "fired"—blurred the line, if not creating striking parallels, between the lynchers and the guns they used. Lynching, in other words, had brutal effects on lynchers.

The imagined white masculine moral virtue that led to lynching was the same thing that eroded white Americans' moral sense. What at first was expressed publicly and in racially specific ways could soon come to know no boundaries. "The beast of prey which turns to destroy its own is not considered less," she wrote in another context, "but more blood-thirsty and ferocious than when it preys on other animals. The taste for blood grows with indulgence, and when other means of satisfying it fail he turns to rend his own household."[71] Violence offers no durable sense of identity, but it entirely infuses one's personality and social relation-ships.[72] People "forget that a concession of the right to lynch a man for a certain crime," Wells told readers, "concedes the right to lynch any person for any crime."[73]

Identifying this interconnected process of black and white dehuman-ization was part of Wells's larger unifying rhetorical objective: the cre-ation of disbelief. The following statement captured this perfectly:

> When that poor Afro-American was murdered, the whites excused their refusal of a trial on the ground that they wished to spare the white girl the mortification of having to testify in court.
>
> This cry has had its effect. It has closed the heart, stifled the con-science, warped the judgment and hushed the voice of press and pulpit on the subject of lynch law throughout this "land of liberty." Men who stand high in the esteem of the public for Christian character, for moral and physical courage, or devotion to the principles of equal and exact justice to all, and for great sagacity, stand as cowards who fear to open their mouths before this great outcry. They do not see that by their tacit encouragement, their silent acquiescence, the black shadow of lawless-ness in the form of lynch law is spreading its wings over the whole country.[74]

Disbelief upends conventional ways of understanding the world. Link-ing the distorted body of the lynched victim with that of the passive citizen in the above passage—whose "closed" heart and "stifled" con-science parallels the lifeless heart of the dead lynched victim whose conscience no longer exists, whose "warped" judgment parallels the contorted body of the lynched victim, whose silence and gaping mouth parallels the lynched victim's limp face—Wells forced American read-ers, who stood by idly without agitating politically while their fellow compatriots were being lynched, to see themselves in jarring ways. If Americans were prepared to ask themselves the questions that such recognition might yield—Is this really what we've become? How can we support this?—Wells hoped that they would find a way to change.

This passage, however, also revealed Wells's thinking about shame. If Douglass in *My Bondage and My Freedom* was optimistic that white males' sense of shame at violating their masculine and racial superiority could create a space for black freedom—Covey was ashamed to let any of his friends know about the fight with Douglass, which allowed Douglass to continue plotting his escape—Wells worried that it would do exactly the opposite. The sense of character deficit that shame conjures could be paralyzing, forcing people to withdraw from critical examination rather than engage in it.[75]

Shame at violating the expectations that arose from the misogynistic view that women were too fragile and too traumatized to speak about the trauma they experienced kept in place, rather than exploded, these misogynistic assumptions.[76] "*The white people won't stand for this sort of thing,*" she wrote, "*and whether they be insulted as individuals or as a race, the response will be prompt and effectual.*"[77] This extended across racial lines. "Even to the better class of Afro-Americans the crime of rape is so revolting," Wells wrote, "they have too often taken the white man's word and given lynch law neither the investigation nor condemnation it deserved."[78] Shame had a chilling effect on democratic deliberation: No one wanted to talk about rape, examine whether it truly occurred, or force the alleged victim to relive her experience because doing this would challenge the expectation of women's lack of agency and threaten the fantasy of male chivalry. Neither lynching nor the masculine myths upon which it rested could ever fully be examined and rejected.[79]

THE BONDS OF INTIMACY

Jim Crow segregation is usually recalled for its tactics of political disenfranchisement, its racially based economic inequality, and the public humiliation to which it subjected Southern blacks. But it was also about the private realm, of which the policing of human intimacy was crucial. Lynching may have been predicated upon the white supremacist fantasy that black men wished to rape white women, but the existence of anti-miscegenation laws made apparent that the mundane fact of interracial relationships was an egregious transgression of the deeply etched line of racial difference. Many whites took this crime to be more sinful than the so-called unspeakable crime of rape.[80]

Wells rendered this line of racial difference fictitious by exposing the inescapable interracial intimacy that existed beyond and against the written law. "In numerous instances where colored men have been lynched on the charge of rape," she wrote, "it was positively known at the time of lynching, and indisputably proven after the victim's death, that the relationship sustained between the man and woman was voluntary and clandestine, and that in no court of law could even the charge of assault have been successfully maintained."[81] Not only was interracial love voluntary, but Wells described how it was frequently instigated by women. Casting women as conscious agents in interracial encounters reversed the male fantasy of women's passivity and undermined the racist myth of black men's uncontrollable hypersexual desire. Wells quoted Mrs. J. C. Underwood of Ohio, who first accused an African American of raping her but eventually confessed that "he made a proposal to me and I readily consented . . . in fact I could have resisted, and had no desire to resist . . . I hoped to save my reputation by telling you a deliberate lie."[82]

Furthermore, Wells depicted how human intimacy could not be completely regulated by racial segregation because intimacy was fundamental to and pervasive in everyday human interactions. Antimiscegenation laws could never stifle the brief but impossible-to-control everyday act of intimacy like the smile, which also became one reason for lynching:

> The truth remains that Afro-American men do not always rape [?] white women without their consent . . . there are many white women in the South who would marry colored men if such an act would not place them at once beyond the pale of society and within the clutches of the law. . . . When men lynch the offending Afro American, [they do

so] not because he is a despoiler of virtue, but because he succumbs to the smiles of white women.[83]

Smiling can be an invitation to friendship or an expression of flirtation; it can also sometimes be quite trivial, nothing more than a reflexive gesture of neighborliness into which one doesn't put much thought.

Here and throughout her writings, Wells transformed desire into something untethered to racial identification. Nowhere was this more apparent than in the example of a white woman, Sarah Clark of Memphis, who "loved a black man and lived openly with him," and "when she was indicted last spring for miscegenation she swore in court that she was *not* a white woman."[84] Desire was not simply a threat to standards of piety and self-control championed by some Progressives. Desire was also a creative force, unleashing the self that racial identity imprisoned in new directions and opening it to new experiences, roles, and possibilities. Strict adherence to race dictated the range of pleasures one could partake in, but adherence to pleasure could remake one's identity, as was clear with Clark's renouncement of her whiteness. As much as this was a form of privilege unequally enacted—as it would have been impossible for Clark's black lover—it nonetheless was an embrace of vulnerability.[85] Race created boundaries defined by hierarchy, while intimacy made one precarious—Clark's connection to a community was much easier and less risky than the connection to her lover, who could have left her at any moment or betrayed her in a much more emotionally devastating way. Choosing the riskier of two options—rejecting whiteness and spurning her community—constituted an acceptance of the unknown along with its dangers and beautiful possibilities.[86]

HOPE AND THE POLITICS OF STRUGGLE

The same year that the founder of the periodical *The New Republic*, Herbert Croly, would crystallize in *The Promise of American Life* (1909) the ideal of political hope that drove the Progressive movement, the

NAACP (National Association for Colored People) was founded partly as a response to government inaction toward lynching. For the American, Croly wrote, "the better future, which is promised for himself, his children, and for other Americans, is chiefly a matter of confident anticipation. . . . The better future is understood by him as something which fulfills itself."[87] For the NAACP and Wells, who was also one of the organization's first signatories (though she did come to believe it to be more moderate and less radical than she had wished), hope instead straddled the line between realistically acknowledging and attending to society's tragic limitations while dreaming of a brighter future to come. As Wells told her readers at the conclusion of *A Red Record*:

> Think and act on independent lines in this behalf, remembering that after all, it is the white man's civilization and the white man's government which are on trial. This crusade will determine whether that civilization can maintain itself by itself, or whether anarchy shall prevail; whether this Nation shall write itself down a success at self government, or in deepest humiliation admit its failure complete; whether the precepts and theories of Christianity are professed and practiced by American white people as Golden Rules of thought and action, or adopted as a system of morals to be preached to, heathen until they attain to the intelligence which needs the system of Lynch Law.[88]

Wells, unlike Croly, had no reason to believe that progress was a given, especially where race was concerned. But, while under threat from the violent uncivil mobs that she denounced, Wells would continue using the pen and the podium to speak against a national racial problem that many Americans did not see as a serious political issue.[89] She spoke to packed halls in England, worked to resuscitate the National Equal Rights League, founded the Negro Fellowship League, and unsuccessfully campaigned for an Illinois state senate seat in 1930. A similar sense of hope informed the NAACP legislative agenda of reform: It successfully persuaded the U.S. House to pass the Dyer Bill in 1922, which would have made lynching a federal crime (before it was filibustered to death in the U.S. Senate), and it was instrumental for drafting the

Costigan-Wagner Bill in 1934, which would have held federal trials for law-enforcement officials who failed to act during a lynching but which floundered after the highest-ranking Democrat in office, President Franklin Delano Roosevelt, refused to lend it his support given his fear of alienating Southern Democrats, who were a crucial part of his governing coalition. Yet, Wells's activism and the activism of the broader antilynching movement to achieve the impossible embodied a sense of hope that understood practical constraints but nonetheless consistently pushed against the boundaries of the dominant enactments of politics, which called for deferring to the logic of what existed rather than aiming toward a future that didn't yet.

EXTRALEGAL VIOLENCE AND THE AMERICAN POLITY

For Americans today, lynching appears to be a distant part of a racist American past that has been slowly, even if unevenly and incompletely, addressed over the past century. This distance has been marked even further through what has become in contemporary American politics the only tactic of grappling with historical racial injustice: the official state apology. Too radical was the prospect of giving monetary reparations to the descendants of lynching victims. So in 2005 the U.S. Senate took a symbolic route, apologizing for the federal government's repeated historic failure to enact federal antilynching legislation.

The event was not without its irony. After all, lynching has not been eliminated from American society. The brutal murder of a fourteen-year-old African American boy, Emmett Till, in Money, Mississippi, in 1955 for smiling at a white woman at a grocery store may now be a distant memory for some, but many still remember the not-so-distant murder of Yusef Hawkins, a sixteen-year-old African American who was beaten and shot to death by a mob of white men in 1989, when he entered a white Italian-American neighborhood, Bensonhurst, in Brooklyn, New York—because the mob suspected that he was dating a local white Italian woman. Even fewer can forget what happened a decade later, in 1998, when three unabashed white supremacists in Jasper, Texas, tied a forty-nine-year-old African American man, James Byrd Jr., to the back of their pickup truck and dragged his body across asphalt for three miles. His crime: walking along the side of the road. As much as a symbolic act, lynching also still works as a powerful symbol: In 2006, several nooses were discovered hanging from trees around a public high school in Jena, Louisiana, after a black student, who was part of the 10 percent black student population there, decided to sit beneath a tree that some of his classmates had somehow deemed the exclusive property of the white student population.

It is correct to associate lynching first and foremost with racism, but the deeper problems that it reflects about American democracy still remain. We are still grappling with the issue of vigilante justice when groups like the Minutemen—citizens with no state-sanctioned authority—patrol the U.S.-Mexico border in search of Mexican migrants or when a neighborhood watchman like George Zimmerman kills an unarmed black teenager, Trayvon Martin, in Sanford, Florida, in 2012, for what he perceived as Martin's suspicious behavior. We have also witnessed the way violence has been used as a public spectacle to police the boundaries of normative ideas about sexuality, like the 1998 violent homophobic killing of a gay Wyoming college student, Matthew Shepard, and to instill fear into populations who do not express these norms, from the Islamophobic attack on a Sikh temple in Oak Creek, Wisconsin, in 2012 by a white supremacist that left six people dead to the more recent Charleston, South Carolina, church shooting, which saw another white supremacist gun down nine African Americans at a historic black church in June 2015.

Without question—compared to the early twentieth century—the American government has taken a much more active role in addressing such violence. In the aftermath of the Civil Rights Act of 1968, many states have put into effect hate-crime laws that—in conjunction with those at the federal level—add harsher penalties for crimes committed with the intention to discriminate against people based on everything from race, gender, sexuality, disability, religion, and ethnicity. Yet one wonders whether such laws are enough when they cannot themselves alter the attitudes toward citizenship.

Wells offers some insights into what shifts might be necessary. Citizens need to acknowledge how instrumental thinking can create apathetic behavior, how popular sovereignty can lead to violence, and how injustice can exist through collective inaction. And they would need to attend to human complexity and vulnerability, all while being cognizant of the political limitations of shame and the power of human intimacy. In Wells's view, such a practice of citizenship was strenuous, but it was necessary for all those concerned with the fate of U.S. democracy. Silence was not an option, as Wells told readers: "Can you remain silent and inactive when such things are done in our community and country? Is your duty to humanity in the United States less binding? What can you do, reader, to prevent lynching, to thwart anarchy and promote law and order throughout our land?"[90]

3

HUEY NEWTON, THE BLACK PANTHERS, AND THE DECOLONIZATION OF AMERICA

An iconic photograph taken in 1967 captured everything Americans thought they knew about Huey P. Newton, the minister of defense and founding member of the Black Panther Party for Self-Defense, which was created in 1966. Seated in a peacock wicker chair, adorned in a leather jacket, white collared shirt, jeans, and his signature beret, tilted to the right, while holding a rifle in his right hand and spear in his left, the twenty-five-year-old Newton looks directly ahead at the camera, unflinching; a zebra skin lies at his feet. This photo was the cultural image of Black Power—aggressive, stoic, and centered on a militant form of self-defense, which tried to combine elements of African and modern culture to liberate black Americans from the repressive American state and capitalist system that was pushing them toward a slow death.[1]

In the late 1960s, few American groups were as militant and loud in their opposition to American society as the Black Panthers. And Americans heard them. White liberals patting themselves on the back about their progressive racial thinking shook with horror at the scene of armed black men in paramilitary gear walking the streets of Oakland. Those relatively few black Americans trying so desperately to integrate into the American middle class rebuked them, but young radicals who were

FIGURE 3.1 Huey Newton sitting in wicker chair, 1967.

Source: Courtesy of Collection Merrill C. Berman.

becoming increasingly disenchanted about the Vietnam War cheered them on.[2]

On one level, the Panthers stood against much in American political culture. Their Marxist call to resist American capitalism was anathema to liberals, many of whom came of age during the postwar economic boom of the 1950s and were schooled in an American history that had always made personal wealth and rugged individualism synonymous with a successful, meaningful existence.[3] The Panther code of armed self-defense countered Martin Luther King Jr.'s plea for nonviolence and James Baldwin's plea for universal love in the name of humanity.[4]

On another level, Panther political practice reflected core elements of the American political tradition. The Panthers' stress on political organization was famously popularized in *The Federalist*, which contended that successful collective action required structured leadership. Their view that political power was more important than ethics and that freedom would be best secured through the factional competition of competing interests extended Madison's arguments.[5] Their conviction that public action centered on the common good needed to be divorced from moral considerations resonated with American civic republicans. Or, to put it differently, the Panthers thought politics needed to be conducted by political moralists rather than moral politicians.[6]

Studying the Panthers from this perspective might lead to a fruitful debate about whether they were more or less like the American version of a Marxist anticolonial Left that spread throughout the Global South in the postwar period or whether they were instead American realists who preferred *what existed* to what *could exist*.[7] Such an exploration misses how Newton and the Panthers revised longstanding and widely held American understandings. Tyranny became something that worked through the unequal organization of physical space. American identity was rendered as deeply unexceptional and amoral. Action was depicted as a willingness to accept the new and unknown. Freedom became dependent upon a radical notion of self-determination. Popular power became manifest through subversive performative acts that played on but aimed to render unsustainable dominant cultural and political formulations. Empathy became a crucial ingredient for enacting horizontal rule, and rage became transformed into a political emotion crucial for justice.

Revising these American ideals was the Panthers' answer to the question the politically mainstream part—what the activist Bayard Rustin in 1965 called the classic phase—of the civil rights movement never fully considered.[8] The Panthers emerged in 1966, just after the passage of the Voting Rights Act (1965) and two years after the Civil Rights Act (1964)—two pieces of legislation that signaled for many Americans the realization of a decade-long struggle for black civil rights. Guaranteeing black Americans equal protection under the law and ensuring their voting rights seemed to make good on the liberal dream of full enfranchisement and the hope of better economic opportunity for all citizens.[9]

But the Panthers weren't easily swayed by this promise. If one major goal of the civil rights movement was to dismantle the barriers for the African American citizens who were already not too far from middle-class American life, then the Panthers' central objective was to create livable conditions for the destitute, for those for whom violence was a fact of everyday life, for those who were enclosed in segregated, crumbling public-housing projects.

Black activists such as King, Rustin, and Fred Shuttlesworth shared the concern of liberal political thinkers as diverse as Locke, Mill, and Madison: How does one create effective political institutions for those who were broadly in a position to enjoy political rights like voting, equal protection under the law, and public respect?[10] The values of political progress, equality, and liberty common to both civil rights and liberal political thought assumed a baseline where one's life was not fundamentally threatened by heart-wrenching poverty that made social mobility impossible, by crippling violence that made political participation difficult, by state-sanctioned police power that could not be reasoned with, and by physical segregation that undermined the possibility for interracial democratic communication. The Panthers, however, were much more concerned with the question Marx posed: How does one get those who were not socially or economically positioned for freedom— for Marx this was expressed through the vastly unequal relationship between workers and those who owned the means of production—raised to that position?

Yet, if Marx's challenge was to create a political theory serviceable for those who labored in factories and for whom political rights were only of secondary importance to economic equality, the challenge for the Panthers was to create a political theory that not only responded to the poor but—following Walker, Douglass, and Wells—to those who were racialized, those who lived within a society that endowed a certain kind of meaning to black life, replete with narratives about black character and identity.

In navigating this fraught terrain, the Panthers countered two narratives of black identity that became crucial for making racial-justice claims during the 1960s. On the one hand, they rejected the narrative of black respectability—the idea of black civic character being defined by the middle-class virtues of industriousness, forbearance, and racial empathy—that was invoked by Douglass and Du Bois and became a central tool used by King and civil rights activists to create the types of political demands that whites were willing to hear.[11] On the other hand, they rejected the narrative of black culture at times implied by Douglass in *My Bondage and My Freedom* but that became popularized by social scientists known as "racial liberals": that after years of racism, black culture was characterized by emasculation and hopelessness.[12]

AMERICAN TYRANNY

Drawing upon the anticolonial revolutionary ideas that had spread throughout the Global South in the postwar period and that were championed by prominent African Americans including Paul Robeson, Max Yergan, and Alphaeus Hunton, who together organized the black diasporic Council on African Affairs (CAA), the Panthers recast American race relations as the struggle between black colonized subjects and white colonizers.[13] For the most devout patriots, America had always been something of what John Winthrop called an exceptional shining city upon a hill, with an ideological commitment to transcendent liberal values that escaped the desires of the flesh. With the Cold War fully entrenched in the 1950s, this vision become orthodoxy for many prominent American intellectuals. "Consensus historians" such as Daniel Boorstin and Arthur Schlesinger Jr. and political scientists such as Louis Hartz spoke with great conviction about the unrivaled way in which Americans had always been irrationally devoted to freedom, political equality, capitalism, and limited government. As Hartz put it, "the storybook truth about American history" is "that the American community is a liberal community."[14]

Had they listened to Newton, these intellectuals would have been scandalized. Newton would often draw on Malcolm X's distinction between "Negro revolution," which was about nonviolent respectability in the United States, and "black revolution," which was about the end of worldwide racial colonialism.[15] But he would also say America was an unexceptional empire that governed through overwhelming fear, unimaginable cruelty, and unending exploitation: "The United States as an empire necessarily controls the whole world either directly or indirectly."[16] African American slavery—which postwar American intellectuals went to great lengths to reconcile with, or excuse from, liberalism—was part of a long history of American colonialism that started with the genocide of Native Americans and continued with the lynching of black men and women, the internment of Japanese Americans, the dropping of atomic bombs on Nagasaki and Hiroshima, and the massacre of Vietnamese during the Vietnam War. Violence was as American as apple pie. "We are forced to conclude," he declared, "that these concentration camps are being prepared for Black people," and that "toward people of color the racist power structure of America has but one policy: repression, genocide, terror, and the big stick."[17]

For the American revolutionaries, the oft-used word "tyranny" had always been viewed as the state's arbitrary deprival of one's (largely political) rights or freedoms.[18] But Newton, like Walker, Douglass, and Wells, retold American history to emphasize its physical effect on bodies in everyday life. Talk of the American liberal project of allowing individual character and labor to govern one's choices seemed laughable when the tyrannical American state intensely focused its violent eye on the bodies of demonized populations. "The government, the social conditions, and the legal documents which brought freedom from oppression [for whites]," he wrote, "had entirely opposite consequences for another portion of the people . . . [they] achieved alienation from the lands of their fathers and slavery."[19] State-sponsored racism made individual freedom from one's body impossible. One was trapped in and by one's skin color. State violence directed toward these bodies made safely roaming freely in the world impossible.

American tyranny was not exactly immune from American liberalism. American public housing was a product of progressive New Deal thinking and ostensibly reflected the commitment to equality of opportunity, providing working-class Americans with affordable homes, which would give them a solid foundation for the American dream of upward mobility.[20] But when public housing was brought into what Newton called the "black ghetto" and its collapsing infrastructure, it became something of a prison. Newton wrote:

> The painful reality of their lives [in the black ghetto] from childhood on reveals that the inequities they encounter are not confined to a few institutions. The effects of injustice and discrimination can be seen in the lives of nearly everyone around them. A brutal system permeates every aspect of life; it is in the air they breathe.[21]

Newton's contemporary, Michel Foucault, asserted in *Discipline and Punish* (1975) that Jeremy Bentham's eighteenth-century Panopticon— which sought to mitigate the coercive nature of discipline by making the prison watchman invisible, so as to allow prisoners to police themselves—was an example of liberal humanism turned repressive.[22] Newton suggested something else: Liberal humanism exercised its repressiveness through state-run low-income housing that destroyed people's health. State oppression existed through a lack of economic resources and through the toxic asbestos and lead that black Americans breathed in their homes. Many black citizens, Newton thus explained, "have been deprived of human dignity, crushed by oppressive forces, and denied their right to live as proud and free human beings."[23]

Newton applied Fanon's recognition in *The Wretched of the Earth* (1961) about the spatial dimensions of colonial power—"It's a world with no space, people are piled on top of the other"[24]—to democratic life. Understanding the centrality of space as essential for robust civil conversation and critical questioning, Newton believed that reasoned reflection would be incredibly difficult, if not impossible, when citizens lived in cramped conditions.[25] He felt the stifling effects of this firsthand when he recalled as an adult the injustice he still felt at being forced to sleep in an incredibly small space as a child: "Whenever I think of people being crowded into a small living space. . . . I still burn with the sense of unfairness I felt every night as I crawled into the cot near the icebox."[26]

Like Douglass—who recognized that slavery deprived people of the very ability to conceptualize their dignity—Hannah Arendt, despite failing to theorize seriously the political theory expressed in the experience of racial slavery, asserted in *The Origins of Totalitarianism* (1951) that the Nazi death camps converted people into lifeless automatons. "The real horror of the concentration and extermination camps lies in the fact that the inmates, even if they happen to be alive, are more effectively cut off from the world of the living than if they had died, because terror enforces oblivion."[27] Both Newton and Arendt understood that such power not only eroded people's rights or security but also their sense of human individuality, but Newton questioned the possibility of starting something new politically, what Arendt described throughout her writings as the principle of "natality," in which, as she put it, "the fact of action is ontologically rooted."[28]

Collective public action by black Americans seemed destined to fail when, as Newton declared in the opening lines of *Revolutionary Suicide* (1973), for black people "life does not always begin at birth. My life was forged in the lives of my parents before I was born . . . racism destroyed our family history."[29] Slaves were born and died anonymously in plantations, while African Americans living in ostensibly free American cities—ones without de jure Jim Crow segregation—were born in ghetto-style concentration camps and died in prisons. In his essay "We Can Change This Country" (1963), Baldwin declared: "Ask yourself what you'd feel like if you lived [in the black ghetto], why you lived there if you did, and why it looks like a concentration camp. I mean the police walking two by two and three by three."[30] Newton experienced what Baldwin only asked white readers to imagine: that the relentless repetition of injustice, domination, and feelings of despair created a sense of hopelessness.

A profound critique of American nationhood was at the center of Newton's thought. At times, he seemed to distinguish between the original promise of America and its ensuing history: "The history of the United States, as distinguished from the promise of the idea of the United States, leads us to the conclusion that our sufferance is basic to the functioning of the government of the United States."[31] But even here Newton's claim was that the measure of American democracy was not its ideals but its history and institutions. He continued: "Thus 200 years later we have an overdeveloped economy which is so infused with the need for profit . . . the free opportunity of all men to pursue their economic ends has been replaced by constraints (confinement) placed upon Americans by the large corporations which control and direct our economy."[32]

At the heart of this historical account of American identity was a critique of American benevolence. Notwithstanding the problematic masculinist language of equating American imperialism with rape, Newton said: "The United States is an empire which has raped the world to build its wealth here. Therefore the United States is not a nation . . . the United States lost its right to claim nationhood when it used its nationalism as a chauvinistic base to become an empire."[33] America was fundamentally not a moral idea but an amoral constellation of real, everyday people and elites who made decisions. The collective institutions these people composed acted with little interest for the public good and were primarily concerned with profit making. Strategically enacting political decisions for the sake of preserving American national interests reflected petty self-interest common to ordinary human beings. This was America, nothing more, nothing less. "If the world does not change," Newton wrote,

> all its people will be threatened by the greed, exploitation and violence
> of the power structure in the United States. . . . The United States is
> jeopardizing its own existence and the existence of all humanity. If

Americans knew the disasters that lay ahead, they would transform this society for the sake of their preservation.[34]

Disclosing how the state's self-professed humanistic projects perpetuated suffering and depoliticization warned black citizens about the false promise of state-sponsored liberation. But shifting perceptions about national identity would be insufficient. Equally necessary was subverting the powerful social and political identities that kept racial injustice intact.

THE POWER OF LANGUAGE

Language became one way the Panthers accomplished this. In a way that made them unique in the American tradition, which, unlike its Western European counterparts, had almost always prioritized deeds over words, the Panthers understood the link between language and politics.[35] Language and power had long been linked in the Western tradition, from Aristotle's *logos*—the fusion of word and reason,[36] to Ludwig Wittgenstein's "language games," those collections of words with family resemblances that create the culture in which individuals live and relate to one another.[37]

For civil rights protesters, words like "freedom now" and "no justice, no peace" became ways to name political aspirations, but for Newton words helped create truth. "Language, the power of the word . . . is not underestimated in our ideology . . . [it is an] important area of raising consciousness," Newton explained, because "words are another way of defining phenomena, and the definition of any phenomenon is the first step to controlling it or being controlled by it."[38]

Walker mobilized words to endow political agency to those he named (who were denied full citizenship), but Newton did it to subvert institutions of social control such as the police, which threatened black freedom. Mirroring the language used to describe slaves—as chattel sold as pieces of meat on the slave market—Newton called the police officer a

"racist pig," to stress the officer's failure of distinguishing between public responsibilities and petty private interests.[39] Not only was the term
"a neutral word" in "racial terms," Newton insisted, but calling "a policeman a pig conveys the idea of someone who is brutal, gross, and
uncaring."[40] Police officers were like the members of the "city of pigs"
Plato described in *The Republic*, which Newton read voraciously and
with which he was deeply impressed, who could not embody the public
virtues of wisdom and justice crucial for rule.[41]

Saying that America was a "fascist" state committing "genocide"
against African Americans living in "concentration camps" patrolled
by "gestapo policemen"[42] also reversed the binary that characterized
postwar human-rights discourse: Americans became Nazis rather than
liberals, hell-bent on exploiting the labor of black Americans, who became the suffering and victimized Jews living in black ghetto-style concentration camps rather than blamed as being culturally responsible
for their marginalized condition.

"All Power to the People" was another core term the Panthers coined,
clearly playing off V. I. Lenin's "All Power to the Soviets."[43] This term not
only named the idea of popular sovereignty but also implied something
not fully developed in Walker's *Appeal*: the idea of radical democratic
respect, which names being responsive to human beings in all their di-
versity and plurality. Here Newton adopted the philosopher Martin
Buber's concept of the "I-Thou" relation for thinking about democratic
life.[44] Buber's plea to approach others spiritually, as if they were transcendent God-like beings rather than things to be objectified, found expression in Newton's thought. As Newton put it, the "idea of man as
God . . . if each man is God, then you must be true to him. . . . As far as
I am concerned, if men are responsible beings, they ought to be responsible to each other."[45] Wells, who insisted on the importance of truthfully
describing the social implications of lynching, would have commended
Newton's view that honesty was crucial for democracy. In the context
of discussing the rationale behind the idea of "All Power to the People,"
Newton declared, "we mean to convey a sense of deep respect and love
for the people, and the idea that the people deserve complete honesty
and truth."[46]

Honesty seemed at odds with the Panther brand of realpolitik. Echoing Malcolm X's realist position, instrumental thinking geared toward political ends seemed infinitely more important than moral behavior.[47] But honesty squares well with popular rule; it necessitates a condition of vulnerability that precludes power from being monopolized. In the course of discussing the Panthers' failed attempt to merge with the SNCC, Newton wrote, "if we supported each other and were honest, I felt that a certain level of trust would be reached. This is very crucial in any relationship . . . since the merger between [the Panthers and SNCC] was susceptible to misrepresentation and misunderstanding."[48] Honesty is essential for an effective democratic politics because it helps create transparency and places individuals in a relationship where they are disclosing things that may be uncomfortable for them to say and hear. Honesty helps ensure that power will be shared and divided between citizens.

PANTHER IDEOLOGY

Altering American understandings of power was only part of what Newton and the Panthers sought to accomplish. Equally crucial for them was developing an alternative notion of power capable of resisting the kind of world that American racial totalitarianism produced. For the Panthers, African American freedom required more than Arendt's call for direct public action in concert, which would involve discussing the nature of the laws that structured their polity rather than issues relating to socioeconomic equality.[49] Freedom, for the Panthers, also depended upon more than the economic resources emphasized by the civil rights movement in the late 1960s. Months before he was assassinated, King, along with the SCLC (Southern Christian Leadership Council), during their "Poor People's Campaign" called for an "Economic and Social Bill of Rights," which made freedom contingent upon a decent job, minimum income, and decent housing for every citizen.[50] King's position countered much of the equal-opportunity discourse of the

1960s that didn't take seriously the idea of equality of results, but it also implied that freedom depended upon giving people better access to obtain property and social assimilation.

The Panthers, however, devised a theory of politics capable of empowering poor black Americans. On some level, the "Ten-Point Program" was nothing if not a continuation of a long American tradition of coopting American founding documents for revolutionary ends. Traditionally, the common rhetorical strategy was to show that the universal "we" at the center of the Declaration of Independence or U.S. Constitution failed to live up to its egalitarian promise. Elizabeth Cady Stanton's Declaration of Sentiments rewrote the Declaration to be applicable for women's political and social equality; Douglass's "What to a Slave Is the Fourth of July?" made it incompatible with slavery.[51]

By trying to revive the American rights of life, liberty, and the pursuit of happiness in the Declaration of Independence, both projects were redemptive. But Newton and his fellow Panther Bobby Seale were more interested in using the revolutionary notion one would find in the Declaration—which asserted that people could legitimately abolish the governments that oppressed them—to rethink American rights. No matter how unconventional and polemical its substance, the Ten Points' expository tone, philosophical justification, and reason-based assertion was much closer to the rhetorical logic of the Declaration than to Walker's *Appeal*. Democracy, the Ten Points implied, meant methodical political analysis and claim making rather than the unending, dizzying Socratic questioning that Walker so eloquently dramatized.

But this new American Bill of Rights was unlike anything Americans had ever seen. Point One, "We want freedom," transformed the First Amendment's call for free speech and assembly—freedoms that placed restrictions upon what government could do to citizens—into freedom as self-determination. Not just the idea of positive freedom that created obligations for government to care for its citizens but the capacious idea of autonomy—where one could personally choose how to guarantee their own flourishing: "We believe that Black people will not be free until we are able to determine our destiny."[52] Point Two defended the right of full employment rather than good jobs—"We believe that the federal government is responsible and obligated to give every man employment or a guaranteed income"—and Point Three called for abolishing the "robbery by the CAPITALIST of our Black Community" rather than re-iterating the right to bear arms found in the Second Amendment. Human safety was about protection from bodily necessities like hunger and ignorance rather than protection from one's neighbors.[53]

This idea was continued in Point Four, the right of decent housing ("housing and the land should be made into cooperatives so that our community, with government aid, can build and make decent housing for its people"), and Point Five, quality education focused on black people's experiences ("We believe in an educational system that will give to our people a knowledge of self").[54] Point Four implied that the Fourth Amendment's right to illegal search and seizure of one's property meant nothing without access to shelter, and Point Five implied that the Fifth Amendment's right to be free from self-incrimination meant nothing if illiteracy reigned supreme. Full citizenship was nothing without the capacity for reason and imagination.[55]

By calling for the right of exempting black men from military service, Point Six replaced the Sixth Amendment's guarantee of a speedy trial and a jury of one's peers with the guarantee that black citizens could become metaphorical jurors who judged America. While reiterating the Second Amendment's right to self-defense, Point Seven's call for an "immediate end to POLICE BRUTALITY and MURDER of Black people" nonetheless stressed that the Seventh Amendment's guarantee of a trial by jury was useless when the state not only neglected but disproportionately inflicted violence upon some of its most vulnerable citizens. Point Eight, which stated, "We believe that all Black people should be released from the many jails and prisons because they have not received a fair and impartial trial,"[56] cast black imprisonment as the cruel and unusual punishment that the Eighth Amendment guarded against, while also radicalizing the very meaning of freedom from state-inflicted cruelty. In this sense, freedom meant not simply making more humane the way the state punished but actually abolishing capital punishment and the prison system because they represented the logical end of an unjust criminal-justice system.

Point Nine's call for the right of African Americans to be tried by juries of their own African American peers suggested that the implied rights guaranteed by the Ninth Amendment would be unequally enjoyed by white citizens and stressed the value of social identity and shared experience for judgment. Finally, while the Tenth Amendment authorized the right of federalism to divide, check, and balance the power vested in state and federal government, the Black Panther Party's Tenth Point summarized the preconditions for ensuring human dignity and exercising one's sovereignty: the right to "land, bread, housing, education, clothing, justice and peace."[57]

REVOLUTIONARY SUICIDE

No less radical than rethinking the conditions for freedom, equally crucial was a rethinking of action, which Newton called "revolutionary suicide." Historically, revolution had been entwined with the specter of violence and the threat of death, from the Jacobin Reign of Terror, to the Bolshevik overthrow of the Russian monarchy, to the Algerian use of guerrilla warfare against their French colonizers. Yet such revolutions never took place in America. There was much to be learned from the famous images of the Constitutional Convention of 1787, where well-dressed middle-class white men discussed ideas rather than spilled blood, using pens rather than swords, to debate the U.S. constitutional structure rather than address its entrenched social inequalities—slavery, gender domination, poverty. As Arendt asserted in *On Revolution* (1963), if the American Revolution was unique, it was only unique because of its exclusive concern with political change. A better organization of government—how political power was divided and administered and to whom it was given—would restore, rather than fundamentally alter, representative rule.[58]

Socialist revolution was always on Newton's mind, but his idea of revolutionary suicide pushed the envelope on American thinking about action. Suicide was, for Newton, more than the romantic sacrifice of oneself for the collective, the deferring of one's individuality for the sake of the collective. It was also not a description of black hopelessness that would result from their oppression by what C. Wright Mills called the "power elite"—the capitalists who controlled the means of economic production, elected officials who controlled public policy, and the white Americans who constructed the normative culture.[59] As Newton explained: "Revolutionary suicide does not mean that I and my comrades have a death wish; it means just the opposite. We have such a strong desire to live with hope and human dignity that existence without them is impossible."[60] Politics was at the forefront of Newton's mind, but throughout *Revolutionary Suicide* there is also a clear sense of existential revolution. While eventually arguing that his youthful existentialism disappeared after his conversion from political naïf to no-nonsense, socialist revolutionary, Newton could never fully dispense with what he learned from his careful readings of Camus, Sartre, and Kierkegaard.[61] Newton's existentialism, which was expressed less through the narrow idea that one could always freely choose one's destiny than through the individual intellectual shift of one's attitudes about the world, mixed with Fanon's understanding of revolution.

Fanon himself was no existentialist, but at the conclusion of *The Wretched of the Earth* (a text to which Sartre would pen a laudatory foreword) Fanon's notion of revolution centralized the idea of a new humanity, what he called a "new history of man"[62]—the idea that although one could never know what a future, utopian society would bring and what possibilities it would allow for, it would certainly be *new*.[63] The opening poem of Newton's autobiography, aptly entitled "Revolutionary Suicide," placed Fanon's utopian vision of a future to come into an American context. Newton wrote:

"Revolutionary Suicide"

By having no family,
I inherited the family of humanity,
By having no possessions,
I have possessed all.

By rejecting the love of one,
I received the love of all.
By surrendering my life to the revolution,
I found eternal life,
Revolutionary Suicide.[64]

Huey P. Newton

One can certainly contest the aesthetic merits of the poem. If the African American essayist and author of the award-winning novel *Invisible Man* (1952), Ralph Ellison, had taken the time to read it, he would have questioned its status as art. Art was evocative and encouraged complex reflection and introspection; by contrast, a cerebral prose style, which echoed the rhetoric of politics—of manifestos, speeches, or political-theoretical treatises—was driven by arguments with which one was asked simply to agree. As Ellison put it, art was defined by its ability to reveal the world's "mad, vari-implicated chaos, its false faces, and on until it surrenders its insight, its truth."[65] Yet, there is something deeply poetic about Newton's poem, which both encourages introspection in the American reader and makes introspection a part of what constitutes exemplary citizenship. Whatever else revolutionary suicide meant for Newton, these lines attest that it meant intellectual rebirth. Rebirth defined the 1960s. Protesting the mass death caused by the Vietnam War, student antiwar activists called for peace, challenging the idea that state violence always needed to be on the table. Hippies called for noninstrumental expression—life for life's sake—not driven by the demands of rigid American corporate culture. Feminists called for gender equality that refused to be suffocated by patriarchy.

Revolutionary suicide, for Newton, was always an existential matter. Suicide was the death of the self that one knew, and it was followed by intellectual rebirth. The violence at the heart of "suicide" was metaphorical. If anything, it was a violent conflict between two opposing forces within one consciousness, between one's attraction to American cultural conventions and their alternatives.

Denounced by critics and celebrated by allies for being an "intellectual," something of an armchair philosopher, Newton added his voice to this discourse. His poem concisely details core elements of Newton's view of exemplary action. First, attachment to a traditional family[66]—with all its fixed hierarchical roles—is replaced with identification with humanity, which knows no boundaries or identity and cuts across gender, race, sexuality, and nation. Despite the internationalist orientation—that of global political struggle—Newton shared with Walker, his version of cosmopolitan humanism went beyond Walker's racial particularism. "Our hopes for freedom then lie in the future," Newton wrote in *Revolutionary Suicide*, "a future which may hold a positive elimination of national boundaries and ties."[67]

Second, what Marx called "commodity fetishism," a thirst for material goods as well as an inability to think outside the intrinsic value of such goods,[68] a view that was propagated during the postwar American culture of consumption, was, for Newton, replaced with what Wells advocated: anti-instrumental thinking and a sense of collective responsibility. Newton concluded *Revolutionary Suicide* by stressing the importance of seeing the interplay between individual and collective responsibility: "There is an old African saying, 'I am we.' If you met an African in ancient times and asked him who he was, he would reply, 'I am we.' This revolutionary suicide; I, we, all of us are the one and the multitude."[69] Resisting such individualism means being emotionally and intellectually receptive—"receiving"—to the love of all and being capable of listening to the vulnerability inherent in that love.

Third, surrendering one's life as one has known it meant a life of constant rebirth, where one was attentive to and responsive to everything percolating within humanity, with its ever-changing shapes and forms. This must have been responsible not only for Newton's call for the Panthers to create coalitions with the gay and feminist movements but his own willingness to acknowledge his homophobia in much more rigorous ways, for instance, than Martin Luther King Jr.[70] "I have hang-ups myself about male homosexuality . . . probably because it is a threat to me," Newton once confessed.[71] Homophobia needed to be rejected, Newton declared, because it was essential to have "respect and feelings for all oppressed people . . . and a person should have the freedom to use his body in whatever way he wants."[72] Moreover, despite using misogynistic tropes, Newton, like Wells before him, expressed attunement to the way the fear of emasculation that could accompany gender equality was responsible for misogyny and gendered violence: "We want to hit the woman or shut her up because we are afraid that she might castrate us, or take the nuts that we might not have to start with."[73]

The idea of revolutionary suicide thus explained Newton's critique of popular black radical ideologies. Newton's personal problems with Ron Karenga ran deep. But for Newton, Karenga's black cultural nationalism, which was expressed in his organization US and the holiday Kwanzaa, expressed a futile cultural response to a structural problem of racial inequality and was misguided in privileging black essentialism, the idea that black people's shared identity was fixed and well defined. As Newton put it, "US was in fact an agency to keep the Black community under control: courses in Swahili and a kind of cultist philosophy were offered. Advertised as a program to free Blacks, Karenga's US in fact exploited them."[74] Moreover, the capacious love of black people expressed in the writings of Stokely Carmichael, who was one of the coauthors of the seminal *Black Power* (1967), was what policed progressive coalitions that could include white American activists. "We consider this viewpoint both racist and suicidal," said Newton, speaking of Carmichael: "If you support a Black man with a gun who belongs to the military arm of your oppressor, then you are assisting in your own destruction."[75] Not only did Newton's critique of black essentialism animate his denunciation of Eldridge Cleaver's homophobia—which was expressed through Cleaver's violent attack on James Baldwin in *Soul on Ice*[76]—but it also inspired a devastating critique of Cleaver's politics. As Newton put it, Cleaver's political thought was "based on a rhetoric of violence," "abounded in either/or absolutes," and was governed by the belief that "transformation could take place only through violence, by picking up and storming the barricades."[77]

Such "reactionary suicide," Newton believed, presupposed fixed identity rather than viewed identity as dependent upon action. Following anarchists such as Emma Goldman, who asserted that direct action is "potent in the environment of the individual. There a hundred forces encroach upon his being, and only persistent resistance will finally set him free,"[78] Newton insisted that direct action had its own logic and demands. The acting person needed to expect the unexpected, be prepared to reimagine themselves and their commitments anew. The action Newton had in mind came not simply from a love of black people but, as he put it, "out of an intense love for the earth, for our brothers, and for justice."[79] Action founded in this kind of capacious love of the world and ideals captured the "revolutionary principle of transformation" and—borrowing Camus's quote, Newton said—worked "to remake the soul of our time."[80]

Throughout his writings, Ellison argued for replacing the standard American romantic view of action with what he called a tragicomic one. Here blind faith in achieving good outcomes through perseverance would be replaced with action that appreciated the inescapability of failure. Ellison wrote: "This has been the heritage of a people who for hundreds of years could not celebrate birth or dignify death, and whose need to live despite the dehumanizing pressures of slavery developed an endless capacity for laughing at their painful experience."[81] Unlike Ellison, however, Newton wanted to replace the romantic American view with one where the self needed to be deconstructed and reconstructed. Action actually expanded people's openness to the world, making them responsive to its ebbs and flows as it was unfolding before them.

SELF-DEFENSE

But is an existential conception of revolutionary suicide adequate for real political change, which requires direct political struggle? Newton didn't believe it was. That's why he and the Panthers devised public tactics to achieve racial equality.[82]

Consider their most famous: self-defense. Walking the streets with gun in hand—for the sake of self-defense—put into practice modern thought's preoccupation with bodily security, which was at odds with the vulnerability found in civil rights protestors' nonviolent pleas for civic love. Notwithstanding the masculinist preoccupation with the phallic instruments of destruction, this public display of guns was nothing if not a subversive attempt to use the symbols of American culture against themselves.

In her ethnocentric, if not overtly racist, critique of Black Power, Arendt misunderstood this dimension of Panther actions. In *On Violence* (1970) she argued that "serious violence only entered the scene with the appearance of the Black Power movement on campuses . . . Negro Students, the majority of them admitted without academic qualities . . . it was clear from the beginning . . . that violence with them was not a matter of theory or rhetoric."[83] Arendt's equation of violence with black students was intellectually irresponsible. But she was right to be concerned that violence could perpetuate more violence. The barrel of the gun may lead not to the conversation essential for pluralistic living but could silence those who wished to speak, much like a bullet travels in one direction, at a particular target, on a fixed route.[84] But taking seriously another of Arendt's claims—the role of public appearance in politics—might lead to a different interpretation. As she wrote, "power preserves the public realm and the space of appearance . . . it is . . . the lifeblood of the human artifice, which, unless it is the scene of action and speech . . . lacks its ultimate *raison d'être*."[85] If public space is where individual artistry can be remembered, then carrying guns in public actually gave disesteemed black citizens a voice—despite the fact that they were segregated from public view and from the institutions of political power.

In a moment of remarkable candidness, Newton expressed the depth of Arendt's misunderstanding of the gun's symbolic role for the Panthers when he told a police officer who was writing a traffic ticket to a local black man that "a gun . . . did not give [the police officer] the right to intimidate [Newton]. The gun did not mean anything, because the people were going to get guns of their own and take away the guns of the police."[86] The gun was less an instrument of intimidation than a symbol steeped in the American cultural mythology of Power with a capital "P." Newton explained: "People respect the expression of strength and dignity displayed by men who refuse to bow to the weapons of oppression. Though it may mean death, these men will fight, because death with dignity is preferable to ignominy."[87]

Policing their neighborhoods communicated the failure of the American liberal system. Suggesting that they would protect themselves and their communities from state violence—a promise that had formed the theoretical rationale for building, as well as the key political objective of, the modern liberal state—made the Panthers into exemplary democratic citizens and exposed how the American state never lived up to its core political promises. By exposing this edifice, the Panthers testified to the way Arendt's dream of nonviolent talk about distinctly political issues such as the organization of the law and Constitution was impossible because physical safety was never guaranteed for all.

Yet momentarily eschewing the question whether armed self-defense is strategically useful or normatively desirable for any liberation practice, we should ask: What kind of statement is it exactly? Beyond making loud and clear that they were real mean men to be reckoned with, the gun expressed that black life mattered, that it was worth protecting. If gun-toting Panthers confirmed Mao's idea that "power grows out of the barrel of the gun," it was the power to make visible a fierce attachment to life rather than death.

But are there no other ways to make this statement? There are. But in 1960s America—a moment when the black body was under threat, subject to assassination, and threatened by white supremacists, gang activity, and police brutality—the Panthers reversed the narrative of black carelessness. To those who would point to African American abject living conditions in public housing as signs of deficient black moral character, as a kind of irreverence for a sense of home, the symbolism of walking around for self-defense made vivid black self-love against that of self-hate, of which suicide was the most extreme result.

POLICING THE POLICE

No Panther tactic, however, was as revolutionary as policing the police. With copies of California state law and Oakland city law in hand, which asserted the legality of citizens monitoring police officers while carrying loaded guns as long as they were openly displayed, Newton and the

Panthers began patrolling their neighborhoods. An illustrative example of this is recounted in Joshua Bloom and Waldo Martin's definitive history of the Panthers, *Black Against Empire*:

> They saw a police car patrolling the area and decided to monitor it. As Bobby Seale later recounted the incident, Newton sped up to within a short residential block behind the car and kept that distance. When the officer turned right, Newton turned right. When the officer turned left, Newton turned left. Newton was armed with a shotgun, Seale with a .45 caliber handgun, and Hutton with an M-1 rifle. A law book sat on the back seat.
>
> Newton took the shotgun from Seale, leapt out of the car, and jacked a round of ammunition into the chamber. He shouted, "Now, who in the hell do you think you are, you big rednecked bastard, you rotten fascist swine, you bigoted racist? You come into my car, trying to brutalize me and take my property away from me. Go for your gun and you're a dead pig." The officer lifted his hands away from his gun while Seale and Hutton jumped out of the passenger side of the car. Seale pulled back the hammer on his .45. The officer backed away from Newton toward his car, where he radioed for backup.
>
> The officer then demanded that Seale hand over his gun, and Seale refused. Newton, Seale, and Hutton would not submit to the police. Citing local ordinances as well as the Second Amendment to the Constitution, they asserted their right to bear arms as long as the guns were not concealed. . . . As soon as Newton pulled over, the officer stopped and burst out of his car, hollering, "What the goddam hell you niggers doing with them goddam guns? Who in the goddam hell you niggers think you are? Get out of that goddam car. Get out of that goddam car with them goddam guns." . . .The officer insisted . . . "I have a right to see the weapon." Newton refused. "Ain't you ever heard of the Fourteenth Amendment of the Constitution of the United States? Don't you know you don't remove nobody's property without due process of law? What's the matter with you? You're supposed to be people enforcing the law, and here you are, ready to violate my constitutional rights. You can't see my gun. You can't have my gun. The only way you're gonna get it from me is to try to take it."[88]

A decidedly American argument about personal rights, equal protection under the law, and private property was expressed through Newton's declaration that the gun and the car were his inalienable property. But also at work here was a subversive critique about the everyday practice of state-sponsored force. Watching the watchers, checking and balancing the state, dramatized that ordinary citizens could replicate state power. State power was thus exposed as neither exceptional nor mysterious. Moreover, a claim about police needing to justify their own democratic legitimacy was made through Newton's invoking the constitutional law of due process and equal protection. Police officers needed to work from within the boundaries of the law, not beyond them. Although the law buttressed police power, reasons needed to be given for the contours of policing practices. Whatever else it could have provoked, policing the police became, for the Panthers, a mechanism for instituting a democratic dialogue about the nature of authority.

First, carving out the right to police the police showed how rights could be invoked through popular assertions that were politically unsanctioned in a way that Douglass and Walker would have certainly approved.[89] Second, like Walker's invocation of black citizenship, Newton's claiming of the right to police the Oakland officers actually reoriented the power of democratic judgment away from the state and placed it upon an ordinary citizen, who became prosecutor, judge, and jury. In Newton's encounter with the white officer, the roles are reversed: The officer becomes the black citizen being policed in his neighborhood, while Newton is an exemplary civic educator—no longer the delinquent, culturally pathological, black criminal male that the officer assumed him to be.

Like Walker, Newton fashioned himself as a Socratic sage, forcing the officer to engage in what King and Baldwin counseled citizens: self-examination. Self-examination, for King, meant attentiveness to one's implication in a universal network of brotherhood, what he called "an inescapable network of mutuality,"[90] while for Baldwin it was locating one's own emotional complexities and desires so as not to project them onto others in the form of racism: "White people will have to ask themselves precisely why they found it necessary to invent the nigger; for the nigger is a white invention, and white people invented him out of the terrible necessities of their own."[91] In contrast, calling upon the officer to acknowledge his racism in the act of policing, Newton urged a citizen turned into an instrument of the state to reflect upon his own thirst for and position of power.

Like Socrates, the public nature of Newton's action was also pedagogic—it was about educating the black community about their rights: "I always carried lawbooks in my car. Sometimes, when a policeman was harassing a citizen, I would stand off a little and read the relevant portions of the penal code in a loud voice to all within hearing distance. In doing this, we were helping to educate those who gathered to observe these incidents."[92] Greater knowledge of one's rights could be empowering, transforming one from a passive bystander to injustice to one who could be greater protected from it.

On the one hand, Newton always professed fidelity to the law rather than some abstract moral concept of justice.[93] In Newton's own words: "The Black Panthers were and are always required to keep their activities within legal bounds. . . . The police [were] invariably shocked to meet a cadre of disciplined and armed Black men coming to the support of the community."[94] On the other hand, his declaration to the police officer in the earlier passage—"What's the matter with you? You're supposed to be people enforcing the law, and here you are, ready to violate my constitutional rights"—illustrated his view that commitment to the idea of "the people" forces one to resist those who unjustly enforce the law. Yet Newton's idea was not found in something like King's version of civil disobedience—where one refuses to follow unjust laws. It was closer to Walker's: directly confronting with searching questions and probing critique those who enforce laws unjustly.

PANTHER COMMUNITY SERVICES

As much anything else, Panther political thought was expressed through their community services, known as "survival programs," which Newton described as having "great importance from the beginning" because the Panthers "always planned to become involved in Black people's daily struggle for survival and sought only the means to serve the community's needs."[95] At its core, these programs treated black Americans as dignified human beings and provided them with the resources essential to becoming full citizens.[96]

Nourishing the hungry and frail body, the Free Breakfast for Children Program, Free Clothing Program, and Free Shoe Program stressed the importance of what contemporary philosophers have called basic resources—"capabilities"—for freedom, which could only be realized through alleviating internal, rather than external, constraints. Led by ex-addicts, Panther health-care clinics combating drug addiction[97] dramatized Douglass's idea that black self-determination was possible[98] and the idea—expressed by Douglass, Walker, and Wells—that all human beings, irrespective of what they did or who they were, had inherent human dignity. Flawed individual behavior could neither fully nor forever monopolize the distinct human being from which it arose. Granting such responsibility to ex-addicts countered the racist image of permanent black delinquency while replacing a punitive approach to suffering with a rehabilitative one.

The Free-Busing-to-Prison Program, for its part, helped solidify black communities. Transportation had always been a powerful political force in the black freedom struggle, from the Underground Railroad to Rosa Parks's refusal to assume second-class citizenship in the back of a segregated Montgomery, Alabama, bus. Providing citizens affordable transportation to prison helped mitigate the emotional and physical boundaries between those who were free and those who were incarcerated—boundaries that militated against mutual understanding, compassion, and solidarity. Equally central to the program was educating people that political power shaped the structure of families, that the absence of black fathers, and the existence of nontraditional families was not based in a corrupt and criminal black culture—as Moynihan's infamous report suggested—but was instead created through political decisions and injustice in the criminal justice system.[99]

Panther schools, known as "Liberation Schools,"[100] transformed education into a tool for critical thinking rather than rote memorization.

Emphasizing the study of black history and white supremacy meant beginning with local knowledge, which put into practice John Dewey's defense of experimental education attentive to both history and lived experience. Moreover, this was about creating within black American education three of Dewey's insights: Education was a form of democracy, it was preparation for democracy, and it was an essential condition for democracy.[101]

Organized mostly by women volunteers, Panther soup kitchens seemed to confirm the misogynist image of black women as those who simply cared for black men via domestic work. But enacting such important grassroots community work for securing black citizenship meant that black women's contributions were deeply political. Finally, the Loans for Welfare Mothers Program communicated Panther awareness of the intersectional nature of oppression—gender along with class and race[102]—while also conveying appreciation for the crucial role black mothers played in the black community.

ETHICS, RAGE, AND DEMOCRACY

Ethics seemed to be irrelevant to Newton's revolutionary political rhetoric and tactics. If anything, stoicism is the disposition most readily associated with Panther revolutionary action. The revolutionary's willingness to follow an ideal to its logical end or sacrifice his or her safety and risk his or her life requires some detachment from emotional reactions, if not neutrality toward them.[103] But Newton's stoicism coexisted with, if it was not superseded by, his ethic of empathetic perspectivalism. He shared Walker's attentiveness to oppositional perspectives, but unlike him, he believed such knowledge was crucial less for self-defense than for engendering solidarity and diminishing animus.

Though Newton was clearly no Baldwin, whose rich and heartfelt meditations on human suffering would bring readers to tears and thereby to action, the compassion with which Newton described hungry African American children was matched only by his awareness of

the way poor whites used racism as a crutch for personal deficiencies—
"many times the poorest White person is the most racist because he is
afraid that he might lose something, or discover something he does not
have"[104]—and that the prison guards Newton encountered during his
time in Alameda County Jail were "victims, too" precisely because "they
have a limited and very crude kind of power [that] tends to corrupt and
brutalize them."[105]

Echoing Douglass's attempt in "The Meaning of July Fourth for the
Negro" to reframe the white American's perception of America by highlighting the slave's perspective,[106] Newton modeled the political importance of understanding opposing views: why young black male citizens
might seriously ponder suicide, for "they have been deprived of human
dignity, crushed by oppressive forces, and denied their right to live as
proud and free human beings,"[107] or why white juries who, unaware that
"many activities defined by the ruling class as criminal are the acts of
poor and exploited people, desperate people, who have no access to the
channels of opportunity," would be incompetent to judge the black de-
fendant before them "because . . . [they do] not understand the circumstances that brought on his actions."[108]

Widespread black suffering moved Newton and the Panthers to feel
rage, the feeling with which they would be popularly associated. For
American racists, unbridled rage had always been seen as central to
black psychology: A weak sense of reason and diminished self-control
created vacillating emotions, which led to a thirst for vengeance.[109] The
irony, however, was that this fictional, white racist narrative of black
rage was itself responsible for what Baldwin called the "rage of the disesteemed."[110] And its tragic consequences would be made clear through
the powerful literary example of the life of Richard Wright's protago-
nist Bigger Thomas, in his novel *Native Son* (1940). Thomas's rage at being
preemptively and wrongfully accused of murder because of white racism facilitated more rage in him, which actually led him to murder.[111]

Yet the Panthers redirected, rather than succumbed to, Thomas's internal rage toward external institutions of racism when they shouted
at police officers, calling them "racist pigs" and "gestapos," and when
they denounced American imperialism, capitalism, and collective white

apathy toward poor black citizens. "I do not think life will change for the better without an assault on the establishment," Newton wrote, "which goes on exploiting the wretched of the earth."[112] What made this all the more striking was that few emotions had been treated with so much contempt in the American tradition as rage. The image of what the philosopher Jürgen Habermas would eventually call "communicative action"—the view that democratic life rested on the rational and respectful exchange of competing truth claims—was arguably the metaphor for exemplary American citizenship.[113] Take, for instance, the Federalists and Anti-Federalists talking about the nature of centralized power in the Constitution, Lincoln and Stephen Douglas debating the politics of abolition, and King telling Americans in 1963 that the egalitarian promise of the Declaration had been left unfulfilled.

In their rhetoric and direct actions, the Panthers refused such cordial debate, instead turning rage into a productive political resource. Cynicism encourages skepticism of the world, but rage embodies vigorous disagreement and polemical confrontation.[114] Rage communicates the gravity and urgency of a situation in a way reason doesn't. Rage suggests that something must be addressed immediately, without any hesitation or rationalizations meant to delay. Like cynicism, rage can more effectively unveil what is behind or obscured by the niceties of social convention, which help obfuscate the scope and nature of problems. But rooted as it so often is in intense volume and pitch, rage—more so than cynicism—demands someone to hear it and look at the person delivering it, and so it is unlike shame and despair, which often encourage something of a depressive state in the person experiencing it. Neither the enraged person nor the enraged claim can be easily ignored.[115]

THE ENDS OF PANTHER POLITICS

Panther political radicalism certainly shortened the movement's public life. Founded in 1966, the party was virtually eliminated from American consciousness by the early 1970s. By the 1980s, after years of FBI attempts at subverting and squashing the organization, with the exception of some local branches throughout the country, very few Panther community programs and schools were left. After being released from jail in 1970 for the manslaughter of an Oakland police officer, John Frey, Newton's life spiraled out of control. For the next twenty years, he suffered from mental illness, was repeatedly accused of violence and even murder, and became severely addicted to crack cocaine. Tragically, Newton died on August 22, 1989, at the young age of forty-seven, after being shot by a drug dealer.

But Newton's ideas have had a life of their own. In response to the killing of black men—Michael Brown, Eric Garner, Freddie Gray, Walter Scott, Tamir Rice, Samuel Du Bose, Laquan McDonald, Alton Sterling, Philando Castile—by police officers, protestors around the United States have chanted slogans that speak to the undeniable dignity of black life: Black Lives Matter! The grassroots organization Copwatch, which began in Berkeley, California, in 1990 and has since spread to many large American cities, polices the police through videotaping their actions and posting the videos on social-media websites for all to see.

Not all of Newton's and the Panthers' ideas are democratically valuable. In addition to rejecting their misogyny and latent homophobia, contemporary activists should also rethink their preoccupation with the right to bear arms. The recent spate of school shootings and ongoing gang violence in the United States have proven that the violent social and human cost of the gun is much greater than its symbolism. Moreover, over the past three decades, the Second Amendment has been monopolized by powerful right-wing lobbying groups such as the NRA (National Rifle Association) to destroy any effort at gun-control legislation. Even the Panthers saw guns as nothing more than strategic tools put in the service of dramatizing the problem of racial inequality. Bearing arms, for them, was a necessity for no other reason than to defend against white racism and police brutality.

Yet activists concerned with energizing democracy can benefit from Newton's and the Panther's ideas. They can better appreciate how state power works its dominion not simply through the denial of political rights or through the warrantless surveillance of citizens but through the structure of the built environment.[116] Activists could better appreciate that exposing the amoral core of American nationhood helps attune citizens to the ever-present possibility of injustice.[117] Democracy depends on concrete socioeconomic resources like quality education, welfare, transportation, food, and shelter, rather than only political rights.[118] Articulating unsanctioned rights can force those who enforce power to justify their power, rather than hide behind its veil.[119] Action must be founded upon a willingness to experience intellectual and political rebirth.[120] Democracy depends upon empathizing with the suffering and divergent experiences of others.[121] Rage is a powerful tool for politicizing injustice and for being heard politically.[122]

Throughout his life, Newton maintained hope that a more socially just world was within reach. Struggling against the unjust could lead to "death," but, he explained, "there is at least the possibility, if not probability, of changing intolerable conditions. This possibility is important, because much of human existence is based upon hope without any real understanding of the odds."[123] This is what animated Newton's lifelong commitment to activism. In the penultimate page of *Revolutionary Suicide*, he framed the difference between reactionary and revolutionary suicide by borrowing a quote of Nietzsche's. "The difference lies in hope and desire. By hoping and desiring, the revolutionary chooses life," Newton wrote. "He is, in the words of Nietzsche, 'an arrow of longing for another shore.'"[124] Taking seriously some of Newton's most valuable insights could help Americans reach a future democratic shore more quickly.

4

ANGELA DAVIS, PRISON ABOLITION, AND THE END OF THE AMERICAN CARCERAL STATE

Over the past thirty years, arguably no American institution has so intensified its reach and power over African Americans than the prison. In the early 1980s, roughly 474,000 men and women were incarcerated in federal and state penitentiaries, but, by the beginning of the 2010s, that number had ballooned to over two million.[1] This rapid growth was no accident but was part of a concerted political effort. Calling for cracking down on crime and increasing law-enforcement authority, Richard Nixon's "law-and-order" discourse in the late 1960s and early 1970s became persuasive to many in the American middle class. By the 1980s, Congress began passing "War on Drugs" legislation, which criminalized low-level drug use and distribution. Little changed in the 1990s. Democratic president Bill Clinton signed into law the Violent Crime Control and Law Enforcement Act of 1994, which increased federal funding for prisons, added over 100,000 police officers, and created harsher sentencing laws, especially for drug offenders. The prison population continued to swell.[2]

The Panthers had expressed concern that an unjust policing and criminal-justice system, which preemptively criminalized black Americans with as much regularity as it exonerated white Americans, was as inimical to American democracy as it was deadly for many people of color. But they never could have fully anticipated that it would congeal to create something of a national prison epidemic—no one could.[3]

Political realism put the Panthers in a good position to understand that tough-on-crime discourse would be politically profitable. Nixon won a contested 1968 presidential contest against the Democratic candidate, Hubert Humphrey, partly by appealing to the racial resentment held by segments of the working-class white American electorate—the use of what the conservative tactician Kevin Phillips called the "Southern Strategy."[4] In 1968, many whites were prepared to support the openly racist Alabama governor, George Wallace, the third-party candidate who won an unprecedented 13 percent of the popular vote.[5] Election seekers on the American left and right—and most recently, the Republican presidential candidate and real-estate mogul Donald Trump—have since followed Nixon's example. Existential fear about crime across the racial spectrum brings many people to the polls and often trumps other political issues.[6] The resulting mass-incarceration system is, however, much easier for whites to support. After all, they understand that those citizens who will be trapped behind its walls will most likely be nonwhite. Not their children or family members.[7]

Racial disparity defines contemporary American mass incarceration. According to one influential sociological interpretation, the prison is the most recent installment of a history of racial oppression, what the sociologist Loïc Wacquant calls the fourth "peculiar" race-based American institution of social control that first began with chattel slavery before continuing through Jim Crow and then the black ghetto.[8] If W. E. B. Du Bois in *The Souls of Black Folk* correctly prophesized the color line to be the defining boundary for distributing rights to black and white Americans in the twentieth century,[9] then the prison is the most obvious manifestation of the color line in the twenty-first century.

Thirty-six percent of the American population is nonwhite, but over 60 percent of the American prison population is of color; some projections indicate that one in three black men born in the United States will be incarcerated at some point in their lives.[10] Incarceration carries direct political implications. Prisons welcome people with open arms but release them with a mark of social deviance. Many states place voting restrictions on felons, and even a short period of time spent incarcerated can destroy one's family and deplete one's social connections, greatly restrict one's prospects for future employment, and create lasting psychological distress.[11]

Mass incarceration has increased in unprecedented ways over the past three decades, but the prison has always been a fixture in America.[12] American democracy, which prides itself on a commitment to human flourishing, seems at odds with prisons. Prisons are structured as hierarchies, they degrade human beings by placing them in cages, and they inflict suffering on people's minds and bodies through disciplinary measures. But punishment and democracy have always been intricately linked in America. Tocqueville only composed *Democracy in America* (1835/1840), after he traveled, along with a fellow Frenchmen, Gustave de Beaumont, across the United States in 1831 to study its prisons. In *Democracy in America*, Tocqueville had little to say about the American prison system, instead spending pages upon pages cataloguing how he was as impressed by the exceptional American spirit of unbridled individualism as he was shocked by the spontaneity with which Americans joined together to form civic associations and the unanimity with which they held their political convictions.[13]

But Tocqueville and Beaumont's now-forgotten report on American prisons, *On the Penitentiary System in the United States: And Its Application in France* (1831), issued a powerful reminder to those who read it: "It must be acknowledged that the penitentiary system in America is severe. While society in the United States gives the example of the most extended liberty, the prisons of the same country offer the spectacle of the most complete despotism. The citizens subject to the law are protected by it; they only cease to be free when they become wicked."[14]

Perhaps unintentionally but nonetheless quite powerfully, these words undercut the very opposition Tocqueville and Beaumont wished to establish between the despotic severity of punishment and the overarching American commitment to a democratic society. What becomes apparent instead is that the very democratic law that protects people's liberty is what creates the prison. John Locke—himself one of the core theoretical inspirations for American liberalism—was among the first thinkers to establish this link years before Tocqueville and Beaumont's study. In his *Second Treatise of Government*, Locke argued that one of the purposes of representative government was to maintain social order by replacing a person's natural right to punish those who committed crimes in the so-called state of nature with an impartial judicial system. In the state of nature, Locke claimed, "the law of nature is . . . put into every man's hands, where every one has a right to punish the transgressors of that law to such a degree, as may hinder its violation."[15]

If the link between punishment and democracy in America is as complex as it is mutually constitutive, how should social movements address it? What alternative visions must they advance? And how should they couch their arguments?

Many antiprison activists have called for substantive prison reform—centering on changing mandatory-sentencing standards such as the infamous "Three Strikes" law, which, in many instances, carries the sentence of life in prison after someone has committed three felonies, or on efforts to decriminalize certain activities, especially drug possession and addiction. Only a small minority, however, have made the much more radical argument for prison abolition.

No thinker over the past thirty years has been as incisive and theoretically sophisticated in such a call than Angela Yvonne Davis. Born in 1944 in segregated Birmingham, Alabama, Davis would go on to receive a doctorate in philosophy under the direction of the Frankfurt School critical theorist Herbert Marcuse before becoming an international cultural and political icon in the early 1970s after being famously placed on the FBI's Most Wanted list.[16] Davis's political-theoretical writings offer a wide range of arguments that deserve attention, ranging from her view that freedom should be understood as an unending condition of struggle, rather than a static good that people are simply given,[17] to her thinking about the excesses of global neoliberal capitalism, which coalesce with, sustain, and are sustained by war and empire,[18] to her reflections on the intersection between gender and race.[19]

No study as of yet, however, has seriously examined the political theory at the heart of what has arguably been one of her life's overarching theoretical projects—a complete rethinking of the American prison system and the regimes of punishment, discipline, control, and security upon which it has always been founded. Not only does this dimension of Davis's work directly address a concrete and pressing political problem—what to do about prisons?—but it also grapples with a host of theoretical questions. For example, what is the relationship between prisons, crime, and democracy? How does punishment relate to freedom and equality? How does political liberalism continue to justify and reproduce a massive system of incarceration?

At its heart, Davis's work—and the grassroots-led abolitionist social organization Critical Resistance, which she cofounded in the late 1990s—answers a broader and more untimely question: How would one articulate a political theory and normative defense of an idea that appears politically impossible?

Raising the possibility of prison abolition over the past two decades was a powerful intellectual intervention, but it was also not entirely out of step from the historical moment in which both Davis and we still reside. It was a response to a reality in which the impossible became possible. From the 1980s through the financial collapse of 2008, not only did the prison population increase in unprecedented ways, but neoliberal privatization measures, which championed the rule of free markets, eroded government regulation of the financial sectors and the social-welfare state, creating an unseen gap of economic inequality between the wealthiest 1 percent of Americans and the other 99.[20] Decrying prison abolition as nothing more than political utopianism thus seems odd. After all, the world abolitionists have been addressing seemed unreal. If anything, especially for many poor citizens of color, this world looked much more like a nightmare from which they could not awaken.

Davis's call for prison abolition followed in the footsteps of earlier nineteenth-century slavery abolitionists, whose utopian calls to end slavery were realized in their own lifetime, and American anarchists, who—with little political success—in the early twentieth century continued to call for an end to state rule, which empowered a military-industrial complex and unfettered capitalism to roam freely. Yet not only did Davis expand the abolitionist vision, which was largely focused on securing equal political rights and dignity for slaves, to include more robust socioeconomic equality, but she was also more attentive than her white anarchist antecedents to the racial and gendered experience of domination.

Countering the culturally widespread American view that punishment was nothing more than a deterrence strategy for crime, Davis stressed that it was an instrument of social control that dehumanized culturally demonized populations. Punishment reproduced existing systems of socioeconomic inequality and fractured spaces of social solidarity for marginalized populations. Punishment was neither natural nor apolitical.

Davis supplemented this analysis with a set of alternative democratic ideals and practices that she believed could most effectively replace prisons. Self-examination of the proclivity to feel apathy toward those suffering in unseen spaces needed to be tethered to a commitment to social interdependence, in which citizens saw themselves and others as requiring socioeconomic resources to flourish. A mode of judgment attentive to the political dimensions of seemingly private forms of violence and that rejected moralistic binaries needed to be adopted. Citizens needed to reimagine themselves as fallible while taking seriously restorative justice practices such as forgiveness, empathy, trust, and reconciliation.

Critical Resistance has developed many of Davis's insights by offering a set of concrete, practical strategies—including workshops, exercises, and toolkits for activists—that aim to deconstruct the notion of criminality and safety. Two tactics of prisoner protest have extended Davis's ideas. Hunger strikers dramatize how the state's use of solitary confinement violates its commitment to protect citizens from cruel and unusual punishment. And jailhouse lawyers use American constitutional guarantees of free speech to carve out the right to defend themselves legally in ways that reclaim their dignity.

PUNISHMENT AND RACE

Very few thinkers have, like Davis, so eloquently countered the view that state-enacted punishment is nothing but a race-neutral, strategic response meant to deter individuals from crime.[21] Central to this criminological position was a theory of individual behavior, which, as famously expressed by the Nobel Prize–winning economist Gary Becker as early as 1968, viewed people as rational actors—as economic man, *homo economicus*. Becker's rational subject could choose when to commit a crime and would calculate whether punishment was a cost worth incurring for the gain of succeeding. "A person commits an offence," he wrote, "if the expected utility to him exceeds the utility he could get by using his time and other resources at his activities."[22] If Becker was right—as many Democrats and Republicans believed him to be—then a spirit of fairness seemed to animate both President Richard Nixon's "law-and-order" rhetoric in the early 1970s and James Q. Wilson and George Kelling's theory of "broken-windows" policing, which argued in the 1980s that low-level criminal offenders such as petty drug dealers, drug addicts, burglars, and the homeless population needed to be swept off the streets. "Social psychologists and police officers tend to agree," they wrote, "that if a window in a building is broken and is left unrepaired, all the rest of the windows will soon be broken."[23] In their own estimate, neither Nixon's nor Wilson and Kelling's defense of punishment was discriminatory—that is, neither was based on gender, race, sexuality, or class background. After all, crime was an equal-opportunity endeavor enacted by profit maximizers who thought it was simply in their self-interest. Punishment, like crime, was thus also something of an equal-opportunity practice.

Davis saw things differently. "The prison," she claimed, "reveals congealed forms of antiblack racism that operate in clandestine ways," but "they are rarely recognized as racist."[24] Like Newton, Davis experienced punishment firsthand when she spent over a year in jail for criminal conspiracy after purchasing a firearm that was used by Jonathan Jackson, a seventeen-year-old African American radical who initiated a tense hostage situation in a California courtroom that led to a confrontation with police, leaving several people wounded and one dead. Although eventually acquitted of these charges, Davis came to understand that punishment disproportionately centered its attention upon and affected certain social groups. She agreed with Michel Foucault that the modern penitentiary had a history—that it was produced through eighteenth-century liberal-humanitarian discourses of rehabilitation and minimizing suffering.[25] But she criticized Foucault for overlooking the way that prisons were built upon and were extensions of racial orders. "A genealogy of imprisonment that would differ significantly from Foucault's," she explained, would "accentuate the links between confinement, punishment and race."[26] Even if one were to concede that there was something "race free" about Becker's notion of the criminal as rational actor, nothing was "race free" about a state-sanctioned system of punishment—informed by a network of policing and prisons—that had long treated acts committed by people of color as criminal offences in ways not identical to how it treated similar acts by white Americans. Even in its earliest forms, punishment was differentially and racially enacted. At the beginning of the nineteenth century, prisons were reserved for reforming and punishing "white wage-earning individuals," but slavery functioned differently:

> Within the institution of slavery . . . racialized forms of punishment developed alongside the emergence of the prison system . . . the deprivation of white freedom tended to affirm the whiteness of democratic rights and liberties. As white men acquired the privilege to be punished in ways that acknowledged their equality . . . the punishment of slaves was corporal, concrete and particular.[27]

Davis followed Wells in shifting attention away from the morality of state-based punishment or the moral culpability of those who committed crimes and onto the effect punishment had upon human beings. She connected what seemed for many Americans completely unconnected: what she called the contemporary "prison-industrial complex" with a history that began with slavery—the complete deprivation of black freedom, the exploitation of black labor, and unchecked violence against black bodies—to the more modified but no less egregious history of the Black Codes, which criminalized acts including vagrancy, breach of contract, and possession of firearms only if they were committed by people of color, and to the rise of the convict-lease system—the provision of prison labor for private companies—that disproportionately affected black Americans under Jim Crow.[28] "As black people were integrated into southern penal systems—and as the penal system became a system of penal servitude," Davis wrote, summarizing the way racialized punishment centered on what Foucault would call regimes that discipline bodies and what Marx would see as the ruthless exploitation of people's labor, "the punishments associated with slavery became further incorporated into the penal system."[29] In short, "both Emancipation and the authorization of penal servitude combined to create an immense black presence within southern prisons and to transform the character of punishment into managing former slaves as opposed to addressing problems of serious crime."[30]

Given the way American punishment was so closely linked to the operations of legal justice, which depended upon and reinforced certain notions of identity, there seemed something misplaced, Davis implied, in the liberal philosopher John Rawls's belief in *A Theory of Justice* (1971) that any concept of justice required individuals to go behind a so-called veil of ignorance—so they had no idea what their identity was or where they would end up socioeconomically, their "class position or social status" or "fortune in the distribution of natural assets and abilities . . . intelligence, strength, and the like."[31] In Davis's view, this was because words helped organize access to citizenship, creating the very truth of disenfranchisement rather than simply describing it. "Criminals" were "constituted as a class," Davis argued, "and, indeed, a class of human beings undeserving of the civil and human rights accorded to others."[32] The term "criminal" was often racialized. "Particularly in the United States," she suggested, "race has always played a central role in constructing presumptions of criminality."[33] From the 1980s onward, American critics of affirmative action had contended that race-conscious public policies such as affirmative action violated the American cultural commitment to colorblindness.[34] But arguably the much bigger problem— that itself affected black opportunities to go to college, get decently paying jobs, have access to affordable housing, and, in some cases, exercise their political right to vote—was that punishment was not colorblind.

The contemporary prison was an institution of social control that not only deprived human beings of freedom but also dehumanized them. As Davis wrote:

Imagine what our lives might have become if we were still grappling with the institution of slavery—or the convict lease system or racial segregation. But we do not have to speculate about living with the consequences of the prison. There is more than enough evidence in the lives of men and women who have been claimed by even more repressive institutions and who are denied access to their families, their communities, to educational opportunities, to productive and creative work, to physical and mental recreation.[35]

The prison, for Davis, was what segregated public housing was for Newton: a highly regulated space that not only restricted individual movement but created something approximating spiritual death.[36] The prison stifled creative work that gave one a sense of meaning, and it destroyed social connection, intimacy, and the potential for critical thought capable of confronting arbitrary formulations of state power. Nowhere was Davis's argument expressed as eloquently as in the writings of Mumia Abu-Jamal, an African American inmate on death row who, over the past thirty years, has become an outspoken prison-abolition advocate and whose conviction, based on highly circumstantial and questionable evidence, and continuing incarceration have become a symbol of racial injustice. Abu-Jamal wrote:

The ultimate effect of noncontact visits is to weaken, and finally to sever, family ties. Through this policy and practice the state skillfully and intentionally denies those it condemns a fundamental element and expression of humanity—that of touch and physical contact—and thereby slowly erodes family ties already made tenuous by the distance between home and prison. Thus prisoners are as isolated psychologically as they are temporally and spatially. By state action, they become "dead" to those who know and love them, and therefore dead to themselves. For who are people, but for their relations and relationships?[37]

For Davis, unlike Abu-Jamal, soul death not only gave rise to social death but also reproduced the system of socioeconomic inequality responsible for rising incarceration rates: "Mass imprisonment generates profits as it devours social wealth," Davis reflected, "and thus it tends to reproduce the very conditions that lead people to prison."[38] States stripping felons of voting rights was just the tip of the iceberg. Prisons were implicated in increasing capitalist profit.

> Corporations producing all kinds of goods—from buildings to electronic devices and hygiene products—and providing all kinds of services—from meals to therapy and healthcare—are now directly involved in the punishment business. . . . It was during the decade of the 1980s that corporate ties to the punishment system became more extensive and entrenched than ever before. But throughout the history of the U.S. prison system, prisoners have always constituted a potential source of profit.[39]

The libertarian valorization of free markets, Davis implied, was a myth.[40] On the one hand, state-regulated institutions funded by taxpayers were crucial for providing public jobs and creating a space for the private economy to flourish when deindustrialization was wreaking havoc on working-class Americans.[41] On the other hand, the capitalist economy depended upon new markets in which cheap and unfree labor could be turned into profit.

Prisons also mirrored another structurally similar state-sanctioned apparatus: the military. "The emergence of an ever expanding, ever more repressive prison system, [and] the economic, political, and ideological stakes in the punishment industry . . . [has] created a set of relations that recapitulate the development of the military industrial complex."[42] The prison, like the American military, provided jobs for many working-class people and was deployed upon populations to create the feeling of safety for the American majority.

Prisons solidified ideologies that perpetuated social inequality: "The institution of the prison has stockpiled ideas and practices that are hopefully approaching obsolescence in the larger society, but that retain all their ghastly vitality behind prison walls."[43] Following black feminists who claimed that sexual violence was a social problem not confined to the privacy of people's homes, Davis cast the prison, which was one of the most public yet deeply segregated-from-view spaces in America, as a microcosm of and productive force for gender inequality.[44] Prisons reinforced the gendered division of citizenship—between public actor and private person —by placing women behind bars in ways that kept masculine political power in place and where, as objects of male desire, their bodies would be objectified and physically abused:[45] "for women, prison is a space in which the threat of sexualized violence that looms in the larger society is effectively anchored as a routine aspect of the landscape of punishment behind prison walls."[46]

Like Walker, Davis thought that punishment fractured solidarity for the racially and socially marginalized. But unlike Walker, she thought this happened not through cultivating competition or ignorance but through creating deeply stigmatized emotions. Wells recognized that shame was a great intensifier: It naturalized and reinforced existing deleterious assumptions about gender roles that facilitated violence— recalling how white men were so ashamed of being emasculated by the imagined black rapist that they wanted to lynch black men with brutal intensity. For Davis, however, shame had more a depressive political function; it led people to disavow those who were stigmatized: "The ideologies that support the prison system demonize those who have been touched by it, and many of us are afraid to admit that we know someone who could be the kind of person who is behind bars."[47] Yet for many white Americans, a willful kind of amnesia—what Baldwin called "racial innocence"—rather than shame led to the relegation of prisons to the back of their minds, which only intensified the brutality experienced by those who lived within prison walls.[48] Davis explained: "The prison-industrial complex has materialized and mushroomed because we have all learned how to forget about prisons; we push them into the background even if they're in our own neighborhoods."[49]

American communitarians such as Robert Bellah and his coauthors, writing in their best-selling *Habits of the Heart* (1985), were convinced that the embrace of a socially unfettered individualism helped erode American civic engagement. At issue for them was not simply "whether self-contained individuals might withdraw from the public sphere to pursue purely private ends, but whether such individuals are capable of sustaining either a public *or* private life."[50] For Davis, however, individualism could become lethal for those behind bars, where it transformed into a radical kind of moral apathy. If no one cared about what was happening, then it would happen over and over again.

Davis's overarching argument was that punishment was not natural. Punishment was filtered through historically contingent factors, which themselves were caught in a milieu of interests entwined with the society in which one lived, and these interests often were always fully apparent to those who held them.

> "Punishment" does not follow from "crime" in the neat and logical sequence offered by discourses that insist on the justice of imprisonment, but rather punishment—primarily through imprisonment (and sometimes death)—is linked to agendas of politicians, the profit drive of corporations, and media representations of crime.[51]

In Davis's view, however, the dynamism of punishment was only matched by that of freedom. Freedom was not defined as a protection from government or as the ability to flourish but was a dynamic idea found in and through struggle. In one of her early philosophy lectures in 1969 at UCLA in a class on black literature, she found this definition in Douglass's *My Bondage and My Freedom*: Freedom was "the goal of an active process, something to be fought for, something to be gained in and through the process of struggle."[52] But freedom's dynamism cut both ways; it was as potent for white supremacy as it was valuable for racial justice. Prisons functioned analogously to racism. The prison, like racism, Davis explained, relieves

> us of the responsibility of thinking about the real issues afflicting those communities from which prisoners are drawn in such disproportionate numbers . . . it relieves us of the responsibility of seriously engaging with the problems of our society, especially those produced by racism and, increasingly, global capitalism.[53]

Prisons, like racism, displaced one's own darker emotions, such as rage and fear, onto stigmatized populations. Gone was the personal responsibility to confront these issues. This constituted an implicit critique of Rousseau, who once asserted that society created self-love (*amour-propre*) and a vicious form of social comparison, which unleashed within people feelings of hatred, competition, and jealousy. "Self-love," he claimed, "leads each individual to place greater value on himself than anyone else, which inspires all the evils that men do to one another."[54] For Davis, unlike Rousseau, the problem was not self-love but rather self-fear. Domination was caused by the very wish to be free of one's darker feelings and personal failures rather than simply the wish to preserve one's own economic or social freedom.

Prisons reminded Americans of their negative freedom of minimal physical mobility but also relieved them of the burden of social engagement that would abolish the excesses of global capitalism and racism so that all people were afforded the ability to flourish. Capturing this tension, Davis noted at once seriously and ironically: "Prisons tell us that we are free. We are able to recognize ourselves as participants in a democracy because we get to look at this institution that has walled off those who are not. And because there are those who are not, by comparing ourselves to them, we know that we are."[55]

PRISON ABOLITION

For Davis, prison abolition depended as much on robust political coalitions and concrete policy goals as it did upon individual ethical transformation. Walker called for cynical scrutiny of political institutions, Douglass for embodied political thinking about freedom, Wells for attentiveness to suffering, and Newton for empathetic perspectivalism. Davis added her voice to this chorus: "If I acknowledge that I am also implicated in the continued patterns of racism, I ask not only how do I help to change those whom I hold responsible for the structures of racism, I ask also: How do I change myself?"[56] Not only did Davis's turn to the personal seem opposed to a structural remedy to racial inequality, but this turn appeared problematic given the cultural discourse of her time. Although the feminist claim "the personal is political" was a powerful strategic intervention in countering the 1960s patriarchal society that refused to see the politics of reproductive rights, by the 1980s conservatives exercised a hegemonic hold over the language of personal responsibility and used that language to expand the prison system. Prisoners were responsible for their crimes; they deserved the ensuing repercussions.

These criticisms cannot be ignored, but they miss an important point. Personal action is both as capacious as it is malleable, defined less by its antithesis to collective action and more by what one does with it. Indeed, the kind of transformation Davis counseled centered on cultivating a utopian imagination in ways that threatened what was practical. Central to this was postulating what Kant called a "regulative ideal"—something that did not yet exist but that served as a transcendental aspiration for which individuals could strive.[57] Asking the question "what if?" and assuming that the impossible could become possible did not mean confusing hope with reality. "The prison," Davis acknowledged, "is considered an inevitable and permanent feature of our social lives . . . in most circles prison abolition is simply unthinkable and implausible."[58] But the very act of asking an unasked question, of assuming what was not realized could be realized, constituted a powerful political-theoretical intervention.

> The most effective abolitionist strategies will contest these relationships and propose alternatives to pull them apart. What, then, would it mean to imagine a system in which punishment is not allowed to become the source of corporate profit? How can we imagine a society in which race and class are not primary determinants of punishment? Or one in which punishment is no longer the central concern in the making of justice?[59]

The act of questioning, for Walker, reflected one's capacity for democratic judgment, while for Davis it inspired an intellectual process for severing the link between the practical and the valuable. Corporate profit needed to be isolated from punishment rather than curtailed through government regulatory practices. Justice needed to be transformed into something that was not about meting out appropriate punishments for alleged crimes but rather what encouraged self-determination and equality. Social statuses like race and class, which were often seen as surmountable barriers to individual achievement, needed to be examined for the way they legitimized state-sanctioned violence.

Something capacious was at the heart of this intellectual work: a holistic political imagination that appreciated the multilayered intersections of personal, social, political, economic, and civic life. Reform sought to improve what existed, while abolition was about entirely reimagining what it might look like:

> A necessary step in winning greater freedom and greater justice is to imagine the world as we want it to be, a world in which women are not assumed to be inferior to men, a world without war, a world without xenophobia, a world without fenced borders designed to make us think of people from Mexico and Latin America as aliens and enemies. It is important to imagine a world in which binary conceptions of gender no longer govern modes of segregation or association, and one in which violence is eliminated from state practices as well as from our intimate lives, in heterosexual and same-sex relationships alike. And, of course, it is important to imagine a world without war.[60]

Abolition depended on a fundamental transformation of the prevalent ideologies. Americans needed to renounce a biologically deterministic view of gender identity that asserted that women's potential was to be found in the household;[61] the idea of national cultural purity, in which white Anglo-Saxon values were to be upheld against all others;[62] and that war was essential for peace.[63]

So too was it necessary to upend the "public-private dichotomy." Violence against women and queer, nonheteronormative populations was, as Davis noted, "still seen as private and personal," but it needed to be seen as informing regimes of punishment.[64] Antiprison activism needed to extend globally, from struggling against torture, which made physical harm a tool for national security, to the "War on Terror," which encouraged domestic racism toward Arab Americans. "Linked to the abolition of prisons," she wrote, "is the abolition of the instruments of war, the abolition of racism, and, of course, the abolition of social circumstances that lead poor men and women to look toward the military as their only avenue of escape from poverty, homelessness, and lack of opportunity."[65] Dismantling American punishment, Davis believed, required what the contemporary philosopher Judith Butler has recently identified as crucial for global responsibility: undoing the discursive and conceptual frames that make certain lives grievable and ungrievable. "To say that a life is injurable, for instance, or that it can be lost, destroyed, or systematically neglected to the point of death," Butler wrote, "is to underscore . . . its precariousness (that life requires various social and economic conditions to be met in order to be sustained as a life)."[66] This meant shattering the vocabulary of normalcy that sponsored an economy of violence—directing it against some and withholding it from others—and an economy of human worth, which was predicated on the notion that certain lives were indispensable and others disposable.

Also necessary was a shift in perspective, from a philosophy of pick-oneself-up-by-the-bootstraps individualism to the idea of social interdependence. The community-to-prison pipeline eroded social resources essential for freedom.[67] A program of decarceration would require the "revitalization of education at all levels, a health system that provides free physical and mental care to all."[68] No less important was the radicalization of American education. Davis shared Dewey's belief that education was the bedrock of democracy: the space where citizens learned to listen and disagree.[69] Dewey devoted his attention to revolutionizing the power relations within the classroom—so students would move from passive to active learners, making ideas matter for their lives—but Davis was concerned with demilitarizing the education system.

> Thus, we need schools—schools that don't feel like prisons. . . . As schoolchildren they are already treated like prisoners. When the message they receive in school is that they live in the world as objects of surveillance and discipline, and that security guards are more important and powerful than teachers, they are clearly learning how to be prisoners.[70]

Nondomination, for Davis, meant not the idea centered on public citizenship—to participate in politics freely and vigorously—but a commitment to creating conditions of nonviolence that enabled creative human development.

In Davis's view, the moral boundaries between those who were free and imprisoned needed to be dismantled. "If we agree to begin to acknowledge that there is no essential difference between people in prison and people in the free world," she wrote, "then we can seek to create more contact between the inside and the outside, and between prison and what prisoners call the 'free world.'"[71] Accepting this idea of equality did not fit into the version of classical liberal thought espoused by Locke. For Locke, the criminal may have been equal to everyone else in terms of their capacity to reason, but when the criminal committed a crime, they existed beyond the reasonable, moral community. "In transgressing the law of nature, the offender declares himself to live by another rule than that of reason and common equity," Locke claimed, "and so he becomes dangerous to mankind."[72]

Unlike Locke, Davis refused to banish those who committed crimes from the realm of reasonableness. If anything, she countered Locke by calling upon citizens to diminish their feelings of moral superiority toward those who transgressed the law. This required adopting a denaturalized and unexceptional view of crime. Crime needed to be seen as nothing more than a social designation connected to the law, which could be unjust.[73]

In the post–civil rights era, a hallmark of American conservative discourse was racializing and sensationalizing crime. In the 1970s and 1980s, Reagan invoked the specter of the "welfare queen" who fraudulently lived off of government's dime, and the Republican presidential candidate George H. W. Bush in 1988 described the mythical black rapist, exemplified by Willie Horton, who, upon being released on a furlough authorized by Massachusetts's Democratic governor, Michael Dukakis, raped a white woman. These images relieved white Americans citizens of the guilt for sending many black people to jail and helped destroy the welfare state—which would be gutted through the Personal Responsibility and Work Opportunity Act of 1996, signed into law by Bill Clinton, and which replaced federal government entitlement programs for the poor with those that were substantially weaker and contingent upon work.[74]

To counter this ideological discourse, Davis recast the meaning of "criminal." Criminal acts cut across racial boundaries and were deeply pervasive in everyday American life. Davis asked: "What is a crime? How do you define a crime? The fundamental legal definition of crime is an action in violation of a law. Whenever you have broken a law you have committed a crime. People generally refer to crimes as felonies, rather than misdemeanors or traffic violations. However, people break the law all the time."[75] Expanding the idea of criminality recalled Walker's earlier attempt to equalize Americans by recalling the inescapable fact of mortality, but Davis's strategy emphasized the way fallibility was an inescapable part of the human condition—something that could never be fully eradicated but only haphazardly managed. A traffic violation, Davis explained, was not morally equivalent to murder, but the forces that inspired one to transgress the law—everything from unchecked desire, to cold-blooded self-interest, to a false sense of necessity—were universal. Arguments about the moral rectitude of punishment provided easy cover for masking the complex dynamics of human behavior. Ideological justification replaced acknowledging harm.

Absolute moral superiority was thus a fiction. Criminality was an elastic concept as universal as it was banal. Prisoners were unexceptional in this fundamental way: They were, like everyone else, ordinary human beings prone to error. One needed to ask whether it was just for people to live the way they did behind bars. Davis asked citizens to consider: "Have you ever looked at a prison and imagined what was happening on the other side of those walls? . . . what it might be like to live under those repressive conditions? . . . that people just like you are in prison, people who may have made one mistake and never had the opportunity to get themselves back on the right track?"[76]

An even more radical practice Davis counseled was striving for greater physical proximity. She dramatized this when she brought her gender-studies class on incarcerated women at San Francisco State University to an actual women's prison. Positioning the prisoners as teachers challenged the expectation shared by students and prisoners that the students would be the ones teaching the inmates. "They taught the students about life in jail," Davis would go on to say, "what went on there, what the major problems were, and they got to choose how the students, those in possession of formal learning, could effectively assist the prisoners. This reversal of assumed hierarchies of knowledge created a radical and exciting learning environment."[77] Undoing assumptions of moral difference entailed placing oneself in a position where one would be forced to rethink one's own agency. Placing in positions of agency those who were disenfranchised challenged one dominant American conservative position of the 1980s and 1990s, advanced most notably by the political scientist Lawrence Mead in *Beyond Entitlement* (1986), which asserted that the state needed to be a paternalistic force that educated the poor into normative standards that would make them capable of exercising full citizenship. Mead wrote that the best hope for solving the "welfare problem" was "to require recipients to function where they already are, as dependents . . . they need to face the requirements, such as work, that true acceptance in society requires."[78] For Davis, prisoners not only had worthwhile local knowledge; that knowledge was also a form of power crucial both for self-determination and for contesting state power.

Equally important for abolition were community reconciliation programs. Taking seriously reconciliation may have appeared odd, given that Davis was a political radical whose political affiliation had once been the Communist Party USA and who endorsed Marx's structural critique of capitalism. But it followed from her understanding of the power of restorative justice. Davis applied to the American context the ideas of the South African philosophers Nelson Mandela and Desmond Tutu, who created the Truth and Reconciliation Commission (TRC) to help postapartheid South Africa complete the transition from minority-white to majority-black rule.[79]

In her conclusion to *Are Prisons Obsolete?* she took intellectual sustenance from the example of Linda and Peter Biehl, who forgave several young black South African men who, while chanting antiwhite slogans, partook in the stoning to death of their daughter, Amy, a white American

Fulbright student visiting the country in 1993. After successfully petitioning the family for amnesty during the proceedings of the TRC in 1998, two of the attackers, Easy Nofemela and Ntobeko Peni, were released from prison. Shortly thereafter, the Biehls invited them to work as instructors for their foundation, which was named after their deceased daughter. One of the perpetrators, Nofemela, eventually told the Biehls, "I know you lost a person you love. I want you to forgive me and take me as your child."[80] Years later, Davis continued,

> Linda Biehl, when asked how she now feels about the men who killed her daughter, said, "I have a lot of love for them." After Peter Biehl died in 2002, she bought two plots of land for them in memory of her husband so that Nofemela and Peni can build their own homes. A few days after the September 11 attacks, the Biehls had been asked to speak at a synagogue in their community. According to Peter Biehl, "We tried to explain that sometimes it pays to shut up and listen to what other people have to say, to ask: 'Why do these things terrible things happen?' instead of simply reacting."[81]

Good reasons exist to be skeptical of restorative justice. For example, it can depoliticize problems by turning them into moral issues.[82] But never did Davis assert that it was superior to political or economic reform. Reconciliation was more about developing an alternative democratic vision of community. In her depiction of the Biehls as exemplary citizens, she did much more than emphasize the importance of social trust.[83] A crucial function of reconciliation, Davis made vivid, was to counter the dominant logic of politics by replacing the thirst for retribution with love, rational self-interest with forgiveness.

Prisons exemplified a theory of democratic society founded on the notion of emotional defensiveness, but the process of working through past trauma interpersonally to repair what had been smashed emphasized mutual vulnerability.[84] Undertaking the emotionally strenuous decision to forgive someone who had committed an unforgivable crime or listening to accusations could remake the moral grammar of the world in which both victims and perpetrators lived. [85] Simply ridding the community of transgressors reified the world while leaving untouched the profound sense of loss that the crime unleashed or the social relations and community values from which it emerged. Reconciliation taught citizens to assume responsibility for collective life, to understand opposing perspectives, and to be capable of doing what once seemed impossible, like empathizing with those who wronged them the most. This helped undermine the binary that punishment encouraged between normal and abnormal, right and wrong, practical and impractical, possible and impossible.

CRITICAL RESISTANCE AND ABOLITIONISM

Over the past two decades, no organization has sought to implement Davis's theoretical insights into a full-fledged political movement like Critical Resistance. Started in 1997, with Davis as one of its cofounders, as a conference meant to address what its organizers called the "prison-industrial complex"—"the overlapping interests of government and industry that use surveillance, policing, and imprisonment as solutions to economic, social and political problems"[86]—by 2001 Critical Resistance was a national political organization with local chapters in New York City, Los Angeles, Oakland, and Portland. It has organized protest campaigns against everything from prison construction to juvenile-detention centers and has called for expanding affordable housing, health-care resources, and addiction-treatment centers. Through its newspaper, *The Abolitionist*, Critical Resistance raises awareness about intersectional oppression based on multiple identity standpoints and challenges American law-and-order rhetoric and the demonizing images of those viewed as deviant. Published since 2005 and written by prison activists, prisoners, and ex-prisoners, it tackles issues including immigration, the national-security state, sexual violence in prison, and the link between capitalism and prisons, with the aims of providing incarcerated people in the United States with a political voice and of raising consciousness about their lives throughout the globe.

Mirroring the Panther Ten-Point Program, Critical Resistance borrows its political philosophy from a text published almost thirty years prior to the group's formation: the Prison Research Education Project's (PREAP) *Instead of Prisons: A Handbook for Abolitionists* (1976).[87] Published in the summer of 2006, the fourth issue of *The Abolitionist* excerpted nine broad perspectives.[88] By invoking a strategy used in various ways by Douglass, Wells, Du Bois, and King, Perspective One described prisons as antithetical to Enlightenment moral principles, upon which U.S. political culture was ostensibly founded and to which it proclaims commitment: "Imprisonment is morally reprehensible and indefensible and must be abolished."[89] Perspective Two cast language as a form of power that could empower or disempower human beings or frame the contours of the institutions that shape their life chances.[90] As it suggested: "The message of abolition requires 'honest' language and new definitions."[91] Perspective Three argued for adopting a restorative conception of justice rather than one based in punishment, claiming that "abolitionists believe reconciliation, not punishment, is a proper response to criminal acts."[92]

Perspective Four—embodying Newton's empathetic perspectivalism—emphasized the difference between institutions of oppression, which had their own logic, and the citizens who populated them, that is, those who worked within them and those who were worked on by them: "Abolitionists work with prisoners but always remain 'nonmembers' of the established prison system."[93] Perspective Five followed anticolonial thinkers that warned against the seduction of paternalism ("Abolitionists are 'allies' of prisoners rather than traditional 'helpers'"), while Perspective Six—taking seriously the notion of radical democracy agency—called for a commitment to prisoner self-determination, suggesting that "abolitionists realize that the empowerment of prisoners and ex-prisoners is crucial to prison system change."[94] Echoing Foucault's theory of power, Perspective Seven argued that power existed everywhere, including in those who were disenfranchised, rather than being restricted to elites.[95] "Power," it claimed, "is available to each of us for challenging and abolishing the prison system." Perspective Eight denaturalized crime, making it productive of social conditions and "mainly a consequence of the structure of society" rather than driven by individual biological failures; Perspective Nine reimagined human flourishing to depend not on self-interest but upon a community founded on what feminists would call an "ethic of care."[96] "Only in a caring community," it said, could "corporate and individual redemption can take place."[97]

Critical Resistance has transformed this philosophy into a policy platform. First, replacing capital punishment with health, "ending the death penalty, and putting appropriate care in place" are ideas that espouse a view of government that ought to nourish rather than simply protect people from physical harm. Second, improving rehabilitation programs for "education, therapy, drug and alcohol treatment, job training, art, athletics and other structured social activities" is a policy that emphasizes the notion of a whole person who cannot be reduced to the crime for which he or she is imprisoned. Third, ending prison-guard brutality and administrative corruption and allowing for prisoners to organize politically "without the threat of punishment" all make the prison subject to democratic accountability and suggest that those languishing within its walls are deserving of the right of freedom of assembly. Fourth, sentences should be reduced and parole opportunities increased. Fifth, state-run responses to harm reduction should be reduced or eliminated and replaced with community programs.[98]

In "The Abolitionist Toolkit," Critical Resistance offers pedagogic material including discussion questions and critical writing and thinking exercises that ask citizens to rethink commonly held theoretical ideals. Deepening Davis's thoughts on the politics of language, in a chapter called "Words Matter: Language and Abolition," Critical Resistance seeks to make serviceable for prison abolition the French poststructuralist philosopher Jacques Derrida's thinking about the power of hierarchical binary oppositions. "We are not dealing with a peaceful coexistence *vis-à-vis* but rather a violent hierarchy," Derrida claimed. "One of the two terms governs the other . . . or has the upper hand."[99] Derrida's name isn't mentioned in the text, but his ideas permeate it. Oppositions such as "guilty v. innocent," "violent v. nonviolent," "criminal v. victim," and "punishment v. justice," so says the toolkit, conjure specific cultural representations that are positioned along a value hierarchy, where the term in the first part of the binary is seen as of a lesser, or more harmful, order.[100] Yet both terms in the binary are intensified precisely because of their opposition: The "criminal" is "criminal" precisely because of the "innocent," and the "innocent" is "innocent" precisely because of the "criminal."

Supplementing this insight into language's role in creating social inequality are critical exercises that aim to make language emancipatory. Marx famously contended that the task of philosophy was not to conceptualize the world philosophically as it was to change it,[101] but Critical Resistance asserts the purpose of language—which Marx himself was uninterested in—is not to describe the world but to change it. "How could you re-phrase this information [concerning the binaries that perpetuate the prison-industrial complex] to be in line with the ideas that no one should be in a cage, and that putting people in cages helps no one?"[102] Words could be subversively resignified by those seeking to trouble extant social identities[103]—examples might include black youth resignifying the language of "nigga" to invoke black solidarity, gay citizens reclaiming "queer" to mean something that counters heteronormative identity, or youth reimagining "punk" as something that resists conformity—the toolkit asks: "Are there ways to use the word 'against itself'—to use it in a way that challenges the way it's most used now?"[104]

This open-ended question embodies the kind of pedagogic democratic ethos, like Walker's, that insists upon everyone's capacity for expressing their own reasoned thoughts—but one term the toolkit calls for rethinking is *safety*. Security has been as central to American political culture as much as any other ideal, but over the past fifteen years, in the wake of the September 11, 2011, terrorist attacks on the World Trade Center and Pentagon, it has arguably become one of the most significant. Not only has this allowed for a doubling down on mass incarceration, but it has legitimized the U.S.-led wars in Afghanistan and Iraq and the construction of an expansive domestic national-security state, which has included warrantless wiretapping programs and the covert surveillance of American citizens.

Critical Resistance confronts the language of safety, rather than abandoning or simply positioning it on a lower normative order than liberty: "Policing and prisons are held up as the only solution, the only way to control problem and create safety. One positive way to talk about what we do is to challenge that idea by talking to people about what really makes our communities safe. What else makes safety?"[105] Critical Resistance's answer to this question, that "tough-on-crime" laws have had "little impact on 'public safety'" severs the link between safety and incarceration.[106] Everyday insecurity is an existential experience for all people—in varying degrees and at different moments in their lives—that can never be fully eradicated by removing certain people from society. So too does Critical Resistance's claim that "random violence is not as common as it's made out to be" challenge the idea that self-interested desires to harm others are central to the human condition.[107] Moreover, its suggestion that "most physical injury happens to people who know each other" describes violence as an interpersonal, temporary problem rather than suggesting that conflict is indiscriminate and ongoing.[108]

Rethinking language is only part of the equation. No less important is implementing the Canadian Aboriginal practice of "circles," which extends Davis's thinking about reconciliation. As a community-based healing process involving two discussion facilitators—those who inflicted the harm and those who were harmed—circles dramatize that moral wrongs are experienced, with clear lines between victims and perpetrators, but that these wrongs can be repaired. After gaining as much information as possible about the circumstances and addressing the competing narratives of the harm—without recourse to the various evidentiary procedures that comprise the state-sanctioned legal trial process and with a diverse array of emotions and concerns that may not be normal in the courtroom—participants decide on the appropriate form of redress, which can range from compensation for lost property to interpersonal mediation.[109] Circumventing the state and embracing self-determination clearly has limitations. Circles have not been used to address murder, they can contain age- or gender-based power imbalances, and they cannot alone change policing and punishment systems or the larger patterns of social inequality that give rise to crime.[110]

But circles provide a regulative ideal for justice that opposes the prison-industrial complex, which defines itself through "punishment, authoritarianism, racism, profit-seeking, and state control," with "personal and social transformation, accountability, equality, fairness, understanding, cooperation, sharing, solidarity, forgiveness, popular participation, and self-determination."[111] Circles can be valuable pedagogically in ways that lead to critical thinking about prisons, even if they cannot replace prisons in the foreseeable future. Critical Resistance urges citizens to adopt circles for a role-playing classroom exercise: to redress a situation in which a high-school student experiences facial deformities for life after being beaten by one of his peers, who himself is regularly beaten by an alcoholic father. Intended less for disclosing that prisons are unjust or that violence is always motivated by tragic social circumstances,[112] this exercise is more about exploring the complex ways that harm becomes manifest, the feelings that it conjures, and the competing ways to address it. The questions ask: "1. What values of principles should guide our circle as we discuss both what happened and how we plan to address it? 2. What happened? How were you affected by what occurred? 3. As much as possible, what can we do to repair the harm that has been done? 4. What can we do to prevent future forms of harm in our community?"[113] Against the prevailing system of legal justice that too often ignores—or even worse, as a way of legitimating itself, intentionally masks the contested narratives and views on authority through which it operates—the questions posed here, which follow insights of critical race theory, transform justice into an ongoing process that is about asking questions rather than answering them, about reflecting upon the values upon which justice should be based.[114]

HUNGER STRIKING AND JAILHOUSE LAWYERING

Critical Resistance aims to empower prisoners, but prisoner protests enrich the theory of prison abolition. Prisoners don't have many tools to protest, but one thing they have is their bodies—a tool that they have used in various hunger strikes. Consisting of thirty thousand strikers statewide and lasting for sixty days, the summer 2013 hunger strike at California Pelican Bay State Prison was not only one of the most famous in recent memory but the largest in history. Protestors mobilized against degrading conditions such as arbitrary solitary confinement, lack of nutritious food, group punishment, and administrative abuse while calling for more creative programming. The strike eventually led to hearings and reform proposals in the California state legislature. This materialized into marginal benefits for those in solitary confinement (like more family visits; permission to use radios and televisions; the use of utensils, bowls, and cups; and underwear) and more significant changes (a more extensive review and oversight of solitary confinement practices).

The Pelican Bay hunger strike, however, was as much a protest tool as it was a statement about the contradictions of American culture. The Panthers' protest was directed outward against police officers; hunger striking is directed inward. The inmate's body becomes the same symbolic weapon that the gun was for the Panthers: It problematized American notions of freedom and bodily security.

Hunger striking replaces the idea of self-defense with self-sacrifice to highlight the intensity of state violence. State violence is so devastating that the only solution is to double down on self-directed violence. The state's commitment to protect a citizen's body as expressed in the Ninth Amendment's protection against cruel and unusual punishment is beyond nonexistent. The state actually does the exact opposite: It destroys the body and mind. By dramatizing how prisoners have commitments to transcendent ideals such as human dignity and justice, hunger striking challenges the idea of a fixed criminal identity—the assumption that those who commit crimes are somehow defined by self-interest or immorality. Like the civil rights protestors who continued to march in the streets despite the racial violence that threatened them and thus reflected their exemplary civic love of America, hunger strikers say that their commitment to democracy is so intense that they are willing to die for it.

Another form of prisoner protest is jailhouse lawyering, which consists of prisoners informally assisting fellow inmates with legal issues related to sentencing, probation, and stay of execution and educating them about their habeas corpus rights.[115] In her foreword to Mumia Abu-Jamal's *Jailhouse Lawyers*, Davis herself applauded the way

> jailhouse lawyers have challenged inhumane prison conditions, and even when they themselves have been unaware of this connection, have implicitly followed the standards of such human rights instruments as the Standard Minimum Rules for the Treatment of Prisoners (1955), the International Covenant on Civil and Political Rights (1966), and the Convention Against Torture, and Other Cruel, Inhuman or Degrading Treatment or Punishment (1984).[116]

Jailhouse lawyers mobilize the principles of international human rights to call attention to and subvert American democracy's unjust outcomes while carving out rights in spaces that do not easily grant them. Challenging the notion that prisoners should be, or the fact that they actually are, barred from public life and the fruits of citizenship, jailhouse lawyers may not always be legally successful, but they reclaim their dignity and that of those they represent through the practice of direct action that Douglass identified over one hundred and fifty years ago in *My Bondage and My Freedom*.

PRISON ABOLITION AND AMERICAN POLITICS

A sober assessment of American politics might lead some to insist that prison abolition seems politically impractical, if not impossible. Perhaps the ideology of socialism—as the recent rise of the Democratic presidential candidate Vermont senator Bernie Sanders illustrates— might have a fighting chance today, even if for much of the twentieth century it was a demonizing epithet reserved only for those who were depicted as antipatriotic atheists. But calls for prison abolition would likely be treated with the same antipathy as earlier twentieth-century anarchist calls to abolish the state. American citizens might concede

Davis's argument that prisons are unjust for the same reasons some agreed with Emma Goldman's critique of the American state, which she called "the greatest criminal, breaking every written and natural law . . . killing in the form of war and capital punishment."[117] Prisons can easily be corrupted by unbridled capitalism, they can undermine individual rights, and they can become purveyors of human suffering. But in the very same breath, even the most progressive citizens would surely temper such concessions with a dose of prudent realism: The price of potential human suffering that prisons create for a relatively small minority of the U.S. population might be morally indefensible, but it is cheaper than the instability that might come from losing such institutions of social control over those who commit crimes.

If this weren't difficult enough, the abolitionist movement faces an even steeper climb because some of the most successful recent arguments for downsizing the prison population—focusing mainly on nonviolent offenders—have failed to address the social factors that compel people to commit crime. Arguments about rational self-interest based in cost-ineffectiveness, which highlight that state-run prisons are too expensive to maintain with taxpayers' hard-earned dollars, have not only given private companies the opportunity to transform punishment into a profit-making enterprise but have left unchanged Americans' reluctance to support rehabilitation programs for the most vulnerable. The beneficiaries of prison-downsizing programs no longer have to live behind bars, but, given the pitiful public investment in state-run social-welfare programs, many are now free to live much like they did before they were incarcerated: homeless or jobless, perhaps suffering from severe mental illness or debilitating drug or alcohol addiction.

Although these obstacles might dishearten even the most optimistic of political radicals, the theory of prison abolition exceeds a narrow political goal. A regulative ideal as much as a political objective, abolition is powerful because it reflects a unique theory of citizenship that calls for the ongoing perfection of tactics and striving toward a horizon that cannot be fully reached; it calls for acknowledging forms of social interconnectedness that are not only obscured and rendered invisible but that sponsor inequality. At the same time, prison abolition draws attention to the power of language for democracy while taking seriously the ethical language of reconciliation.

As foreign as they might be to the mainstream of the American tradition, perhaps these alternative practices of citizenship, alongside prison abolition, might not seem so foreign if, as abolitionists insist, Americans actually began the direct action championed by thinkers as diverse as anarchists such as Goldman, pragmatists such as Dewey, transcendentalists such as Thoreau, liberals such as King and, of course, Walker, Douglass, Wells, and Newton. Prison abolitionists share a core insight with all these thinkers: that the feasibility of any political project depends less on argumentatively sound reasoning than on the process by which one attempts to realize this project in the world.

Action is therefore not simply a testing ground for a prepackaged theoretical truth but creates new truths. Action can challenge one's capacity to withstand what appears insurmountable and to realize what appears unrealizable. It is almost as if the very unlikelihood that prison abolition would ever succeed today or even ten years from now requires those few Americans who are serious about the project to keep acting as if it were possible now. Indeed, Davis's and the prison-abolition movement's call to end mass incarceration today recall the words of King. In "Letter from a Birmingham Jail," he chastised Alabama clergymen who, borrowing the novelist William Faulkner's advice in the 1950s, told black civil rights protestors to be patient in their racial justice struggle so as not to alienate potentially sympathetic moderate whites. King's words are still as relevant now as they were then:

> We must use time creatively, in the knowledge that the time is always ripe to do right. Now is the time to make real the promise of democracy and transform our pending national elegy into a creative psalm of brotherhood. Now is the time to lift our national policy from the quicksand of racial injustice to the solid rock of human dignity.[118]

CONCLUSION

The Future of Resistance

W hat are the larger conclusions we can draw from the history of African American resistance? What might this history tell us about the nature of African American intellectual life, American culture and democracy, and the meaning of resistance itself? How should we understand the present and future of African American resistance in the United States?

First, there are several ways to explain African American resisters' unique strategy of engaging American culture and the particular counternarratives they advanced. One explanation is that African American resisters—like the most ardent of American patriots—could never fully escape engaging with the trope of American exceptionalism. Exceptionalism is the idea that there is something peculiar about American identity: that it is progressive, freedom loving, and marked by a remarkable degree of consistency between the ideal and the practice of democracy.[1] Another explanation, however, is that rather than personally subscribe to what Jerry Watts calls "the hegemonic rhetorics of America,"[2] African American resisters engaged these rhetorics strategically because they were pragmatically aware of the way American politics is limited by them.[3] This interpretation is more apt given that—more often than not—resisters described American ideals in subversive ways. If anything, exceptionalism, for them, was not a reference to the moral benevolence or political genius of American liberalism but of the violence of American racism; democracy was not narrowly constrained to a procedural practice that was about voting and political participation but had more of a social-democratic texture.

The existential act of resistance itself, which is dialectically intertwined with the forces it is criticizing and with which it is breaking, can also help explain why African American resisters revised American ideals in the ways that they did. What makes resistance radical is also what can make it conservative. The resister may seek to articulate a new understanding of rights, freedom, social equality, political power, and human dignity, but the goal of successfully conveying these claims to an audience might also temper their radical potential. Real-world political achievements require strategic concessions that resisters unconsciously acknowledge. The more resisters borrow dominant forms of claim making, the more powerfully these claims register; the more they name goals that are within the bounds of political possibility, the more likely these goals will be taken seriously.[4] Here lies one fundamental paradox of resistance: Without the new vocabulary resisters create, the possibility of radical change will always be dismissed in favor of gradual reform. Yet the more effectively resistance carves out a new vocabulary for politics, the less likely it will be heard.

The resister's commitment to racial justice can also explain the contours of resistance in political thought. Insofar as racial justice names a condition in which racism is eliminated and freedom is achieved for all individuals and groups, it seems plausible why African American resisters favor the theoretical principles of solidarity based on shared political interests, a plural notion of the good, a notion of democratic agency where one is endowed the authority to determine one's own life choices, the inclusion of as many voices as possible, and the embrace of direct action that challenges existing inequalities.[5]

Finally, the long history of American injustice might help explain the texture of African American resistance. American racial inequality is unfortunately but one variation on a cyclical theme that seems to be the rule rather than the exception in America.[6] Evidence abounds, from the shameless socioeconomic marginalization of and sexual violence toward women, to the vociferous xenophobic attacks on immigrants and the unabashed demonization of LGBT populations, to the big-business assault on the rights of the American working class. Sometimes African American resisters have fallen prey to perpetuating these injustices— sexism, homophobia, classism, and even racism. But more often than not they tie their thinking to a critique of these injustices, exposing how racism is abetted by them in ways that compromise democracy.

But awareness of this history also encourages African American resisters to treat with cynicism claims of goodwill or progress. And it encourages them to be sensitive toward spaces where robust critique and utopian imagination can thrive. The more one expects injustice to be lurking around the corner, the more likely one will seize on those fugitive moments of opportunity to make claims that are generally outside conventional wisdom. African American resistance thought thus shares a certain affinity with what the political theorist Sheldon Wolin has identified as the essence of democracy: that it is a "fugitive" practice as ephemeral as it is powerful.[7]

RESISTANCE AND THE LIMITATIONS OF AMERICAN DEMOCRACY

Appreciating the rich intellectual history of African American resistance can also shed insights on American democracy. Widespread backlash from much of the white electorate, political elites, and even segments of the black population against slave abolition, the antilynching movement, the Panthers, and prison abolitionists seems to confirm that the American public is deeply invested in the values of procedural democracy, elite rule, capitalism, and the notion of negative liberty.[8] Any perceived threats to these institutions are treated with skepticism, if not overt hostility.

But this cannot eradicate something powerful that defines democracy. In democracy, the idea of "the people" is a performative category, which is always more and less than each of its existing iterations and whose meaning depends on the particular movements who claim to speak on its behalf.[9] At the same time, the tension between core democratic ideals lends itself to political struggle. After all, if too much democratic freedom may undermine equality and too much sovereignty can threaten the commitment to plurality, then democracy will always be a product of ongoing political contestation that can never be fully completed.[10]

American resisters clearly have their work cut out for them. But these tensions ensure that resistance will always have a future because democracy is, on some level, as much science fiction as reality, a futuristic fantasy where more than what is initially imagined can become possible.

BLACK LIVES MATTER AND THE FUTURE OF RESISTANCE

A case in point: Just when a new wave of African American resistance seemed unlikely, the future arrived full steam in the form of Black Lives Matter (BLM), which has come to prominence in the wake of the tragic series of police killings of unarmed African American men—Michael Brown, who was shot to death by a white police officer, Darren Wilson, in Ferguson, Missouri, and Eric Garner, who was strangled to death by another white officer, Daniel Pantaleo, and other black males killed by police officers across the nation: Tamir Rice in Cleveland, Freddie Gray in Baltimore, Walter Scott in North Charleston, Samuel DuBose in Cincinnati, and Laquan McDonald in Chicago.

Founded as the Twitter hashtag #BlackLivesMatter by three queer black women activists, Patrisse Cullors, Alicia Garza, and Opal Tometi, in the aftermath of the 2013 acquittal of George Zimmerman, a neighborhood watchman who, invoking Florida's "stand-your-ground" law, shot and killed an African American male youth, seventeen-year-old Trayvon Martin, in Sanford, Florida, in 2012, the movement has since become an international force, engaging in direct political actions aimed to eliminate everything from race-based police brutality and mass incarceration to socioeconomic inequality and unjust immigration policy. Black Lives Matter's populist language and youth-directed activism built upon the energy of the anti-inequality movement Occupy Wall Street, which in 2012 brought into relief the way the neoliberal privatization efforts and trickle-down economic theories of the past thirty years have only intensified the longstanding gap between the superrich, the "1 percent" of the population, and the overwhelming majority, the "99 percent."

But if Occupy Wall Street highlighted the way citizens of all identities were dominated by corporate greed and the excesses of global capitalism, Black Lives Matter takes seriously the particular normative value of black life—in an American society that has, at best, aimed to render unexceptional the distinct experience of black people in the United States or, at worst, has sought to eradicate systematically black people's dignity. As the organization's website declares, "Black Lives Matter is an ideological and political intervention in a world where Black lives are systematically and intentionally targeted for demise. It is an affirmation of Black folks' contributions to this society, our humanity, and our resilience in the face of deadly oppression."[11] BLM has mobilized in response to the painful reality once expressed by the Panthers but more recently by the African American journalist Ta-Nehisi Coates's National Book Award–winning and bestselling *Between the World and Me* (2015): The black American body has always been and still is degraded, and it is seen as expendable and as a potential receptacle of state-sponsored violence. Coates writes:

> Perhaps there has been, at some point in history, some great power whose elevation was exempt from the violent exploitation of other human bodies. If there has been, I have yet to discover it. But this banality of violence can never excuse America, because America makes no claim to the banal.[12]

Black Lives Matter has not yet claimed responsibility for any major legislative proposals, but its ongoing agitation on college campuses, at political campaign events, and throughout city streets has upended the narrative that African American political activism for social egalitarianism died with the black freedom movements of the 1960s. Black Lives Matter refuses to embrace what the African American intellectual Cornel West argued in the early 1990s was the post–civil rights era's black political quietism, which was caused by the problem of "black nihilism"—the disorientation and sense of political despair—and which cut against the tragicomic sense of hope that had once animated black political struggle.[13]

To be sure, vibrant political black activity has existed in several prominent examples over the past fifty years. But even those moments have left something to be desired in the pursuit of a radical democratic agenda. There was the black electorate's involvement in Jesse Jackson's 1984 bid for the White House, the Nation of Islam's Million Man March on Washington, D.C., in 1995, and then, unexpectedly, the election of the first African American president, Barack Obama in 2008 and in 2012. But even these movements had pedestrian, if not deeply problematic, political objectives. Jackson and Obama were mainstream black Democrats who eschewed any commitment to racial egalitarianism—appearing as moderates on racial equality compared to someone like Martin Luther King Jr. in his least radical moments.[14] The Nation of Islam, led by Louis Farrakhan, was not only openly sexist—the Million Man March was literally marketed toward and composed of black men trying to redeem their lost masculinity—but also homophobic and anti-Semitic, and it proffered a deeply conservative notion of picking oneself up by one's bootstraps, reminiscent of earlier black nationalists including Booker T. Washington and Marcus Garvey.[15]

It is also striking that a sizeable portion of African American public intellectual life—notwithstanding obvious exceptions like West, Coates, Michael Eric Dyson, and Melissa Harris-Perry—has been dominated by black conservatives such as Shelby Steele, Bill Cosby, and John McWhorter. Though different in their arguments, they preach a secular vision of Farrakhan's notion of black self-help and espouse a commitment to the American ideals of equality of opportunity and "colorblindness." They call for ending affirmative-action programs and balk at any talk of state-led race-based redistributive efforts.[16]

Although Black Lives Matter has done most of its political work through direct actions and community organizing, we can already begin to see the glimmers of how the movement is an important intervention in the history of African American resistance. First, no black political movement in recent memory that has received so much public attention has made intersectional analysis so central to its politics. As activists declare: "We are guided by the fact that Black Lives Matter, all Black lives, regardless of actual or perceived sexual identity, gender identity, gender expression, economic status, ability, disability, religious beliefs or disbeliefs, immigration status or location."[17] Following the insights of queer black difference feminists such as the Combahee River Collective and the poet-philosopher Audre Lorde, Black Lives Matter has brought into relief an intersectional perspective on domination, understanding that the lived experience of differently oppressed identities creates unique obstacles for human flourishing and requires remedies that cannot be one-size-fits-all. Like Wells and Davis before them, BLM activists refuse to interpret domination in universal and abstract terms, while critiquing and bringing attention to the masculinism (which was at times espoused by Walker, Douglass, and Newton) and homophobia (which Newton sometimes expressed) that still saturates American culture. Furthermore, BLM brings into a contemporary context Wells's insights about the link between chivalry, violence, and myths about femininity and Davis's thinking about capitalism, prisons, imperialism, and gender inequality—at a moment when gender inequality is sustained through the national assault on reproductive rights, the intensification of a rape culture on college campuses, the continued assaults on socioeconomic programs for black women across the United States, and the demonization of many trans and gay citizens of color.

Second, BLM rejects the dichotomy between performance and politics. The movement's declaration "Black Lives Matter" is often shouted when activists publicly intervene in unsanctioned and ephemeral ways. For example, BLM protestors interrupted the progressive Democratic presidential hopeful Bernie Sanders's rally in Seattle, Washington, on August 8, 2015, to call upon attendees to acknowledge the ongoing structural racism in Seattle and to participate in a moment of silence for

Michael Brown. On November 21, 2015, in a Birmingham, Alabama, rally for the conservative Republican hopeful Donald Trump, a BLM protestor intervened before being kicked and punched by the attendees, to the approval of the candidate—to draw attention to Trump's overtly racist rhetoric and policy proposals.

Much more so than Walker, Douglass, Wells, Newton, and Davis, BLM transforms public space into a theater meant to educate and alienate an audience from their most deeply cherished beliefs. Like French avant-garde artist-activist-intellectuals in the 1960s, the so-called situation-ists, who were directly involved in and whose ideas helped inspire the May '68 student movements in France,[18] BLM understands the way public spectacle (BLM protestors have also worn T-shirts and placed duct tape on their mouths with the movement's declaration) commands attention and disrupts notions of civility. So too does the very utterance "Black Lives Matter!" subversively articulate the normative value of black life in a society that continues to deny it; it also calls attention to the fact that there is still a need to articulate this claim—at a moment many white Americans see as "postracial," where racism is only occa-sional and no longer deeply ingrained in American culture nor latently present in American politics.

Third, and perhaps most important, BLM political resistance is as physical as it is virtual—enacted through Internet-based social-networking tools such as Facebook, the messaging service Twitter, and the image-sharing service Instagram. By connecting a community of citizens who might otherwise not have been politicized in traditional ways—like community meetings, rallies, marches, protests, petitions, canvassing—BLM social-media activism realizes Walker's and Doug-lass's idea that a community is ephemeral and constantly evolving. By using a short Tweet, a Facebook message, or some kind of mobile ap-plication to mobilize potential protesters in a matter of hours, BLM cre-ates spontaneous and disruptive direct actions that would have been embraced by Newton and the Panthers.

BLM tries to make social media into a platform of serious contesta-tion about divergent political discourse. They do this through a kind of micropolitics, which dramatizes what the French philosophers Gilles

Deleuze and Félix Guattari called a "rhizomatic" structure of politics, where loosely connected and disparate political activities would replace those with firmly defined hierarchies, strategies, directives, rules, and organizational structures.[19]

But what makes BLM's use of social media so valuable can also have deleterious effects. Identifying with a movement's message virtually can serve as a substitute for real-world action, and micropolitical acts can lack macropolitical demands. Furthermore, although social media can mobilize political emotion—doing digitally what Wells did through print and what Newton and the Panthers did through policing the police—these emotions can never be fully contained in the social sphere. BLM indignation about the degradation of black life only heightens some black Americans' sense of despair about the possibility of substantive change, while inspiring some white Americans to declare a love of white as well as black life—"All Lives Matter"—an assertion that obviously misses both the intentional irony of BLM's slogan and responds with hostility toward its race consciousness.

Yet BLM could benefit from embracing the political ideas of earlier African American resisters. Knowing how state power deprives citizens of a sense of creativity and self-worth to lead fulfilling lives can bolster BLM thinking about the scope of racial injustice. Words like "neoslavery" or "racial terrorism" can help activists draw public attention to the way the state is implicated in eroding freedom and in creating fear in black populations. Cultivating an embodied form of political thinking that maintains empathy toward a plural range of experiences and that engages opposing worldviews can deepen the practice of democratic judgment. Appreciating the way action is about accepting new political possibilities and coalitions and allowing these to disclose things that would alter one's perceptions of reality can help activists struggle in more creative, democratic, and sustainable ways. Subverting discourses of American exceptionalism and not shying away from deploying emotions in public, to encourage moral outrage or to politicize further a reality that appears incontestable, can deepen BLM political rhetoric.

The tactics of black politics have always been contested: Booker T. Washington endorsed social accommodation and rugged individualism, Martin Delany and Malcolm X called for black separatism, and Du Bois and King called for political agitation. Yet the overarching concern of black politics across the ideological divide has been the quest for black dignity and self-determination amid white supremacy. The continued existence of racial inequality will encourage dissatisfaction and dissent, critique and direct action. Political hope may come from knowing that the next resistance movement is around the corner. But the crucial political task is to translate the ideas and demands that emerge from resistance into a coherent program that would create a more democratic nation in which all Americans would want to live.

NOTES

INTRODUCTION: THE POLITICAL THOUGHT OF
AFRICAN AMERICAN RESISTANCE

1. U.S. Department of Defense, *Department of Defense Dictionary of Military and Associated Terms*, Joint Publication 1-02, http://www.dtic.mil/doctrine/new_pubs /jp1_02.pdf, 206.

2. See George Frederickson, *Racism: A Short History* (Princeton, N.J.: Princeton University Press, 2009); George Frederickson, *The Black Image in the White Mind: The Debate on Afro-American Character and Destiny* (Wesleyan, Conn.: Wesleyan University Press, 1987).

3. Herman Melville, "Bartleby the Scrivener: A Story of Wall Street" (1853), in *Great Short Works of Herman Melville* (New York: Harper Perennial, 2004), 39–74.

4. See Plato, *The Republic*, trans. C. D. C. Reeve (Indianapolis, Ind.: Hackett, 2004); Thomas Hobbes, *Leviathan* (1651), ed. Richard Tuck (Cambridge: Cambridge University Press, 1991).

5. Much of this literature is historical. Among others, see E. P. Thompson, *The Making of the English Working Class* (New York: Vintage, 1966); Joan Scott, *Gender and the Politics of History* (New York: Columbia University Press, 1999). An early pioneer of this in the history of slavery was Herbert Aptheker, *American Negro Slave Revolts* (1943; New York: International Publishers, 1983); Eugene Genovese, *From Rebellion to Revolution: Afro-American Slave Revolts in the Making of the Modern World* (Baton Rouge: Louisiana State University Press, 1992).

6. G. W. F. Hegel, *The Phenomenology of Spirit* (1807), trans., A. V. Miller (New York: Oxford University Press, 1977), 111–118; Karl Marx and Friedrich Engels, "The Manifesto of the Communist Party" (1848), in *The Marx-Engels Reader*, ed. Robert C. Tucker (New York: Norton, 1978), 469–500. For Thoreau, see Nancy L. Rosenblum,

"Thoreau's Democratic Individualism," in *A Political Companion to Henry David Thoreau*, ed. Jack Turner (Lexington: University Press of Kentucky, 2009), 15–38; for Mahatma Gandhi, see *The Essential Writings of Mahatma Gandhi*, ed. Raghavan Iyer (New Delhi: Oxford University Press, 1991); for King, see Martin Luther King Jr., "A Letter from a Birmingham Jail" (1963), in *A Testament of Hope*, ed. James M. Washington (San Francisco: HarperCollins, 1986), 293.

7. See James C. Scott, *Weapons of the Weak: Everyday Forms of Resistance* (New Haven, Conn.: Yale University Press, 1987); James C. Scott, *Domination and the Arts of Resistance: Hidden Transcripts* (New Haven, Conn.: Yale University Press, 1993).

8. See Michel Foucault, "Truth and Power," in *The Foucault Reader*, ed. Paul Rabinow (New York: Pantheon, 1984), 51–75.

9. Michel Foucault, "Power and Sex," in *Michel Foucault: Politics, Philosophy, Culture: Interviews and Other Writings, 1977–1984*, ed. Lawrence Kritzman (New York: Routledge, 1988), 123.

10. Genovese, *From Rebellion to Revolution*; Steven Hahn, *A Nation Under Our Feet: Black Political Struggles from the Rural South to the Great Migration* (Cambridge, Mass.: Belknap, 2005); Stephanie M. H. Camp, *Closer to Freedom: Enslaved Women and Everyday Resistance in the Plantation South* (Chapel Hill: University of North Carolina Press, 2004).

11. Ralph Ellison, "Change the Joke and Slip the Yoke" (1958), in *The Collected Essays of Ralph Ellison*, ed. John Callahan (New York: Modern Library, 1995), 100–112.

12. Robin D. G. Kelley, *Race Rebels: Culture, Politics, and the Black Working Class* (New York: Free Press, 1996).

13. Melissa Victoria Harris-Lacewell, *Barbershops, Bibles, and BET: Everyday Talk and Black Political Thought* (Princeton, N.J.: Princeton University Press, 2006); Imani Perry, *Prophets of the Hood: Politics and Poetics in Hip Hop* (Durham, N.C.: Duke University Press, 2004).

14. See Jeffrey B. Ferguson, "Race and the Rhetoric of Resistance," *Raritan* 28, no. 1 (Summer 2008): 4–32.

15. Richard Iton, *In Search of the Black Fantastic: Politics and Popular Culture in the Post–Civil Rights Era* (New York: Oxford University Press, 2011), 102.

16. In his critique of Neil Roberts, *Freedom as Marronage* (Chicago: University of Chicago Press, 2015), Charles Mills wonders whether it makes sense to transform what Roberts calls "flight," or what could also broadly be labeled resistance, into a distinct genre of political thought and practice because it can be said to exist everywhere. Charles Mills, "Review of *Freedom as Marronage*, by Neil Roberts," *Journal of French and Francophone Philosophy—Revue de la philosophie française et de langue française* 23, no. 2 (2015): 145–149.

17. Political resistance movements are unlike what we might describe as cultural resistance movements, which would find exemplary expression in James Baldwin's and Ralph Ellison's essays or in the work of the various writers associated with the Harlem Renaissance, such as Nella Larsen, Zora Neale Hurston, Jean Cane, and Langston Hughes. Of course, I acknowledge the contested nature of the term "political" and agree with the argument of the political theorist Jacques Rancière that politics is

foundationally defined through disagreement and contestation. While I do take this expansive definition seriously, I also try to isolate, in the broadest sense, how a study of resistance that centers on traditional political goods associated with government and collective life is distinct from one that focuses on culture, even though the two are often difficult to disentangle. On this understanding of the "political," see Jacques Rancière, *Dis-agreement: Politics and Philosophy* (Minneapolis: University of Minnesota Press, 2004); and Anne Norton, *Ninety-Five Theses on Politics, Culture, and Method* (New Haven, Conn.: Yale University Press, 2004).

18. See Bayard Rustin, "From Protest to Politics: The Future of the Civil Rights Movement" (1964), in *Time on Two Crosses: The Collected Writings of Bayard Rustin*, ed. Devon Carbado and Don Weise (San Francisco: Cleis, 2004), 116–129.

19. Loïc Wacquant, *Deadly Symbiosis: Race and the Rise of the Penal State* (London: Polity, 2009).

20. For a short philosophical analysis of radicalism, which, admittedly, is as amorphous as the idea of resistance, see Paul McLaughlin, *Radicalism: A Philosophical Study* (New York: Palgrave MacMillan, 2012).

21. For the best book on the political thought of civil rights, see Richard H. King, *Civil Rights and the Idea of Freedom* (New York: Oxford University Press, 1992). Other important books on King include Eric J. Sundquist, *King's Dream* (New Haven, Conn.: Yale University Press, 2009); and George M. Shulman, *American Prophecy: Race and Redemption in American Political Culture* (Minneapolis: University of Minnesota Press, 2008), 97–130.

22. See in particular "The American Dream," "My Trip to the Land of Gandhi," "Where Do We Go From Here?," "A Time To Break the Silence," "The Drum Major Instinct," "Black Power Defined," and "A Testament of Hope," in *A Testament of Hope.*

23. Historians have vigorously debated the meaning of the so-called long civil rights movement, which arguably began as early as black workers' struggles in the 1930s and 1940s and extended past King with the rise of the Black Nationalism and encompassed the democratic struggles waged by black activists such as Hamer, Baker, and Forman and Robert Moses. For what has become a classic statement on the long civil rights movement, see Jacquelyn Dowd Hall, "The Long Civil Rights Movement and the Political Uses of the Past," *Journal of American History* 91, no. 4 (2005): 1233–1263. For one of the most important accounts of the tradition of democratic organizing in Mississippi, of which Baker and Forman were crucial, see Charles M. Payne, *I've Got the Light of Freedom: The Organizing Tradition and the Mississippi Freedom Struggle* (Berkley: University of California Press, 1995).

24. For such sociological interpretations, which largely though not exclusively center on the civil rights movement, see Frances Fox Piven and Richard Cloward, *Poor People's Movements: Why They Succeed, and How They Fail* (New York: Vintage, 1978), 181–264; Doug McAdam, *Political Process and the Development of Black Insurgency, 1930–1970* (Chicago: University of Chicago Press, 1982). Also see Aldon Morris, *The Origins of the Civil Rights Movement: Black Communities Organizing for Change* (New York: Free Press, 1986).

25. See, in particular, Jeffrey C. Alexander, *The Civil Sphere* (New York: Oxford University Press, 2008), 265–394.

26. John Skrentny, *The Minority Rights Revolution* (Cambridge, Mass.: Belknap, 2004); Joseph Luders, *The Civil Rights Movement and the Logic of Social Change* (New York: Cambridge University Press, 2010).

27. Here I am thinking of the work of Neil Roberts, who has argued that resistance breeds a political theory of freedom. He has shown that Frederick Douglass and Angela Davis (as well as the Afro-Caribbean intellectual Edouard Glissant) creolize standard views of freedom—which, in their haste to debate the merits of positive or negative liberty, miss the understanding of freedom as flight, as continuing and ongoing struggle. I extend Roberts's focus by showing how African American resisters fundamentally altered time-honored American understandings of various political ideas. See Roberts, *Freedom as Marronage*. More broadly, however, this book contributes to the burgeoning field of theorizing the relationship between race and political theory. This literature includes Lawrie Balfour, *Evidence of Things Not Said: James Baldwin and the Promise of Democracy* (Ithaca, N.Y.: Cornell University Press, 1999); Lawrie Balfour, *Democracy's Reconstruction: Thinking Politically with W. E. B. Du Bois* (New York: Oxford University Press, 2011); Shulman, *American Prophecy*; Stephen H. Marshall, *The City on the Hill from Below: The Crisis of Prophetic Black Politics* (Philadelphia: Temple University Press, 2011); Jack Turner, *Awakening to Race: Individualism and Social Consciousness in America* (Chicago: University of Chicago Press, 2012); Danielle S. Allen, *Talking to Strangers: Anxieties of Citizenship After Brown v. Board of Education* (Chicago: University of Chicago Press, 2004); Alex Zamalin, *African American Political Thought and American Culture: The Nation's Struggle for Racial Justice* (New York: Palgrave Macmillan, 2015); Robert Gooding-Williams, *In the Shadow of Dubois: Afro-Modern Political Thought in America* (Cambridge, Mass.: Harvard University Press, 2011); Tommie Shelby, *We Who Are Dark: The Philosophical Foundations of Black Solidarity* (Cambridge, Mass.: Belknap, 2005); Eddie Glaude Jr., *In a Shade of Blue: Pragmatism and the Politics of Black America* (Chicago: University of Chicago Press, 2008).

28. For historical studies of black nationalism, see Wilson J. Moses, *The Golden Age of Black Nationalism, 1850–1925* (New York: Oxford University Press, 1988); Sterling Stuckey, *The Ideological Origins of Black Nationalism* (Boston: Beacon, 1972); Peniel E. Joseph, *Waiting 'Til the Midnight Hour: A Narrative History of Black Power in America* (New York: Holt, 2006). For a study of black nationalism that details how it has always been a historically evolving rather than timeless ideology and political practice responsive to currents in American politics, see Dean E. Robinson, *Black Nationalism in American Politics and Thought* (Cambridge: Cambridge University Press, 2001). For a study of the core categories of black political thought—black disillusioned liberal, socialist, Marxist, conservative, radical egalitarian, and black feminist, see Michael C. Dawson, *Black Visions: The Roots of Contemporary African-American Political Ideologies* (Chicago: University of Chicago Press, 2001). For a study of the black radical orientations—"black prophetic" and "black heretic"—see

Anthony Bogues, *Black Heretics, Black Prophets: Radical Political Intellectuals* (New York: Routledge, 2003). For black Marxism see Cedric J. Robinson, *Black Marxism: The Making of the Black Radical Tradition* (Chapel Hill: University of North Carolina Press, 2000).

29. Historians might be leery of any book that seeks to place political ideas in a historical context. After all, this historical contextualization, which spans almost two hundred years, does not do justice to the specific nuances of the historical changes of political parties and electoral alignments, the American judiciary, public norms of citizenship, and voting patterns. Situating resistance historically, however, is more about showing how resistance ideas were responses to particular intellectual debates within a specific historical milieu. In every case, the ideas of African American resistance motivate the choice of historical contextualization.

30. For the relationship between political theory and political vision, which informs my own understanding of political theory, see Sheldon Wolin, *Politics and Vision* (Princeton, N.J.: Princeton University Press, 2006). In a certain sense, however, my historical orientation is also partially indebted to the so-called Cambridge school of political theory of historical contextualism. See Quentin Skinner, *Visions of Politics* (Cambridge: Cambridge University Press, 2002); J. G. A. Pocock, *Political Thought and History: Essays on Theory and Method* (Cambridge: Cambridge University Press, 2008). Finally, it should be noted that this book is squarely in the tradition of political theory rather than political philosophy, with a specific concern with the ways in which black political thought can help energize contemporary citizenship. Political theorists begin with and try to scrutinize the fact of politics—as it is and has existed historically—while political philosophers are interested in comprehensive and rigorous analysis of the conceptual validity and normative viability of certain political claims. Particularly, this book continues a project that has used African American political thought to refine, complicate, and enlarge thinking about democratic citizenship. See, in particular, Allen, *Talking to Strangers*; Turner, *Awakening to Race*; and Nick Bromell, *The Time Is Always Now: Black Thought and the Transformation of U.S. Democracy* (New York: Oxford University Press, 2013). While my book is informed by many of their important insights, it differs in its focus both on relatively neglected figures and on specifically showing how they expand thinking in the American tradition.

31. Louis Hartz, *The Liberal Tradition in America: An Interpretation of American Political Thought Since the Revolution* (New York: Harcourt, Brace and Jovanovich, 1991); Richard Hofstadter, *The American Political Tradition and the Men Who Made It* (New York: Vintage, 1989); Daniel J. Boorstin, *The Genius of American Politics* (Chicago: University of Chicago Press, 1953).

32. In this sense, liberalism is found in everything from the founding debates between the Federalists and Anti-Federalists over the scope of government power and the nature of political representation, to slaveholders and abolitionists debating the constitutionality and morality of slavery, to Gilded Age individualists and Progressives debating the role of government in social life, to Cold War conservatives and social

liberals debating the value of democracy. One can certainly argue that liberalism is a contested tradition or that there is no such thing as a singular liberal tradition— only multiple liberalisms. But proponents of the liberal-tradition thesis insist that, compared to its Western European counterpart, there is a surprising lack of political imagination in the United States, which is centered on Lockean liberalism. For a brief survey of the complexity of liberalism, see Michael Freeden, *Liberalism: A Short Introduction* (New York: Oxford University Press, 2015).

33.   See Rogers Smith, *Civic Ideals: Conflicting Visions of Citizenship in U.S. History* (New Haven, Conn.: Yale University Press, 1999); Anne Norton, *Alternative Americas: A Reading of Antebellum Political Culture* (Chicago: University of Chicago Press, 1986); Michael Rogin, *"Ronald Reagan," the Movie: And Other Episodes in Political Demonology* (Berkley: University of California Press, 1988).

34.   For the argument that civic republicanism was central to the American Revolution, see Gordon Wood, *The Creation of the American Republic, 1776–1787* (Chapel Hill: University of North Carolina Press, 1998).

35.   The canonical view of power in the American tradition, which views it from an institutional perspective, is expressed by thinkers as diverse as Alexander Hamilton in his defense of a unitary executive in "Federalist no. 70" (1788), in Alexander Hamilton, James Madison and John Jay, *The Federalist*, ed. Terence Ball (Cambridge: Cambridge University Press, 2003), 344; slaveholders such as John C. Calhoun in his defense of a so-called concurrent majority, in which all vested social interests have veto power over major political decisions, in *A Disquisition on Government: And Selections from the Discourse* (1848; Indianapolis, Ind.: Hackett, 1995); Progressives such as Herbert Croly in his defense of a strong regulatory government in *The Promise of American Life* (1909; Princeton, N.J.: Princeton University Press, 2014); and conservatives such as William F. Buckley in *God and Man at Yale* (Washington, D.C.: Regnery, 1951), which expresses his view linking religion and political rule.

36.   In this way Walker, Douglass, Wells, Newton, and Davis implicitly rejected the view of the American pluralist tradition that tried to create false equivalencies within it, arguing that power occurs when different groups, irrespective of the magnitude of their resources, exercise their collective voice and interests. For the pluralist tradition, see James Madison, "Federalist no. 10" (1787), in *The Federalist*, 40–46; Robert Dahl, *Who Governs? Democracy and Power in an American City* (New Haven, Conn.: Yale University Press, 1961).

37.   For American social democratic thought, see Walt Whitman, *Democratic Vistas* (1871; Iowa City: University of Iowa Press, 2010); Ralph Waldo Emerson, *Nature and Selected Essays*, ed. Larzer Ziff (New York: Penguin, 2003); John Dewey, *The Public and Its Problems* (1927; Athens, Ohio: Swallow, 1991); and Jane Addams, *The Jane Addams Reader*, ed. Jean Belthke Elshtain (New York: Basic Books, 2001).

38.   For surveys of the American tradition that capture this point, see Hofstadter, *The American Political Tradition*; Louis Menand, *The Metaphysical Club: A Story of Ideas in America* (New York: Farrar, Straus and Giroux, 2002); John Patrick Diggins, *The Lost Soul of American Politics: Virtue, Self-Interest, and the Foundations of Liberalism* (New York: Harper Collins, 1984).

39. For the civic republican view of community, see John Adams, *Revolutionary Writings, 1775–1783*, ed. Gordon S. Wood (New York: Library of America, 2011); Thomas Paine, *Collected Writings* (New York: Library of America, 1995). For American individualism, see William Graham Sumner, *On Liberty, Society, and Politics: The Essential Essays of William Graham Sumner*, ed. Robert C. Bannister (Indianapolis: Liberty Fund, 1992); Ralph Waldo Emerson, "Self Reliance" (1841), in *Nature and Selected Essays*, 175–204; Henry David Thoreau, *Walden* (1854; New Haven, Conn.: Yale University Press, 2006). For communitarianism, see Robert N. Bellah, Richard Madsen, William M. Sullivan, and Ann Swidler, *Habits of the Heart: Individualism and Commitment in American Life* (Berkeley: University of California Press, 1985).

40. See Abraham Lincoln, "First Lincoln-Douglass Debate, Ottawa, Illinois" (1858), in *Speeches and Writings, 1832–1858*, ed. Roy P. Basler (New York: Library of America, 1989), 512.

41. A notable defender of this view is the American philosopher John Rawls, who argues that the appropriate way to think about justice is for rational subjects to go behind a "veil of ignorance" in the "original position." See John Rawls, *A Theory of Justice* (Cambridge, Mass.: Belknap, 1971).

42. This is the approach that Harold Cruse takes in his famous study *The Crisis of the Negro Intellectual* (1967; New York: NYRB, 2005).

43. See Jerry Gafio Watts, *Amiri Baraka: The Politics and Art of a Black Intellectual* (New York: New York University Press, 2001), 10. See also Jerry Gafio Watts, *Heroism and the Black Intellectual: Ralph Ellison, Politics, and Afro-American Intellectual Life* (Chapel Hill: University of North Carolina Press, 1994).

44. For a survey of major currents in democratic theory, see Ian Shapiro, *The State of Democratic Theory* (Princeton, N.J.: Princeton University Press, 2006).

45. For recent discussions about the idea of "the people" in democracy, see Jason Frank, *Constituent Moments: Enacting the People in Postrevolutionary America* (Durham, N.C.: Duke University Press, 2009); Edmund Morgan, *Inventing the People* (New York: Norton, 1988); and Bruce Ackerman, *We The People*, vol. 1: *Foundations* (Cambridge, Mass.: Harvard University Press, 1993). For an important discussion about how this works for black politics, through the example of W. E. B. Du Bois's political thought, see Melvin Rogers, "The People, Rhetoric, and Affect: On the Political Force of Du Bois's *The Souls of Black Folk*," *American Political Science Review* 106, no. 1 (2012): 188–203.

46. African American resisters provide a rich empirical case study of Michael Hanchard's important thesis that black political thought provides important resources for political theory because of its unique and sustained concern with racism, oppression, and colonization. See Michael Hanchard, "Contours of Black Political Thought: An Introduction and Perspective," *Political Theory* 38, no. 4 (2010): 512.

47. African American resisters are implicitly in dialogue with care theorists, such as Joan C. Tronto, *Caring Democracy: Markets, Equality, and Justice* (New York: New York University Press, 2013), and those concerned with global responsibility, such as Judith Butler, *Frames of War: When Is Life Grievable?* (New York: Verso, 2009); Judith Butler, *Precarious Life: The Powers of Mourning and Violence* (New York: Verso, 2004).

48. African American resisters are important interlocutors for thinkers concerned with the normative requirements and conditions for democracy. See Amartya Sen, *Development as Freedom* (Oxford: Oxford University Press, 1999); Martha Nussbaum, *Sex and Social Justice* (Oxford: Oxford University Press, 1999); Iris Marion Young, *Inclusion and Democracy* (New York: Oxford University Press, 2000); and Amy Gutmann and Denis Thompson, *Democracy and Disagreement* (Cambridge, Mass.: Belknap, 1996).

49. For the radical democratic position, see Frank, *Constituent Moments*; for the liberal-constitutional perspective see Jürgen Habermas, *The Postnational Constellation: Political Essays* (Cambridge, Mass.: MIT Press, 2001).

50. For some of the most recent debates about the nature of black politics, see Gooding-Williams, *In the Shadow of Du Bois*; Shelby, *We Who Are Dark*; Glaude, *In a Shade of Blue*.

51. These resisters call into question liberal discourses that still dominate American politics and culture, discourses of paternalism, law and order, safety and bodily security, and those that champion the adequacy of housing policy and systems of crime and punishment. In this way they partake in ongoing conversations about the relationship between liberalism and democracy. For a discussion of this in the American context, see Norton, *Alternative Americas*. For a conceptual study of British liberalism and the politics of empire, see Uday S. Mehta, *Liberalism and Empire: A Study in Nineteenth-Century British Liberal Thought* (Chicago: University of Chicago Press, 1999); for liberal social-contract theory and exclusion, see Charles Mills, *The Racial Contract* (Ithaca, N.Y.: Cornell University Press, 1997).

52. The work of these African American resisters deepens a burgeoning literature on "affect" theory. For a good survey of the field, see Melissa Gregg and Gregory J. Seigworth, eds., *The Affect Theory Reader* (Durham, N.C.: Duke University Press, 2010).

53. For a survey of this turn to mourning, see David Eng and Davis Kazanjin, eds., *Loss: The Politics of Mourning* (Berkley: University of California Press, 2002); and Butler, *Precarious Life*.

54. For studies that address racially based income inequality, see Melvin L. Oliver and Thomas M. Shapiro, *Black Wealth, White Wealth: A New Perspective on Racial Inequality* (New York: Routledge, 2006). For racially based education inequalities, see Amanda E. Lewis and John B. Diamond, *Despite the Best Intentions: How Racial Inequality Thrives in Good Schools* (New York: Oxford University Press, 2015). On the politics of postracialism see Imani Perry, *More Beautiful and More Terrible: The Embrace and Transcendence of Racial Inequality in America* (New York: New York University Press, 2011). Racial injustice today no longer explicitly centers as much on the political problem of de jure segregation, legal discrimination, and social humiliation that King and the civil rights movement's political theory, for example, sought to address. For King, the question was, quite broadly, how to create a society where black Americans are not discriminated against and can reap the fruits of the American dream, with all its promises of economic upward mobility and political voice. Today, the question is: How do we address the vast racial structural and socioeconomic

disparity—from jobs to income to life expectancy—that continues to create a system in which black citizens are marginalized?

55. For this interpretation of Baldwin, Ellison, and Morrison see Zamalin, *African American Political Thought and American Culture*.

56. For the idea of nonviolent coalition building, see Rustin, "From Protest to Politics." For the vitality of difference politics, see Audre Lorde, *Sister Outsider: Essays and Speeches* (New York: Crossing Press, 2007).

57. I am thinking of figures such as the black separatist Martin Delany, the black feminist Maria Stewart, the black communist Hubert Harrison, and Malcolm X. For the best examination of Delany, see Shelby, *We Who Are Dark*, 24–59. For Stewart, see Valerie C. Cooper, *Word, Like Fire: Maria Stewart, the Bible, and the Rights of African Americans* (Charlottesville: University of Virginia Press, 2012). For Harrison see Jeffrey B. Perry, *Hubert Harrison: The Voice of Harlem Radicalism, 1883–1918* (New York: Columbia University Press, 2011). For Malcolm X, see Saladin Ambar, *Malcolm X at Oxford Union: Radical Politics in a Global Era* (New York: Oxford University Press, 2014).

58. Their arguments are neither policy focused—those that advocate sentencing reforms, greater leniency toward nonviolent offenders, fewer privatized prisons, and more humane prison conditions—nor those that are diagnostic and explanatory, which try to account for the rise of mass incarceration over the past forty years and ask whether it is inherently racist. For the policy argument, see Michelle Alexander, *The New Jim Crow: Mass Incarceration in the Age of Colorblindness* (New York: The New Press, 2010). For the critical-diagnostic interpretation, see Loïc J. D. Wacquant, *Prisons of Poverty* (Minneapolis: University of Minnesota Press, 2009); Ruth Wilson Gilmore, *Golden Gulag: Prisons, Surplus, Crisis, and Opposition in Globalizing California* (Berkley: University of California Press, 2007).

59. In doing this, these resisting figures deepen contemporary thinking about the politics of policing, which has been receiving increased interest as of late from political theorists. But rather than focus on policy they provide an alternative political theory and set of normative values that would address the inequalities that arise from policing practices. For political theorists who have tackled contemporary policing policy, see Bernard E. Harcourt, *Illusion of Order: The False Promise of Broken Windows Policing* (Cambridge, Mass.: Harvard University Press, 2005). For a sociological interpretation, see David Garland, *The Culture of Control: Crime and Social Order in Contemporary Society* (Chicago: University of Chicago Press, 2003).

60. The classic, even if now dated, book on de facto segregation is still Douglas S. Massey and Nancy A. Denton, *American Apartheid: Segregation and the Making of the Underclass* (Cambridge, Mass.: Harvard University Press, 1993). For a more recent study, see Adrienne Brown and Valerie Smith, *Race and Real Estate* (New York: Oxford University Press, 2015).

61. For thinking centered on agonistic forms of communication, see William Connolly, *Identity/Difference: Democratic Negotiations of Political Paradox* (Ithaca, N.Y.: Cornell University Press, 1991); Bonnie Honig, *Political Theory and the Displacement of*

Politics (Ithaca, N.Y.: Cornell University Press, 1993); Chantal Mouffe, *Agonistics: Thinking the World Politically* (New York: Verso, 2013); and Chantal Mouffe, *The Democratic Paradox* (New York: Verso, 2000).

1. DAVID WALKER, FREDERICK DOUGLASS, AND THE ABOLITIONIST DEMOCRATIC VISION

1. See Herbert Aptheker, *American Negro Slave Revolts* (1943; New York: International Publishers, 1983); Steven Hahn, *A Nation Under Our Feet: Black Political Struggles from the Rural South to the Great Migration* (Cambridge, Mass.: Belknap, 2005). David Brion Davis in *Inhuman Bondage: The Rise and Fall of Slavery in the New World* (New York: Oxford University Press, 2006) does an excellent job of placing U.S. slave revolts in a global context, especially in relation to rebellions in the Caribbean around the same time.

2. Eric J. Sundquist reports that rumors soon spread that Turner's body was boiled and was used as an oil, which became known as "Nat's Grease." See Eric J. Sundquist, *To Wake the Nations: Race in the Making of American Literature* (Cambridge, Mass.: Belknap, 1993), 82.

3. For what still remains one of the best accounts of the rebellion, see Herbert Aptheker, *Nat Turner's Slave Rebellion* (New York: Dover, 2006).

4. Political freedom, Hannah Arendt believed, constituted the genius of the American Revolution, as opposed to the French Revolution, which was concerned with social equality. Hannah Arendt, *On Revolution* (New York: Penguin, 2006), 49–106.

5. For an excellent account of the historiography of American slavery, see Peter Kolchin, *American Slavery: 1619–1877* (New York: Hill and Wang, 2003).

6. Although unified by the goal of abolishing slavery, the ideas of various abolitionists were complex and diverse. Some abolitionists were more conservative; others were more radical. Some cared deeply about a robust vision of equality; others did not. My aim in this chapter is less to identify the political commitments of various strains of abolitionism and more to highlight a unique line of political-theoretical reasoning that emerges from two important black abolitionists. Focusing on the political ideas of black abolitionists in particular is especially important given that abolitionism was, in the popular American imagination, usually connected to white figures like William Lloyd Garrison and John Brown. For an account of the complex ideas about the meaning of abolitionism, see Andrew Delbanco, *The Abolitionist Imagination* (Cambridge, Mass.: Harvard University Press, 2012), 1–56. For a wonderful history that illustrates the complexity as well as the exchanges between white abolitionists such as Gerrit Smith and John Brown and black abolitionists such as James McCune Smith and Douglass, while examining the way these figures tried to force Americans to think about slavery from the perspective of the slave, see John Stauffer, *The Black Hearts of Men: Radical Abolitionists and the Transformation of Race* (Cambridge, Mass.: Harvard University Press, 2004).

7. For the best account of this in Walker, see Peter Hinks, *To Awaken My Afflicted Brethren: David Walker and the Problem of Antebellum Slave Resistance* (State College, Penn.: Penn State University Press, 1996). For one of the best accounts of Douglass's political thought, especially focusing on his "Fourth of July" speech, see Charles Mills, "Whose Fourth of July? Frederick Douglass and 'Original Intent,'" in *Frederick Douglass: A Critical Reader*, ed. Bill Lawson and Frank Kirkland (New York: Wiley-Blackwell, 1999), 104–105. In particular, Mills asserts that Douglass's four theses are that (1) natural law is a moral and jurisprudence issue; (2) the original intent of the founders is crucial, and so is the Constitution's antiracism and anti-white supremacy; (3) there is inconsistency between founding principles and racial inequality; and (4) one should maintain optimism that blacks will be accepted.

8. To be sure, during the 1850s, Douglass seemed to become disillusioned with moral suasion and became increasingly willing to defend violent resistance. For this interpretation, see Frank M. Kirkland, "Enslavement, Moral Suasion, and Struggles for Recognition: Frederick Douglass's Answer to the Question—'What Is Enlightenment?'" in Lawson and Kirkland, *Frederick Douglass*, 243–310.

9. Mia Bay argues that Walker was one of the first Afrocentrists. She asserts: "In addition to endorsing the Egyptian ancestry and Hamitic descent of the black race, Walker raised another subject that would loom large in nineteenth-century black ethnology, namely, the racial character of white people." Mia Bay, *The White Image in the Black Mind: African American Ideas About White People* (New York: Oxford University Press, 2000), 35.

10. Bernard R. Boxill asserts: "In fact Douglass's opposition to black emigrationism went deeper. Although he agreed with its view that citizenship was vitally important in the modern world, he believed that its pessimism about the prospects for black citizenship in the US stemmed from a misunderstanding of the nature of national feeling." Bernard R. Boxill, "Douglass Against the Emigrationists," in Lawson and Kirkland, *Frederick Douglass*, 22.

11. For an analysis of the African American prophetic tradition, in which Walker could be placed, see George M. Shulman, *American Prophecy: Race and Redemption in American Political Culture* (Minneapolis: University of Minnesota Press, 2008).

12. There is speculation that Walker himself may have been involved. Hinks, *To Awaken My Afflicted Brethren*, 30.

13. The historian John Stauffer notes that the Missouri Compromise "was a crucial turning point that destroyed the successes of the early abolition movement." This was because "the Missouri Compromise marked the beginning of a transformation in American society. It pointed to signs of a new era in reform, including a shift in visions of citizenship and community and in definitions of national and cultural boundaries. This transformation took many forms: the emergence of a national market economy; rapid westward expansion, which became the battleground of slavery; and a blurring of God's law and national law." See John Stauffer, "Fighting the Devil With His Own Fire," in Delbanco, *The Abolitionist Imagination*, 71–72.

14. David Walker, *Appeal, in Four Articles; Together with a Preamble, to the Coloured Citizens of the World, but in Particular, and Very Expressly, to Those of the United States of America*, 45. Available from the University Library of the University of North Carolina-Chapel Hill, *Documenting the American South*, http://docsouth.unc.edu/nc/walker/menu.html.

15. Ibid., 49.

16. Thomas Jefferson, "Declaration of Independence" (1776), http://www.archives.gov/exhibits/charters/declaration_transcript.html.

17. Thomas Paine, *Common Sense*, in *Paine: Political Writings*, ed. Bruce Kuklick (New York: Cambridge University Press, 2000), 28.

18. This is Stephen Marshall's insightful observation. Stephen H. Marshall, *The City on the Hill from Below: The Crisis of Prophetic Black Politics* (Philadelphia: Temple University Press, 2011), 28–29.

19. This is Melvin Rogers's astute argument. He notes, referring to Walker: "His use of key terms—citizen and appeal—exemplify the ways blacks constituted themselves as political actors at the very moment their ability to do so was called into question or denied. The use of those terms, I contend, brings into sharp relief a presupposition of democratic politics—namely, that ordinary individuals are capable of judging their social world—to which he means to awaken his audience, especially his African American audience." Melvin Rogers, "David Walker and the Political Power of the Appeal," *Political Theory* 43, no. 2 (2015): 209.

20. Walker, *Appeal*, 5. In this way, we can also say that Walker was something of a protoanarchist—almost a century before it would grip the imagination of some Americans in the early twentieth century—by calling black Americans to do what its most influential theorist, Emma Goldman, said was its hallmark: "[it] urges [us] to think, to analyze, to investigate every proposition." Emma Goldman, *Red Emma Speaks: An Emma Goldman Reader*, ed. Alix Kate Shulman (Amherst, Mass.: Humanity, 1996), 63–64.

21. In this sense, Walker wanted to tell black readers what Kant had answered in his 1784 essay, "What Is Enlightenment?": "Have courage to use your own understanding!" Immanuel Kant, "An Answer to the Question: What Is Enlightenment?" in *Political Writings*, ed. H. S. Reiss (Cambridge: Cambridge University Press, 1991), 54. Walker's own view that black people should be granted the intellectual and moral authority to judge political problems, despite not being granted the political authority to do this in politics or society, must have come from his acquaintance with the black lumber workers of his childhood; the closely knit black community in Boston, filled with artisans and literate small-shop owners; and his knowledge of the maroon colonies—runaway slaves who lived autonomously. For a more systematic development of Walker's idea of judgment in the *Appeal*, especially in relation to larger discussions about black politics and democratic theory, see Rogers, "David Walker and the Political Power of the Appeal."

22. Walker, *Appeal*, 6.

23. Ibid., 13.

24. Ibid., 33.

25. Ibid., 81–82.

26. Ibid., 14.

27. This term comes from Orlando Patterson, *Slavery and Social Death: A Comparative Study* (Cambridge, Mass.: Harvard University Press, 1982).

28. Walker, *Appeal*, 19.

29. Walker commentators such as Stephen Marshall and Eddie Glaude are right to read the *Appeal* as foundationally a Christian text, one that used messianic religion to instill hope for liberation in black people. But at the same time, as I show, the religiously infused language of morality itself did powerful work in the text. See Marshall, *The City on the Hill from Below*, 26–56; and Eddie Glaude, *Exodus! Religion, Race, and Nation in Early Nineteenth-Century Black America* (Chicago: University of Chicago Press, 2000), 34–43.

30. Walker, *Appeal*, 19–20.

31. Walker thus followed the example set forth by St. Paul, who roamed the streets of what he saw as a corrupt Roman Empire while reciting Jesus's ethical teaching, and anticipated Thoreau, who, decades after the *Appeal* was published, refused to pay poll taxes as a protest against U.S. imperialism and slavery. See Paul, "The Epistle of Paul, Apostle to Romans," in *The Bible: Authorized King James Version with Apocrypha* (Oxford: Oxford University Press, 2005), 189–205; Henry David Thoreau, "Resistance to Civil Government," in *The Higher Law: Henry David Thoreau on Civil Disobedience and Reform*, ed. Wendell Glick (Princeton, N.J.: Princeton University Press, 2004), 63–90.

32. Walker, *Appeal*, 86.

33. The most obvious characteristic of cynicism—a systematic philosophical doctrine that was born in ancient Greece—is its defensive emotional posture. A cynic is someone who is preemptively skeptical or dismissive of what appears before them. For a good, though not exhaustive, introduction to the philosophy of cynicism, see William Desmond, *Cynics* (New York: Routledge, 2014).

34. Walker, *Appeal*, 4.

35. See "Brutus no. 2," in *The Complete Anti-Federalist*, ed. Herbert J. Storing (Chicago: University of Chicago Press, 1981), 1:373. For the definitive, even if brief, text on Anti-Federalist political thought, see Herbert J. Storing, *What the Anti-Federalists Were For: The Political Thought of the Opponents of the Constitution* (Chicago: University of Chicago Press, 1981).

36. Walker, *Appeal*, 56.

37. Ibid., 58.

38. This position was made most famous by the political scientist Louis Hartz in his 1955 classic *The Liberal Tradition in America*. Hartz was wrong to see American slavery as an aberration in the family of American liberalism that fell into the dustbin of history only seventy-five years after the ratification of the Constitution—as if white supremacy and racism died after the Civil War ended. But Hartz was nonetheless astute to draw attention to the way slavery was often justified in liberal terms. Louis Hartz,

The Liberal Tradition in America: An Interpretation of American Political Thought Since the Revolution (1955; New York: Harcourt, Brace and Jovanovich, 1991), 8, 145–172. For a speech that expresses the slaveholder view, see John C. Calhoun, "Speech on the Reception of Abolition Petitions, Delivered in the Senate, February 6th, 1837," in *Speeches of John C. Calhoun, Delivered in the House of Representatives and in the Senate of the United States*, ed. Richard R. Cralle (New York: Appleton, 1853), 625–633.

39. Walker, *Appeal*, 17. Also see Thomas Jefferson, *Notes on the State of Virginia* (Boston: Lily and Wait, 1832), esp. "Query XIV," 135–156.

40. Walker, *Appeal*, 18.

41. James W. Ceaser makes a convincing case that there are two views of nature in *Notes* that characterize Jefferson's thought. On the one hand, there is the modern notion of natural-rights thinking—from Hobbes to Locke—which views rights as inalienable, as being present from birth. On the other hand, there is the popular notion of nature developed by naturalists such as Linnaeus and Buffon, which tried to classify human beings on the basis of certain, hereditary traits. For Ceaser, Jefferson's project was at once to "establish political regimes that recognize natural rights and that employ race as a fundamental criterion for defining the make-up of political communities." James W. Ceaser, "Natural Rights and Scientific Racism," in *Thomas Jefferson and the Politics of Nature*, ed. Thomas S. Engerman (Notre Dame, Ind.: University of Notre Dame Press, 2000), 167.

42. Thomas Jefferson, "Letter to Samuel Kercheval," in *American Political Thought*, ed. Theodore Lowi and Isaac Kramnick (New York: Norton, 2008), 373.

43. Walker thus anticipates agonistic democrats such as Connolly, Honig, and Mouffe.

44. Walker, *Appeal*, 17–18.

45. To be sure, later in this speech Lincoln would gesture toward the way slavery was at odds with the Declaration of Independence's commitment to political equality, but this was only a gesture, not a call for abolishing slavery. Abraham Lincoln, "First Lincoln-Douglass Debate, Ottawa, Illinois" (1858), in *Speeches and Writings, 1832–1858*, ed. Roy P. Basler (New York: Library of America, 1989), 495–535. It was also this aspect of Lincoln's early thinking about slavery that embodied Madison's question in "Federalist no. 10"—What is the best and most practical and pragmatic way to address a political problem and achieve political order, with all its competing violent minority or majority factions that threatened individual property rights, freedom, and personal security? See James Madison, "Federalist no. 10" (1787), in Alexander Hamilton, James Madison and John Jay, *The Federalist*, ed. Terence Ball (Cambridge: Cambridge University Press, 2003), 40–46.

46. Walker, *Appeal*, 5. Walker could never completely render himself immune from the criticism that the fundamentalism integral to his assertions about the moral necessity of abolition could be at odds with the liberal idea of pluralism, which does not assume any substantive conception of the good. For an excellent survey and unique conceptualization of the relationship between liberalism and pluralism, see William A. Galston, *The Practice of Liberal Pluralism* (New York: Cambridge University Press, 2004).

47. Walker, *Appeal*, 25.
48. The position of sentimentalism was most famously defended by David Hume, *A Treatise of Human Nature* (New York: Oxford University Press, 2000). Hume, unlike Walker, was completely unconcerned with the problem of responding to slavery— and at times actually argued that what he called "the Negro race" lacked civilization and was "naturally inferior" to whites. For a discussion of this, see Naomi Zack, *Philosophy of Science and Race* (New York: Routledge, 2002), 15.
49. Walker, *Appeal*, 7.
50. Ibid., 8.
51. Compare Walker to Machiavelli, who turned to history in *The Prince* to remind rulers how remembering past moments of what he saw as the great political skill (*virtu'*) of individuals such as Moses, Cyrus, Romulus, and Theseus would enable rulers to rule better in the present, but Walker did it to highlight exceptional brutality. Niccolò Machiavelli, *The Prince*, trans. David Wootton (Indianapolis, Ind.: Hackett, 1995), 18.
52. Walker, *Appeal*, 9.
53. Good empirical evidence suggests that American black enslavement was historically unique not because of the extent or intensity of its domination but through the unique theory of racism that sought to justify it. See George Frederickson, *Racism: A Short History* (Princeton, N.J.: Princeton University Press, 2009), 49–96.
54. One of Walker's protégés, the African American woman abolitionist Maria Stewart, was much better than him on gender, bringing to relief the way black patriarchy degraded black women. But her brand of exceptionalism, unlike Walker's, centered on the special connection African Americans had to God. See Valerie C. Cooper, *Word, Like Fire: Maria Stewart, the Bible, and the Rights of African Americans* (Charlottesville: University of Virginia Press, 2012), 3.
55. Walker, *Appeal*, 3.
56. Ibid., 4.
57. See John C. Calhoun, "Speech on the Reception of Abolition Petitions," in *Speeches of John C. Calhoun*, 225. For an excellent overview of proslavery ideology, see Eugene D. Genovese, *The World the Slaveholders Made: Two Essays in Interpretation* (Hanover, Conn.: Wesleyan University Press, 1988).
58. George Fitzhugh, *Sociology for the South, or the Failure of Free Society* (Richmond: A. Morris, 1854), 223.
59. Walker, *Appeal*, 31.
60. Ibid., 16.
61. Ibid., 12.
62. Elizabeth Fox-Genovese and Eugene D. Genovese, *The Mind of the Master Class: History and Faith in the Slaveholders' Worldview* (New York: Cambridge, 2005), 105.
63. Hamilton, "Federalist no. 70," in *The Federalist*, 342.
64. Ibid., 346.
65. Walker, *Appeal*, 22.
66. Ibid., 24.
67. Ibid., 25.

68. Ibid., 23.

69. Ibid., 26.

70. This point anticipates Foucault. See Michel Foucault, "Truth and Power," in *The Foucault Reader*, ed. Paul Rabinow (New York: Pantheon, 1984), 51–75. In offering this interpretation of Walker's insights about the consequences of ignorance, I deepen Marshall's view that Walker's idea of ignorance goes beyond liberal pluralists and humanists. For Marshall, in showing how ignorance forces one to misidentify one's true interests, Walker believes its chief problem is not a paucity of intellectual resources necessary for personal growth and economic success. See Marshall, *City on a Hill from Below*, 40.

71. Walker, *Appeal*, 28.

72. Madison, "Federalist no. 10," 45.

73. "To fight accusations of racism," Mia Bay contends that "Walker himself drew on arguments of eighteenth century environmentalism, which were drawn from eighteenth century naturalism. Bay, *The White Image in the Black Mind*, 36.

74. Marshall worries about this possibility in *City on a Hill from Below*, 56–57.

75. Walker, *Appeal*, 70.

76. Ibid., 30.

77. Aristotle, *The Politics*, trans. Ernest Barker (Oxford: Oxford University Press, 1995), 11–13. It should also be noted that the Federalist and Anti-Federalist views of human nature did not always help matters. Using an obviously convoluted logic, which assumed that human beings could be seen as property, slaveholders often justified slavery by saying it was in their self-interest to protect their property.

78. John Locke, *Second Treatise of Government*, ed. C. B. Macpherson (Indianapolis, Ind.: Hackett, 1980), 8–13.

79. However, Walker seemed at times to agree with Rousseau's view. Jean-Jacques Rousseau, "Discourse on the Origin and Foundations of Inequality Among Men" (1755), in *Political Writings*, ed. Alan Ritter and Julia Conaway Bondanella (New York: Norton, 1987), 28–29.

80. Walker, *Appeal*, 20.

81. Ibid., 21.

82. Ibid., 68–69.

83. Ibid., 45.

84. Sandra M. Gustafson argues that Walker critiqued American republicanism but also tried to propose a new "multiracial" republic—engaging America, rather than fleeing from it. Sandra M. Gustafson, *Imagining Deliberative Democracy in the Early American Republic* (Chicago: University of Chicago Press, 2011), 139.

85. Walker, *Appeal*, 34.

86. Garry Wills argues that happiness for Jefferson in the Declaration of Independence was much more about participation in collective life, rather than an individual pursuit. Gary Wills, *Inventing America: Jefferson's Declaration of Independence* (New York: Mariner, 2002), 248–258.

87. Walker, *Appeal*, 34.

88. Indeed, as David Brion Davis writes, because of the fact that there weren't even more slave revolts in the nineteenth century, many whites believed that "slaves were contended with their lot." Davis, *Inhuman Bondage*, 206.

89. See John Adams, *Revolutionary Writings, 1775–1783*, ed. Gordon S. Wood (New York: Library of America, 2011); and Thomas Paine, *Collected Writings* (New York: Library of America, 1995).

90. See Karl Marx and Friedrich Engels, "Manifesto of the Communist Party," in *The Marx-Engels Reader*, ed. Robert C. Tucker (New York: Norton, 1978), 469–500.

91. Walker, *Appeal*, 35.

92. David Howard-Pitney contends that "it is ironic that this earliest expression of messianic black nationalism in America should have sprung up in such close proximity to Anglo-American nationalism ... [this] signals their virtually complete acceptance of and incorporation into the national cultural norm of millennial faith in America's promise." David Howard-Pitney, *The African American Jeremiad: Appeals for Justice in America* (Philadelphia: Temple University Press, 2005), 12.

93. Walker, *Appeal*, 62.

94. Ibid., 85.

95. For this argument, see Maxwell Burkey and Alex Zamalin, "Patriotism, Black Politics, and Racial Justice in America," *New Political Science* 38, no. 3 (2016): 371–389. For another valuable critique of patriotism, see Steven Johnston, *The Truth About Patriotism* (Durham, N.C.: Duke University Press, 2007). For those who find sustenance from patriotism for social justice, see Rogers Smith, *Stories of Peoplehood: The Politics and Morals of Political Membership* (New York: Cambridge University Press, 2003); Richard Rorty, *Achieving Our Country: Leftist Thought in Twentieth-Century America* (Cambridge, Mass.: Harvard University Press, 1999).

96. Stephen Kantrowitz argues that "Walker was a revolutionary of a different and arguably more terrifying kind than the one who generally haunted the imaginations of Southern state officials. Rather than seeking to overthrow the American republic, Walker sought to claim a place in it." Stephen Kantrowitz, *More Than Freedom: Fighting for Black Citizenship in a White Republic, 1829–1889* (New York: Penguin, 2013), 29.

97. Walker, *Appeal*, 5.

98. Ibid., 75.

99. See Hinks, *To Awaken My Afflicted Brethren*, 115.

100. Waldo E. Martin rightly contends that "the guiding assumption unifying Douglass's thought was an inveterate belief in a universal and egalitarian brand of humanism. His seemingly innate commitment to the inviolability of freedom and the human spirit best exemplified this overarching assumption." Waldo E. Martin, *The Mind of Frederick Douglass* (Chapel Hill: University of North Carolina Press, 1984), ix. Peter C. Myers, in contrast, reads Douglass as a natural-rights theorist and believes that his argument lives on in contemporary black conservatives like Thomas Sowell, Shelby Steele, and John McWhorter. Peter C. Myers, *Frederick Douglass: Race and the Rebirth of American Liberalism* (Lawrence: University Press of Kansas, 2008).

101. Frederick Douglass, *My Bondage and My Freedom*, in *The Autobiographies* (New York: Library of America, 1994), 171.

102. Ibid., 189.

103. Ibid., 107–124.

104. Ibid., 238. My discussion deepens Buccola's interpretation of what Douglass meant by slavery but more clearly than Buccola dramatizes the way such domination impacts slave agency. See Nicholas Buccola, *The Political Thought of Frederick Douglass: In Pursuit of American Liberty* (New York: New York University Press, 2012), 14–28.

105. The most famous of these was Stanley Elkins, *Slavery: A Problem in American and Institutional Life* (Chicago: University of Chicago Press, 1959).

106. Jack Turner asserts that "there is a principle uniting Douglass's self-reliant individualism and his insistence in the aftermath of the Civil War that the federal government was obligated to provide material assistance to freed people: liberal democratic governments must not only secure the rights of citizens against interference, but also ensure that the material rudiments of self-help are universally available." Jack Turner, *Awakening to Race: Individualism and Social Consciousness in America* (Chicago: University of Chicago Press, 2012), 49.

107. Henry David Thoreau, "Resistance to Civil Government," in *The Higher Law: Henry David Thoreau on Civil Disobedience and Reform*, ed. Wendell Glick (Princeton, N.J.: Princeton University Press, 2004), 65.

108. My argument here deepens Eric Sundquist's influential interpretation of *My Bondage and My Freedom*. He writes: "In revising his life story while immersing it rhetorically in the ideology of the Revolution, Douglass at once engaged the ancestral masters in struggle and made their language and principles his weapons of resistance." But while Sundquist's focus is primarily on Douglass's cultural politics—he writes, for instance, "transfiguring his slave narrative into a text of revolution became an act in which Douglass's literacy, the ability to command through manipulating the 'signs of power' in a public arena, was resurrection"—my approach is about the revolutionary way Douglass conceptualizes dignity. Sundquist, *To Wake the Nations*, 30, 124.

109. Douglass, *My Bondage and My Freedom*, 283.

110. For this interpretation, see Susan Buck-Morss, *Hegel, Haiti, and Universal History* (Pittsburgh, Penn.: University of Pittsburgh Press, 2009).

111. G. W. F. Hegel, *The Phenomenology of Spirit*, trans. A. V. Miller (1807; New York: Oxford University Press, 1977), 117.

112. Compare this point with Bernard R. Boxill, who argues that "when Douglass claimed that a man without power was without 'the essential dignity of humanity' he was relying on the fact that a person's power does not only depend on her ability to cause trouble, but also, and perhaps and more crucially, on her firm conviction that there is value in risking her life in fighting for her rights." Boxill, "Douglass Against the Emigrationists," 38. Also see Lewis R. Gordon, who argues that "the existential dimension of the situation was such that it collapsed reflective, conceptual reality. It broke through the saturated composition of skewed racist reality." Lewis R. Gordon, "Douglass as an Existentialist," in *Frederick Douglass*, 221.

113. Douglass, *My Bondage and My Freedom*, 269.

114. Ibid., 274.

115. Commentators such as Margaret Kohn, while astutely showing that Douglass draws on and complicates Hegel's notion of the struggle for recognition and especially the productive political dimension of fear, miss the political centrality of anguish, or what we could also call despair. Margaret Kohn, "Frederick Douglass's Master-Slave Dialectic," *Journal of Politics* 67, no. 2 (2005): 497–514. Furthermore, by drawing attention to the way various emotions such as anguish and madness do political work, I am implicitly departing from Robert S. Levine's interpretation of Douglass as solely advocating what he calls "temperate revolutionism." In the Covey encounter, Levine sees a great deal of emotional restraint and control, which serve as a counterpoint to the white slaveholder's emotionally driven violence toward slaves. Levine may be right to say that temperate revolutionism may be one motivation behind Douglass's politics and his call for reform, but I do not believe this is the case in *My Bondage and My Freedom*—a text written in the 1850s, when Douglass explicitly turns away from a staunch defense of nonviolence. Robert S. Levine, *Martin Delany, Frederick Douglass, and the Politics of Representative Identity* (Chapel Hill: University of North Carolina Press, 1997), 101–130.

116. For this distinction in Douglass's thought see Nicholas Buccola, "The Essential Dignity of Man as Man," *American Political Thought* 4, no. 2 (Spring 2015): 228–258.

117. My suggestion is that Douglass offers a perspective on dignity that is traditionally overlooked by contemporary commentators: that the recognition of dignity depends on direct action. For contemporary theorists of dignity, see George Kateb, *Human Dignity* (Cambridge, Mass.: Harvard University Press, 2011); and Michael Rosen, *Dignity* (Cambridge, Mass.: Harvard University Press, 2012). Furthermore, although Gooding-Williams correctly highlights the way dignity in *My Bondage and My Freedom* "expresses a slave's struggle to constrain the power of arbitrary interference. It is a display to others of a slave's ability to help himself, his ability to struggle," he nonetheless does not sufficiently foreground Douglass's insight that dignity is performative, opting instead to focus on the way dignity is necessary for self-respect and for the respect of others. See Robert Gooding-Williams, *In the Shadow of Du Bois: Afro-Modern Political Thought in America* (Cambridge, Mass.: Harvard University Press, 2011), 181.

118. Douglass, *My Bondage and My Freedom*, 283.

119. Ibid., 284.

120. Ibid., 286.

121. This interpretation is legitimate and should be acknowledged as reflecting something troubling about Douglass's own thought. Neil Roberts, for instance, accuses Douglass of failing to see how his theory of freedom as flight actually undermines his own troubling masculinism. Neil Roberts, *Freedom as Marronage* (Chicago: University of Chicago Press, 2015), 84. I agree with Roberts, even though Levine astutely points out that one way to understand Douglass's invocation of "man" is as a universal term meant to designate all of humanity—men and women—and the opposite of nonhuman,

rather than as the antithesis of woman. See Robert S. Levine, *Martin Delany, Frederick Douglass and the Politics of Representative Identity* (Chapel Hill: University of North Carolina Press, 1997), 130. Of course, Douglass's own masculinism did not prevent him from supporting political equality for women. For this point see Martin, *The Mind of Frederick Douglass*, 136–164.

122. There is still some debate about whether Douglass's defense of violent slave resistance in "Is it Right and Wise to Kill a Kidnapper?" (1854) represented an irreversible turning point in his abolitionism, replacing the idea of nonviolence and moral suasion with violence. For a survey of this and an ultimate defense of the argument that there is a consistency between Douglass's two positions, see Frank Kirkland, "Enslavement, Moral Suasion, and Struggles for Recognition," in Lawson and Kirkland, *Frederick Douglass*, 246.

123. Douglass, *My Bondage and My Freedom*, 286.

124. For the best account of Douglass's unique theory of "comparative freedom" as part of the idea of freedom as marronage, see Roberts, *Freedom as Marronage*, 74–88.

125. Ralph Waldo Emerson, "Self Reliance" (1841), in *Nature and Selected Essays*, ed. Larzer Ziff (New York: Penguin, 2003), 178.

126. For an argument that treats Emerson's idea of self-reliance as political, see Jack Turner, "Self Reliance and Complicity: Emerson's Ethics of Citizenship," in *A Political Companion to Ralph Waldo Emerson*, ed. Alan M. Levine and Daniel S. Malachuk (Lexington: University of Kentucky Press, 2011), 125–151.

127. Compare my point with Nick Bromell, who argues that "for Emerson, what is ultimately at stake is personal integrity, the freedom to think for oneself in order to be who one is. For Douglass, what is at stake is the success of a struggle to achieve social conditions that make personal freedom possible in the first place. For Douglass knows from experience something Emerson could know only theoretically, if he knew it at all: the historical reality of unfreedom and the historical contingency of freedom. Thinking his way forward from this experience, he finds the tension between the universal and the contingent, the abstract and the particular, the eternal and the historical much more fraught than does Emerson." Nick Bromell, "'A Voice from the Enslaved': The Origins of Frederick Douglass's Political Philosophy of Democracy," *American Literary History* 23, no. 4 (2011): 712.

128. Gooding-Williams is right that one core dimension of Douglass's thinking about freedom is non-domination. See Gooding-Williams, *In the Shadow of Du Bois*, 170.

129. In this sense, Douglass's goal was much broader than, as Nicholas Buccola points out, to "convince his fellow Americans to purge the narrowness and selfishness from their love of liberty. His aim, in short, was to persuade the American people to accept a new liberal creed that would replace narrowness with egalitarianism and selfishness with humanitarianism." Buccola, *The Political Thought of Frederick Douglass*, 1.

130. John C. Calhoun, *A Disquisition on Government: And Selections from the Discourse* (Indianapolis, Ind.: Hackett, 1995), 3.

131. Douglass, *My Bondage and My Freedom*, 285.

132. This practice seems to anticipate what the political scientist Michael Hanchard, building on James Scott's notion of "infrapolitics," calls "quotidian politics." Michael Hanchard, *Party/Politics: Horizon in Black Political Thought* (New York: Oxford University Press, 2006), 55–64. For a textured interpretation of Douglass's notion of solidarity, which my reading supports, see Gooding-Williams, who, contrasting Douglass with Du Bois, says that Douglass "lets us see that African American politics need not be the expression of an antecedently given, kinship and descent-based identity that the participants have in common. Indeed, he suggests that African American politics is possible where no such identity exists." Gooding-Williams, *In the Shadow of Du Bois*, 187.

133. Douglass, *My Bondage and My Freedom*, 287.

134. For an exploration of the link between black slavery and white freedom, through a case study of colonial Virginia, see Edmund S. Morgan, *American Slavery, American Freedom* (New York: Norton, 1975).

2. IDA B. WELLS, THE ANTILYNCHING MOVEMENT, AND THE POLITICS OF SEEING

1. Lynching is a term that evades as much definition as the connotations its powerful images conjure. Christopher Waldrep notes: "The word lynching cannot be defined. It is rhetoric, and because it is rhetoric, almost any act of violence can potentially be a 'lynching.'" Christopher Waldrep, *African Americans Confront Lynching: Strategies of Resistance from the Civil War to the Civil Rights Era* (Lanham, Md.: Rowman and Littlefield, 2009), xiii.

2. For the literature on lynching, which is mostly historical, see Michael J. Pfeifer, *Rough Justice: Lynching and American Society, 1874–1947* (Urbana: University of Illinois Press, 2004); Jonathan Markovitz, *Legacies of Lynching: Racial Violence and Memory* (Minneapolis: University of Minnesota Press, 2004); Amy Wood, *Lynching and Spectacle: Witnessing Racial Violence in America, 1890–1940* (Chapel Hill: University of North Carolina Press, 2009); Stewart E. Tolnay and E. M. Beck, *A Festival of Violence: An Analysis of Southern Lynchings, 1882–1930* (Urbana: University of Illinois Press, 1995); W. Fitzhugh Brundage, *Lynching in the New South: Georgia and Virginia, 1880–1930* (Urbana: University of Illinois, 1993).

3. "If lynching was a national crime, it was also a southern obsession." Brundage, *Lynching in the New South*, 1.

4. For Wells and gender, see Hazel Carby, *Reconstructing Womanhood: The Emergence of the Afro-American Woman Novelist* (New York: Oxford University Press, 1989), 113–115. Also see Crystal Nicole Feimster, *Southern Horrors: Women and the Politics of Rape and Lynching* (Cambridge, Mass.: Harvard University Press, 2009), which partly focuses on the link between Wells's antirape and antilynching crusades. For her status as truth teller, see Patricia A. Schechter, *Ida. B. Wells-Barnett and American Reform, 1880–1930* (Chapel Hill: University of North Carolina Press, 2001).

5. For this argument see Anthony Bogues, *Black Heretics, Black Prophets: Radical Political Intellectuals* (New York: Routledge, 2003), 47–68. Bogues asserts that for Wells "practical activity is critical practical activity, which confronts the ideas and practices of the old order. Wells-Barnett's writings mark a different stage in the African-American tradition. Her essays on lynching are interventionist texts in which the issues about the referential functions of language are replaced with notions about language and writing as truth claims. If the slave narratives in their literary form were badges of reason, then Wells-Barnett's writings were polemical and sociological excursions" (48). See also Mia Bay, *To Tell the Truth Freely: The Life of Ida B. Wells* (New York: Hill & Wang, 2010).

6. Scholarly interpretations of lynching have largely failed to consider the way it presents a serious problem for politics. One camp has considered lynching's causes, which range from way it provided working-class whites a way to instill fear in the black labor force to those that stress how it helped enforce white supremacy and American manhood in ways much more powerful than Jim Crow laws. Amy Wood argues: "It was the spectacle of lynching, rather than the violence itself, that wrought psychological damage, that enforced black acquiescence to white domination." Wood, *Lynching and Spectacle*, 2. See also Markovitz, *Legacies of Lynching*. Another camp has considered its cultural significance as a ritual that tapped into and reflected anxieties about interracial life and was part of a burgeoning visual culture in which witnessing became a key way of producing a sense of white community when such a community was being fractured internally. For this interpretation see Pfeifer, *Rough Justice*; and Tolnay and Beck, *A Festival of Violence*. Tolnay and Beck argue: "We suspect that whites lynched African-Americans when they felt threatened in some way—economically, politically, or socially" (3).

7. Part of the goal of this chapter is to show political theorists how studying antilynching thinking can actually be fruitful for democratic life precisely because of what lynching reflects about democracy. For one of the few texts that tries to examine carefully what lynching, as a form of noncivil disobedience, can tell us about the rule of law, violence, and political action, see Jennet Kirkpatrick, *Uncivil Disobedience: Studies in Violence and Democratic Politics* (Princeton, N.J.: Princeton University Press, 2008), 62–90. Kirkpatrick is interested in understanding how we can conceptualize the way Southern lynch mobs' sense of morality differed from the more traditional practices of civil disobedience like the civil rights movement. But my concern is to understand what conception of citizenship is most adequate for addressing the problem that lynching—or any form of vigilante violence—poses for and reflects about democracy.

8. The best way to understand Wells's social predicament as a black woman is through what Patricia Hill Collins calls an "interlocking system of oppression," where one is oppressed and marginalized in different ways through various aspects of their identity, such as race, gender, and sexuality. Patricia Hill Collins, *Black Feminist Thought: Knowledge, Consciousness, and the Politics of Empowerment* (New York: Routledge, 1990). In that book, Collins, like many scholars, stays at the level of asserting that

Wells was a critical public intellectual, but I aim throughout the chapter to clarify her unique political theoretical contributions.

9. Ida B. Wells, "Woman's Mission" (1885), in *The Light of Truth: Writings of an Anti-Lynching Crusader*, ed. Mia Bay (New York: Penguin, 2014), 15.

10. Ibid., 14.

11. See Sarah Grimké, *Letters on the Equality of the Sexes, and Other Essays*, ed. Elizabeth Ann Bartlett (New Haven, Conn.: Yale University Press, 1988).

12. Ida B. Wells, "Lynch Law in America" (1900), in *The Light of Truth*, 401. Wells's racist statement, in many ways, confirms Rogers Smith's thesis that various elements of American political culture—liberal, civic republican, and racial ascriptivist—find their way into the thought of individual American thinkers. Rogers Smith, *Civic Ideals: Conflicting Visions of Citizenship in U.S. History* (New Haven, Conn.: Yale University Press, 1999).

13. For this argument, see Aristotle, *The Politics*, trans. Ernest Barker (Oxford: Oxford University Press, 1995), 16.

14. Abraham Lincoln, "First Lincoln-Douglass Debate, Ottawa, Illinois" (1858), in *Speeches and Writings, 1832–1858*, ed. Roy P. Basler (New York: Library of America, 1989), 512.

15. See Martin R. Delany, *Martin R. Delany: A Documentary Reader*, ed. Robert S. Levine (Chapel Hill: University of North Carolina Press, 2003); Booker T. Washington, "The Standard Printed Version of the Atlanta Exposition Address," in *The Booker T. Washington Papers*, ed. Louis R. Harlan (Urbana: University of Illinois Press, 1972), 583–588. For Crummell's political thought, see Wilson Jeremiah Moses, *Creative Conflict in African American Thought* (New York: Cambridge University Press, 2004), 83–140.

16. Ida B. Wells, "The Requirements of Southern Journalism" (1893), in *The Light of Truth*, 92.

17. Ida B. Wells, "Booker T. Washington and His Critics" (1904), in *The Light of Truth*, 440.

18. Ida B. Wells, "Functions of Leadership," in *The Light of Truth*, 8.

19. Wells, "The Requirements of Southern Journalism" (1893), 91.

20. Ibid., 89.

21. For a contemporary iteration of this problem of speaking for others, see Linda Alcoff, "The Problem of Speaking for Others," *Cultural Critique* 20 (1992): 5–32.

22. William James, *On a Certain Blindness in Human Beings* (New York: Penguin, 2009), 4.

23. Ida B. Wells, *A Red Record* (1895), in *The Light of Truth*, 308.

24. Ida B. Wells, "Lynch Law in All Its Phases" (1894), in *The Light of Truth*, 112. Wells counters understandings of publics that deemphasize emotion in favor of rationality. Wells shared Walker's Humean view about the power of moral sentiment and Douglass's view about the way it provided a sense of one's own limitations and deepest commitments. For those contemporary theorists who take emotional life in politics seriously, see Iris Marion Young, *Inclusion and Democracy* (New York: Oxford University Press, 2000).

25. Wells, "Lynch Law in All Its Phases" (1894), 113.

26. In their quasi-messianic mission of transforming humanity, Progressives saw government as the perfect tool for curbing sex work and alcohol addiction, for expanding women's suffrage, and for dealing with poverty. For a history of the Progressive movement, see Michael McGerr, *A Fierce Discontent: The Rise and Fall of the Progressive Movement in America, 1870–1920* (New York: Free Press, 2003). In his classic study, Robert H. Wiebe argued that Progressives responded to and sought to address the radical social disruptions caused in the aftermath of the Gilded Age, such as the urbanization of life, the nationalization of politics, and the industrialization of the American economy. See Robert H. Wiebe, *The Search for Order: 1877–1920* (New York: Hill & Wang, 1967).

27. For one of the classic texts on the Gilded Age, see Sean Dennis Cashman, *America in the Gilded Age* (New York: New York University Press, 1984).

28. William Graham Sumner, *What Social Classes Owe to Each Other* (New Haven, Conn.: Yale University Press, 1925), 20–21.

29. William Graham Sumner, "The Absurd Effort to Make the World Over," in *War and Other Essays*, ed. Albert Galloway Keller (New Haven, Conn.: Yale University Press, 1911), 200.

30. Wells, "Lynch Law in All Its Phases," 105.

31. Karl Marx, "Economic and Philosophic Manuscripts of 1844," in *The Marx-Engels Reader*, ed. Robert C. Tucker (New York: Norton, 1978), 75.

32. Wells, *A Red Record*, 256.

33. Wells, "Lynch Law in America," 394.

34. Quoted in Ida B. Wells, "Lynching and the Excuse for It" (1901), in *The Light of Truth*, 409.

35. Ibid.

36. For the idea that the idea of the people in democracy is an open category, see Claude Lefort, *Democracy and Political Theory* (Minneapolis: University of Minnesota Press, 1989). For the rich literature on the meaning of popular identity, see Edmund Morgan, *Inventing the People* (New York: Norton, 1988); Margaret Canovan, *The People* (New York: Polity, 2005); Ernesto Laclau, *On Populist Reason* (New York: Verso, 2005).

37. Gustave Le Bon, *The Crowd: A Study of the Popular Mind* (New York: MacMillan, 1897), 8.

38. Ida B. Wells, "Bishop Tanner's 'Ray of Light'" (1892), in *The Light of Truth*, 54.

39. In his now classic, even if outdated and contested study, of the late nineteenth- and early twentieth-century age of Populism, the historian Richard Hofstadter argued that this period was defined by conspiratorial and oppositional dichotomous thinking that centered not only on economic issues but on racial ones. A latent but no less significant strain of nativism existed throughout many Populist arguments. See Richard Hofstadter, *The Age of Reform* (New York: Vintage, 1955).

40. The historian Michael Kazin captures this national mood, which also informed some Populist thinking. The Populists, Kazin writes, "spoke about the state as the creation

and property of people like themselves. Greedy, tyrannical men had usurped that birthright." Michael Kazin, *The Populist Persuasion: An American History* (Ithaca, N.Y.: Cornell University Press, 1998), 42.

41. Wells, *A Red Record*, 257.

42. Emile Durkheim, *The Division of Labor in Society* (New York: Free Press, 2014), 63–67.

43. John Locke, *Second Treatise of Government*, ed. C. B. Macpherson (Indianapolis, Ind.: Hackett, 1980), 63–64.

44. Wells, "Bishop Tanner's 'Ray of Light,' " 53.

45. Alexis de Tocqueville, *Democracy in America*, ed. Harvey Mansfield and Delba Winthrop (Chicago: University of Chicago Press, 2000), 490.

46. Wells, *Southern Horrors*, 78.

47. Wells, "Lynch Law in All Its Phases," 111.

48. Wells, *A Red Record*, 307

49. For the history of the social thought of Progressivism, especially how it intersected with social science and social justice thinking, see James T. Kloppenberg, *Uncertain Victory: Social Democracy and Progressivism in European and American Thought, 1870–1920* (New York: Oxford University Press, 1988).

50. Ida B. Wells, *Southern Horrors: Lynch Law in All Its Phases* (1892), in *The Light of Truth*, 58.

51. Wells, *A Red Record*, in *The Light of Truth*, 299–306.

52. Ibid., 281.

53. Jürgen Habermas, *The Theory of Communicative Action* (Boston: Beacon, 1984).

54. William James, *The Meaning of Truth: A Sequel to Pragmatism*, in *Writings, 1902–1910*, 826.

55. In this way, Wells must have also understood what the German sociologist Max Weber argued in his lecture, "Science as a Vocation," (1917), was the central limitation of scientific inquiry: science could at best explain the world but never specify the values for why the questions it raised in the first place where of normative importance. See Max Weber, "Science as a Vocation," in *The Vocation Lectures*, trans. Rodney Livingston and eds. David Owen and Tracy B. Strong (Indianapolis: Hackett, 2004).

56. Wells, "Lynch Law in All Its Phases," in *The Light of Truth*, 109.

57. Wells, *A Red Record*, 237.

58. Ibid., 97.

59. Wells, *Southern Horrors*, 68.

60. Wells, *A Red Record*, 228.

61. Ida B. Wells, *Mob Rule in New Orleans: Robert Charles and His Fight to the Death* (1900), in *The Light of Truth*, 365.

62. Wells, *A Red Record*, 265.

63. Wells, *Mob Rule in New Orleans*, 387–388.

64. Stanley Cavell, *The Claim of Reason: Wittgenstein, Skepticism, Morality, and Tragedy* (New York: Oxford University Press, 1979), 418–419.

65. Upton Sinclair, *The Jungle* (New York: Dover, 2001), 112–113.

66.   Ida B. Wells, *Lynch Law in Georgia* (1899), in *The Light of Truth*, 324–325.

67.   This anecdote is told in David Levering Lewis's seminal biography of Du Bois, *W. E. B. Du Bois: A Biography* (New York: Holt, 2009), 162–164.

68.   See W. E. B. Du Bois, *The Souls of Black Folk* (New York: Oxford University Press, 2007).

69.   These arguments were being asserted in well-known publications like *The Atlantic Monthly* and by the American Economic Association. Jackson Lears, *Rebirth of a Nation: The Making of Modern America, 1877–1920* (New York: Harper Collins, 2009), 104.

70.   Wells, *A Red Record*, 282.

71.   Wells, "Bishop Tanner's 'Ray of Light,'" 53.

72.   Of course, one could accuse Wells of problematically deploying the same human/animal binary that Sinclair used and worry about the moralistic way in which she assumed that lynching members of one's own race was somehow more vicious than doing it to others. After all, violence is violence. For an examination and critique of how this human/animal binary functions in Western philosophy, see Jacques Derrida, *The Animal That Therefore I Am*, trans. David Willis (New York: Fordham University Press, 2008).

73.   Wells, *A Red Record*, 225.

74.   Wells, *Southern Horrors*, 70–71.

75.   For an account that argues that shame ought to be our favored normative response to the problem of racial injustice, see Christopher Lebron, *The Color of Our Shame: Race and Justice in Our Time* (New York: Oxford University Press, 2013). As the discussion in this chapter shows, Wells both dramatized the value of shame for racial justice while also creatively stressing its limitations.

76.   One can certainly argue that Wells's feminism was especially evident through the way she brought into relief how lynching worked through a manipulation of black and women's sexuality—an argument that scandalized many Progressives. Hazel Carby writes: "Wells's analysis of lynching and her demystification of the political motivations behind the manipulation of both black male and white female sexuality led her into direct confrontation with individuals who considered themselves progressive." Carby, *Reconstructing Womanhood*, 113.

77.   Wells, *Southern Horrors*, 73.

78.   Ibid., 71.

79.   Wells shares Martha Nussbaum's skepticism of the democratic value of shame for public life. But unlike Nussbaum, who worries about its moralism and wish to hide human vulnerability, Wells highlights how it precludes deliberative reflection in the first place. For Nussbaum's critique, see her *Hiding from the Law: Disgust, Shame, and Humanity* (Princeton, N.J.: Princeton University Press, 2004), 13.

80.   Brundage writes that "the 'unspeakable crime'—rape—gripped the imaginations of whites to a far greater extent than any other crime." Brundage, *Lynching in the New South*, 58.

81.   Wells, *A Red Record*, 225.

82. Ibid., 271.

83. Wells, *Southern Horrors*, 62.

84. Ibid., 63–64.

85. Willfully renouncing absolute fidelity to one's race amounted to an early example of what some critics have recently identified as the process by which one becomes a "race traitor." See Noel Ignatiev and John Garvey, eds., *Race Traitor* (New York: Routledge, 1996).

86. The contemporary idea of the abolition of whiteness is detailed in Joel Olson, *The Abolition of White Democracy* (Minneapolis: University of Minnesota Press, 2004), 125–146.

87. Herbert Croly, *The Promise of American Life* (1909; Princeton, N.J.: Princeton University Press, 2014), 5.

88. Wells, *A Red Record*, 309.

89. In a sense, Wells's activism anticipated what Cornel West would later call "tragicomic hope." See Cornel West, "Black Strivings in a Twilight Civilization," in *The Cornel West Reader* (New York: Basic Civitas Books, 1999), 118.

90. Wells, *A Red Record*, 308.

3. HUEY NEWTON, THE BLACK PANTHERS, AND THE DECOLONIZATION OF AMERICA

1. For a general history of the Black Power moment, of which the Panthers were part, see Peniel E. Joseph, *Waiting 'Til the Midnight Hour: A Narrative History of Black Power in America* (New York: Holt, 2006).

2. This history is exquisitely detailed in Joshua Bloom and Waldo E. Martin, *Black Against Empire: The History and Politics of the Black Panther Party* (Berkeley: University of California Press, 2014), 1–17.

3. Their arguments at times drew on Marx's so-called early humanism as well as his scientific account of capitalism and arguments about socialism. See Karl Marx and Friedrich Engels, *The Marx-Engels Reader*, ed. Robert C. Tucker (New York: Norton, 1978). For a study of this postwar consumer culture, see Lizabeth Cohen, *A Consumer's Republic: The Politics of Mass Consumption in Postwar America* (New York: Knopf, 2003).

4. Martin Luther King Jr., "I Have a Dream" (1963), *A Testament of Hope*, ed. James M. Washington (San Francisco: HarperCollins, 1986), 217–221. For Baldwin's influential discussion of love, see *The Fire Next Time*, in *Collected Essays*, ed. Toni Morrison (New York: Library of America), 291–331.

5. See James Madison, "Federalist no. 10" (1787), in Alexander Hamilton, James Madison and John Jay, *The Federalist*, ed. Terence Ball (Cambridge: Cambridge University Press, 2003), 40–46.

6. For this distinction in Kant's thought, see Immanuel Kant, *Political Writings*, ed. H. S. Reiss (Cambridge: Cambridge University Press, 1991), 117–118.

7.   If not completely dismissed out of hand as a culturally fashionable yet fringe move-
     ment lacking any serious political philosophy, the few serious studies of the Panthers
     have largely focused on the political utility of their arguments about American capi-
     talism, colonialism, and black self-determination. For sociological and political
     interpretations, see Doug McAdam, *Political Process and the Development of Black
     Insurgency, 1930–1970* (Chicago: University of Chicago Press, 1982), esp. chap. 8; and
     Jeffrey O. G. Ogbar, *Black Power: Radical Politics and African American Identity* (Bal-
     timore, Md.: Johns Hopkins University Press, 2005). For a historical interpretation,
     see Joseph, *Waiting 'Til the Midnight Hour*; and Judson Jeffries, ed., *Black Power in
     the Belly of the Beast* (Urbana: University of Illinois Press, 2005). For the best account
     of Newton's political theory, which primarily places him in conversation with Hobbes
     and Locke and pan-African anticolonial movements, see Judson Jeffries, *Huey P.
     Newton: The Radical Theorist* (Jackson: University of Mississippi Press, 2002).

8.   King's vision, before his more social-democratic turn in the late 1960s, was not the
     only part of civil rights political thought but represented its most politically main-
     stream and publicly visible articulation. It is this understanding of civil rights
     thought that informs the backdrop for this chapter's discussion about the Panthers.
     For a history of the "long" civil rights movement, see Jacquelyn Dowd Hall, "The
     Long Civil Rights Movement and the Political Uses of the Past," *Journal of American
     History* 91, no. 4 (2005): 1233–1263.

9.   For a comprehensive history of the civil rights movement, see Robert Weisbrot, *Free-
     dom Bound: A History of the Civil Rights Movement* (New York: Norton, 1990).

10. This is clearly a simplified view of one core liberal project of modernity, of which
     there are many liberalisms and many modernities. My interpretation here is largely
     informed by Sheldon Wolin, *Politics and Vision* (Princeton, N.J.: Princeton Univer-
     sity Press, 2006); and Quentin Skinner, *The Foundations of Modern Political Thought*,
     vol. 1: *The Renaissance*, and vol. 2: *The Age of Reformation* (Cambridge: Cambridge
     University Press, 1978).

11. This is something that many African American intellectuals have struggled with. For
     a history of this, see Manning Marable, *Black Leadership* (New York: Columbia Uni-
     versity Press, 1998); and Kevin Kelly Gaines, *Uplifting the Race: Black Leadership,
     Politics, and Culture in the Twentieth Century*, 2nd ed. (Chapel Hill: University of
     North Carolina Press, 1996).

12. One of the most notable was Daniel Patrick Moynihan's "The Negro Family: The Case
     for National Action" (1965). For the politics of the "Moynihan Report," see Lee Rain-
     water and William L. Yancey, *The Moynihan Report and the Politics of Controversy*
     (Cambridge, Mass.: MIT Press, 1967). For a survey of how the report was itself part
     of a long history of pathologizing African Americans, see Daryl Michael Scott, *Con-
     tempt and Pity: Social Policy and the Image of the Damaged Black Psyche, 1880–1996*
     (Chapel Hill: University of North Carolina Press, 1997).

13. Penny M. Von Eschen writes: "The sense that African Americans shared a common
     history with Africans and all peoples of African descent had long been an important
     part of African American thought, but the global dynamics unleashed by World

War II brought it to the forefront of black American politics and animated political discourse at an unprecedented level." For a history of black American anticolonialism, which preceded the Panthers, see Penny M. Von Eschen, *Race Against Empire: Black Americans and Anticolonialism 1937–1957* (Ithaca, N.Y.: Cornell University Press, 1997), 7.

14. Louis Hartz, *The Liberal Tradition in America: An Interpretation of American Political Thought Since the Revolution* (New York: Harcourt, Brace and Jovanovich, 1991), 3. See also Daniel Boorstin, *The Americans: The Colonial Experience* (New York: Random House, 1958); Arthur Schlesinger Jr., *The Vital Center: The Politics of Freedom* (1949; New Brunswick, N.J.: Transaction, 1998).

15. Malcolm X, "Message to the Grassroots" (1963), in *African American Political Thought*, vol. 2: *Confrontation vs. Compromise: 1945 to the Present*, ed. Marcus D. Pohlmann (New York: Routledge, 2003), 115–130.

16. Huey P. Newton, "Speech Delivered at Boston College: November 8, 1970," in *The Huey P. Newton Reader*, ed. David Hilliard and Donald Weise (New York: Seven Stories, 2002), 169.

17. Huey P. Newton, "Executive Mandate No. 1: May 2, 1967," in *To Die for the People: Selected Writings and Speeches*, ed. Toni Morrison (New York: Random House, 1972), 7.

18. For a history of the discourse of the American Revolution, see Bernard Bailyn, *The Ideological Origins of the American Revolution* (Cambridge, Mass.: Belknap, 1992).

19. Huey P. Newton, "To the Revolutionary People's Constitutional Convention: September 5, 1970," in *To Die for the People*, 158.

20. For a brief history of American public-housing politics and policy, see R. Allen Hays, *The Federal Government and Urban Housing* (Albany: SUNY Press, 2012).

21. Huey P. Newton with J. Herman Blake, *Revolutionary Suicide* (New York: Harcourt, Brace and Jovanovich, 1973), 42.

22. Michel Foucault, *Discipline and Punish: The Birth of the Prison*, trans. Alan Sheridan (New York: Vintage, 1995).

23. Newton, *Revolutionary Suicide*, 4.

24. Frantz Fanon, *Wretched of the Earth* (New York: Grove, 2005), 4.

25. For Aristotle's conception of the *agora*, see Aristotle, *The Politics*, trans. Ernest Barker (Oxford: Oxford University Press, 1995).

26. Newton, *Revolutionary Suicide*, 16.

27. See Hannah Arendt, *The Origins of Totalitarianism* (New York: Harcourt, 1951), 443.

28. Hannah Arendt, *The Human Condition* (Chicago: University of Chicago Press, 1958), 247.

29. Newton, *Revolutionary Suicide*, 11.

30. James Baldwin, "We Can Change This Country" (1963), in *Cross of Redemption: Uncollected Writings*, ed. Randall Kenan (New York: Vintage, 2010), 62.

31. Newton, "To the Revolutionary People's Constitutional Convention," in *To Die for the People*, 158.

32. Ibid.

33. Newton, *Revolutionary Suicide*, 180.

34. Ibid., 4.

35. This claim, of course, might be viewed as an oversimplification because, especially in the past thirty years, American political thinkers such as Judith Butler and Hannah Pitkin have emphasized the relationship between language and politics. Yet both drew on European sources: Butler draws on the work of thinkers such as Jacques Derrida and Jacques Lacan, while Pitkin draws on Ludwig Wittgenstein. See Judith Butler, *Gender Trouble: Feminism and the Subversion of Identity* (New York: Routledge, 1990); Hannah Pitkin, *Wittgenstein and Justice: On the Significance of Ludwig Wittgenstein for Social and Political Thought* (Berkeley: University of California Press, 1973). To put it in a different way, the pragmatic strain in American political thought, which emphasizes experience and practice, is much more prominent than the metaphysical one. Classic pragmatists include John Dewey, William James, and C. S. Pierce, but those who are concerned with what we might call pragmatic politics and who give language very little due include Alexander Hamilton, John Adams, James Madison, Abraham Lincoln, John C. Calhoun, Elizabeth Cady Stanton, Frederick Douglass, and Robert Dahl, to name only some of the most prominent.

36. See Aristotle, *Rhetoric*, trans. W. Rhys Robert (New York: Dover, 2004).

37. On this relationship, especially as it relates to politics, see Pitkin, *Wittgenstein and Justice*.

38. Newton, *Revolutionary Suicide*, 163. Newton's own words echoed Hobbes's view that words in the state of nature should be taken as seriously as any actions. See Thomas Hobbes, *Leviathan* (1651), ed. Richard Tuck (Cambridge: Cambridge University Press, 1991), 88.

39. Newton's point was also an implicit critique of Madison's argument for elite rule. See "Federalist no. 10," 40–46.

40. Newton, *Revolutionary Suicide*, 166.

41. Plato, *The Republic*, trans. C. D. C. Reeve (Indianapolis, Ind.: Hackett, 2004), 51–52.

42. Huey P. Newton, "The Correct Handling of a Revolution: July 20, 1967," in *To Die for the People*, 15.

43. For Lenin's political thought, see Vladimir I. Lenin, *The State and Revolution* (1917), in *Essential Works of Lenin*, ed. Henry M. Christman (New York: Dover, 1987).

44. Martin Buber, *I and Thou*, trans. Walter Kaufmann (New York: Touchstone, 1971).

45. Newton, *Revolutionary Suicide*, 168, 170.

46. Ibid., 168–170.

47. For Malcolm X's political thought, see Robert Terrill, ed., *The Cambridge Companion to Malcolm X* (New York: Cambridge University Press, 2010); Manning Marable, *Malcolm X: A Life of Reinvention* (London: Penguin, 2012).

48. Newton, *Revolutionary Suicide*, 164.

49. See Arendt, *The Human Condition*, esp. chap. 2, 22–79. Also see Hannah Arendt, *On Revolution* (New York: Penguin, 1963), 49–106, 207–274. Not surprisingly, Arendt's approval of civil rights protestors acting collectively was only matched by the scorn she felt about their focus on social equality—the right to be treated with dignity and respect in public schools, in public playgrounds, and on public transportation.

50. For a recent history of this, see Gordon K. Mantler, *Power to the Poor: Black-Brown Coalition and the Fight for Economic Justice, 1960–1974* (Chapel Hill: University of North Carolina Press, 2015).

51. Elizabeth Cady Stanton, "The Seneca Falls Declaration of Sentiments and Resolutions" (1848), in *American Political Thought*, ed. Theodore Lowi and Isaac Kramnick (New York: Norton, 2008), 529–533. Frederick Douglass, "The Meaning of July Fourth for the Negro," in *Selected Speeches and Writings*, ed. Philip S. Foner and Yuval Taylor (Chicago: Lawrence Hill, 1999), 188–206.

52. Huey P. Newton and Bobby Seale, "The Ten-Point Program," in *To Die for the People*, 3.

53. Ibid.

54. Ibid., 4.

55. Ibid.

56. Ibid., 4–5.

57. Ibid., 5.

58. Arendt, *On Revolution*, 49–106.

59. See C. Wright Mills, *The Power Elite* (New York: Oxford University Press, 1956).

60. Newton, *Revolutionary Suicide*, 5.

61. See ibid., 69–76.

62. Fanon, *Wretched of the Earth*, 238.

63. This position also bore similarities to Marx and Engels's view of communist society. See Marx and Engels, "Manifesto of the Communist Party," in *The Marx-Engels Reader*, 469–500.

64. Newton, "Revolutionary Suicide," in *Revolutionary Suicide*.

65. See Ralph Ellison, "The World and the Jug" (1963), in *The Collected Essays of Ralph Ellison* (New York: Modern Library, 1995), 154.

66. To be sure, this aspiration was not fully realized in Newton's life. Newton himself had a mixed position on marriage and family. On the one hand, he said that "As I grew older . . . I began to see that the bourgeois family can be an imprisoning, enslaving, and suffocating experience. . . . Marriage usually becomes one more imprisoning experience within the general prison of society." On the other hand, he said: "These contradictions have been solved by the values of the Black Panther Party and by the Party's communal life. The closeness of the group and the shared sense of purpose transform us into a harmonious, functioning body, working for the destruction of those conditions that make people suffer. Our unity has transformed us to the point where we have not compromised with the system; we have the closeness and love of family life, the will to live in spirit of cruel conditions." Newton, *Revolutionary Suicide*, 91, 96.

67. Ibid., 208.

68. See Karl Marx, *Capital*, vol. 1: *A Critique of Political Economy*, trans. Ernest Mandel (New York: Penguin, 1993), 81–95.

69. Newton, *Revolutionary Suicide*, 332.

70. James Baldwin's biographer, James Campbell, recounts how King refused to let Baldwin participate in the 1963 March on Washington because he thought he would be best equipped to lead a "homosexual movement," rather than a political one. See

James Campbell, *Talking at the Gates: A Life of James Baldwin* (New York: Viking, 1991), 176.

71. Huey P. Newton, "The Women's Liberation and Gay Liberation Movements: August 15, 1970," in *To Die for the People*, 154.

72. Ibid., 152–153.

73. Ibid., 152.

74. Newton, *Revolutionary Suicide*, 275. For a political history of Karenga and US, see Scot Brown, *Fighting for US: Maulana Karenga, The US Organization, and Black Cultural Nationalism* (New York: New York University Press, 2003).

75. Newton, *Revolutionary Suicide*, 157.

76. Eldridge Cleaver, *Soul on Ice* (New York: Delta, 1991), 122–138.

77. Newton, *Revolutionary Suicide*, 331.

78. Emma Goldman, "Anarchism: What It Really Stands For," in *Red Emma Speaks: An Emma Goldman Reader*, ed. Alix Kate Shulman (Amherst, Mass.: Humanity, 1996), 64.

79. Newton, *Revolutionary Suicide*, 331.

80. Ibid.

81. Ralph Ellison, "Blues People" (1964), in *Collected Essays*, 286. This idea is more fully detailed in Alex Zamalin, *African American Political Thought and American Culture: The Nation's Struggle for Racial Justice* (New York: Palgrave Macmillan, 2015), 90–94.

82. For a sense of Panther projects throughout their communities, see Judson Jeffries, *Comrades: A Local History of the Black Panther Party* (Bloomington: Indiana University Press, 2007).

83. Arendt, *On Violence*, 120.

84. Ibid., 142–155.

85. Arendt, *The Human Condition*, 204. For the canonical argument about appearance and politics, see Niccolò Machiavelli, *The Prince*, trans. David Wootton (Indianapolis, Ind.: Hackett, 1995), 49–51, 54–55.

86. Newton, *Revolutionary Suicide*, 77.

87. Ibid., 112.

88. Quoted from Bloom and Martin, *Black Against Empire*, 44–47.

89. For such a performative theory of rights in contemporary political theory, see Karen Zivi, *Making Rights Claims: A Practice of Democratic Citizenship* (New York: Oxford University Press, 2011).

90. Martin Luther King Jr., "A Letter from Birmingham City Jail," in *A Testament of Hope*, 290.

91. James Baldwin, "The White Problem" (1964), in *The Cross of Redemption*, 97.

92. Newton, *Revolutionary Suicide*, 121.

93. This resonated with earlier generations of civic republicans. See John Adams, *Revolutionary Writings, 1775–1783*, ed. Gordon S. Wood (New York: Library of America, 2011); and Thomas Paine, *Collected Writings* (New York: Library of America, 1995).

94. Newton, *Revolutionary Suicide*, 122.

95. Ibid., 330.

96. My sense of these programs is based on Bloom and Martin, *Black Against Empire*; and Jeffries, *Comrades*.

97. Bloom and Martin, *Black Against Empire*, 188.

98. Frederick Douglass, "What Are the Colored People Doing for Themselves" (1848), in *Political Thought in the United States: A Documentary History*, ed. Lyman Tower Sargent (New York: New York University Press, 1997), 187–189.

99. Bloom and Martin, *Black Against Empire*, 190.

100. See Daniel Perlstein, "Black Panther Party Liberation Schools," in *Encyclopedia of African American Education*, ed. Kofi Lomotey (New York: Sage, 2010), 100–102.

101. John Dewey, *Democracy and Education* (New York: The Free Press, 1997).

102. For the black feminist argument about the "interlocking systems of oppression," see Patricia Hill Collins, *Black Feminist Thought: Knowledge, Consciousness, and the Politics of Empowerment* (New York: Routledge, 1990).

103. This view is captured in Seneca's famous text, *Letters from a Stoic*, trans. Robert Campbell (New York: Penguin, 1969).

104. Newton, *Revolutionary Suicide*, 152

105. Ibid., 249.

106. Douglass, "The Meaning of July Fourth for the Negro," 188–206.

107. Newton, *Revolutionary Suicide*, 4.

108. Ibid., 260.

109. See George Frederickson, *Racism: A Short History* (Princeton, N.J.: Princeton University Press, 2009), 49–97.

110. James Baldwin, "Stranger in the Village," in *The Price of the Ticket: Collected Nonfiction, 1948–1985* (New York: St. Martin's Press, 1985), 83.

111. Richard Wright, *Native Son* (New York: Harper and Row, 1940).

112. Newton, *Revolutionary Suicide*, 5.

113. See Jürgen Habermas, *The Theory of Communicative Action* (Boston: Beacon, 1984).

114. See William Connolly, *Identity/Difference: Democratic Negotiations of Political Paradox* (Ithaca, N.Y.: Cornell University Press, 1991); Bonnie Honig, *Political Theory and the Displacement of Politics* (Ithaca, N.Y.: Cornell University Press, 1993); Chantal Mouffe, *Agonistics: Thinking the World Politically* (New York: Verso, 2013).

115. Much of what the Panthers did with rage is also theoretically expressed in Audre Lorde, "The Uses of Anger: Women Responding to Anger," in *Sister Outsider: Essays and Speeches* (New York: Crossing, 2003), 124–133.

116. They anticipate contemporary radical geographers like David Harvey, *Social Justice in the City* (Athens: University of Georgia Press, 1973); Neil Smith, *Uneven Development: Nature, Capital, and the Production of Space* (Athens: University of Georgia Press, 1984); and Ruth Wilson Gilmore, *Golden Gulag: Prisons, Surplus, Crisis, and Opposition in Globalizing California* (Berkley: University of California Press, 2007).

117. See Rogers Smith, *Stories of Peoplehood: The Politics and Morals of Political Membership* (New York: Cambridge University Press, 2003); and Richard Rorty, *Achieving Our Country: Leftist Thought in Twentieth-Century America* (Cambridge, Mass.: Harvard University Press, 1999).

118. This challenges the political theory of democratic proceduralism, most famously expressed by Robert Dahl, *A Preface to Democratic Theory* (New Haven, Conn.: Yale University Press, 1956).

119. In doing this, the Panthers make vivid what the political theorist Clarissa Rile Hayward describes as a "de-facing" of power, revealing how it is dispersed through all sorts of institutions and everyday norms. See Clarissa Rile Hayward, *De-Facing Power* (New York: Cambridge University Press, 2000).

120. Here the Panthers anticipate radical democratic theorists who, like Alan Keenan, argue that democracy is an ongoing project that resists political closure. See Alan Keenan, *Democracy in Question: Democratic Openness in a Time of Political Closure* (Palo Alto, Calif.: Stanford University Press, 2003).

121. They contribute to a growing literature that considers ethics, race, and democracy. See Jack Turner, *Awakening to Race: Individualism and Social Consciousness in America* (Chicago: University of Chicago Press, 2012); Danielle S. Allen, *Talking to Strangers: Anxieties of Citizenship After Brown v. Board of Education* (Chicago: University of Chicago Press, 2004); Zamalin, *African American Political Thought*.

122. Although Nick Bromell doesn't mention the Panthers in his discussion of rage and democracy, their practice deepens some of his arguments in *The Time Is Always Now: Black Thought and the Transformation of U.S. Democracy* (New York: Oxford University Press, 2013).

123. Newton, *Revolutionary Suicide*, 5.

124. Ibid., 332.

4. ANGELA DAVIS, PRISON ABOLITION, AND THE END OF THE AMERICAN CARCERAL STATE

1. See Bureau of Justice Statistics, "Prison Population Counts," http://www.bjs.gov/index.cfm?ty=tp&tid=131.

2. Michelle Alexander, *The New Jim Crow: Mass Incarceration in the Age of Colorblindness* (New York: The New Press, 2010).

3. For a survey of this history as well as the way it is linked to the notion of racial formation, see Michael Omi and Howard Winant, *Racial Formation in the United States* (New York: Routledge, 2014).

4. Kevin Phillips, *The Emerging Republican Majority* (Princeton, N.J.: Princeton University Press, 2015).

5. Dan T. Carter, *The Politics of Rage: George Wallace, The Origins of the New Conservatism, and the Transformation of American Politics* (Baton Rouge: Louisiana State University Press, 2000).

6. For a discussion of the way the black middle class was instrumental in pushing for more punitive drug-sentencing laws, see Michael Javen Fortner, *Black Silent Majority: The Rockefeller Drug Laws and the Politics of Punishment* (Cambridge, Mass.: Harvard University Press, 2015).

7. See Alexander, *The New Jim Crow*, and the literature on critical race studies, which finds an excellent survey in Richard Delgado and Jean Stefancic, *Critical Race Theory: An Introduction* (New York: New York University Press, 2012).

8. Loïc Wacquant, *Deadly Symbiosis: Race and the Rise of the Penal State* (London: Polity, 2009).

9. W. E. B. Du Bois, *The Souls of Black Folk* (New York: Oxford University Press, 2007), 26.

10. The Sentencing Project, "Fact Sheet: Trends in U.S. Corrections" (2014), http://sentencingproject.org/doc/publications/inc_Trends_in_Corrections_Fact_sheet.pdf.

11. Andrew Dilts, *Punishment and Inclusion: Race, Membership, and the Limits of American Liberalism* (New York: Fordham University Press, 2014).

12. For a historical overview of prisons in the United States, especially the way they interact with American political institutions, see Naomi Murakawa, *The First Civil Right: How Liberals Built Prison America* (New York: Oxford University Press, 2014); Marie Gottschalk, *The Prison and the Gallows: The Politics of Mass Incarceration in America* (New York: Cambridge University Press, 2006).

13. See Alexis de Tocqueville, *Democracy in America*, ed. Harvey Mansfield and Delba Winthrop (Chicago: University of Chicago Press, 2000).

14. Gustave de Beaumont and Alexis de Tocqueville, *On the Penitentiary System in the United States: And Its Application in France* (Carbondale: Southern Illinois University Press, 1979), 79.

15. John Locke, *Second Treatise of Government*, ed. C. B. Macpherson (Indianapolis, Ind.: Hackett, 1980), 9.

16. For more on Davis's life, see Angela Davis, *An Autobiography* (New York: Random House, 1974).

17. See Neil Roberts's interpretation of this dimension of Davis's thought, which is part of his theory of what he calls "freedom as marronage." Neil Roberts, *Freedom as Marronage* (Chicago: University of Chicago Press, 2015), 53–58.

18. For this point, see Angela Davis, *Abolition Democracy: Beyond Empire, Prisons, and Torture* (New York: Seven Stories, 2011).

19. For this, see Angela Davis, *Women, Race, and Class* (New York: Vintage, 1983).

20. For a history of neoliberalism, see David Harvey, *A Brief History of Neoliberalism* (New York: Oxford University Press, 2007).

21. The history of this American culture of fear is captured well in Jonathan Simon, *Governing Through Crime: How the War on Crime Transformed American Democracy and Created a Culture of Fear* (New York: Oxford University Press, 2007).

22. Gary S. Becker, "Crime and Punishment: An Economic Approach," *Journal of Political Economy* 76, no. 2 (1968): 176. For an interpretation and critique of the relationship between agency, free markets, and punishment, see Bernard E. Harcourt, *The Illusion of Free Markets* (Cambridge, Mass.: Harvard University Press, 2011).

23. James Q. Wilson and George L. Kelling, "Broken Windows: The Police and Neighborhood Safety," *Atlantic Monthly* 249, no. 3 (1982): 31.

24. Angela Y. Davis, *Are Prisons Obsolete?* (New York: Seven Stories, 2003), 25.

25. Michel Foucault, *Discipline and Punish: The Birth of the Prison*, trans. Alan Sheridan (New York: Vintage, 1995).

26. Angela Davis, "Racialized Punishment and Prison Abolition," in *The Angela Y. Davis Reader*, ed. Joy James (New York: Blackwell, 1998), 97.

27. Ibid.

28. Davis, *Are Prisons Obsolete?*, 28–31.

29. Ibid., 31.

30. Davis, "Racialized Punishment and Prison Abolition," 99.

31. John Rawls, *A Theory of Justice* (Cambridge, Mass.: Belknap, 1971), 11.

32. Davis, *Are Prisons Obsolete?*, 28.

33. Ibid.

34. For a history of this retreat from race-conscious public policies, see Stephen Steinberg, *Turning Back: The Retreat from Racial Justice in American Thought and Policy* (Boston: Beacon, 1995).

35. Davis, *Are Prisons Obsolete?*, 38.

36. Ironically, the prison was a place that, for all their talk of freedom and government nonintervention, neoconservatives such as Irving Kristol in the early 2000s believed needed to continue to exist. See Irving Kristol, *The Neoconservative Persuasion: Selected Essays, 1942–2009* (New York: Basic Books, 2011).

37. Mumia Abu-Jamal, *Live from Death Row* (New York: Harper Perennial, 1996), 10–12.

38. Davis, *Are Prisons Obsolete?*, 16–17.

39. Ibid., 88.

40. For the most intellectually rigorous philosophical defense of libertarianism, see Robert Nozick, *Anarchy, State, and Utopia* (New York: Basic Books, 1974).

41. For a survey of the various causes and meanings of deindustrialization in America, see Jefferson Cowie and Joseph Heathcott, eds., *Beyond the Ruins: The Meanings of Deindustrialization* (Ithaca, N.Y.: Cornell University Press, 2003).

42. Angela Davis, "Race, Crime, and Punishment," in *The Meaning of Freedom: And Other Difficult Dialogues* (San Francisco: City Lights, 2013), 55.

43. Davis, *Are Prisons Obsolete?*, 83.

44. For an excellent collection of writings by black feminist authors including Audre Lorde, Michele Wallace, and Patricia Hill Collins, see Joy James and T. Denean Sharpley-Whiting, eds., *The Black Feminist Reader* (New York: Wiley-Blackwell, 2000).

45. For the way this division between public and private functions in liberal political thought, see Carole Pateman, *The Disorder of Women: Democracy, Feminism, and Political Theory* (Cambridge: Polity, 1989), 120.

46. Davis, *Are Prisons Obsolete?*, 77–78.

47. Angela Davis, "The Prison-Industrial Complex," in *The Meaning of Freedom*, 51.

48. Baldwin's view on racial innocence is made clear in the first essay of *The Fire Next Time*, in *Collected Essays*, ed. Toni Morrison (New York: Library of America), 291–294.

49. Davis, "The Prison-Industrial Complex," 50.

50. Robert N. Bellah, Richard Madsen, William M. Sullivan, and Ann Swidler, *Habits of the Heart: Individualism and Commitment in American Life* (Berkeley: University of California Press, 1985), 143.

51. Davis, *Are Prisons Obsolete?*, 112.

52. Angela Davis, "Unfinished Lecture on Liberation – II" (1969), in *The Angela Y. Davis Reader*, 55.

53. Davis, *Are Prisons Obsolete?*, 16.

54. Jean-Jacques Rousseau, "Discourse on the Origin and Foundations of Inequality Among Men" (1755), in *Political Writings*, ed. Alan Ritter and Julia Conaway Bondanella (New York: Norton, 1987), 25.

55. Angela Davis, "Racism: Then and Now," in *The Meaning of Freedom*, 125.

56. Angela Davis, "Race, Power, and Prisons Since 9/11," in *The Meaning of Freedom*, 84.

57. Immanuel Kant, *Critique of Pure Reason*, trans. Paul Guyer and Allen Wood (Cambridge: Cambridge University Press, 1999).

58. Davis, *Are Prisons Obsolete?*, 9.

59. Ibid., 107.

60. Davis, "Racism: Then and Now," 132–133.

61. For this view, see Phyllis Schlafly, *The Power of the Positive Woman* (New York: Arlington House, 1977).

62. See Samuel Huntington, *Who Are We? The Challenges to America's National Identity* (New York: Simon and Schuster, 2004).

63. For a history of this, which is part of the tradition of neoconservatism, see Justin Vaïsse, *Neoconservatism: The Biography of a Movement* (Cambridge, Mass.: Belknap, 2011).

64. Angela Davis, "Report from Harlem," in *The Meaning of Freedom*, 33.

65. Davis, *Abolition Democracy*, 112.

66. Judith Butler, *Frames of War: When Is Life Grievable?* (New York: Verso, 2009), 14.

67. For the "capability approach," see Amartya Sen, *Development as Freedom* (Oxford: Oxford University Press, 1999); and Martha Nussbaum, *Sex and Social Justice* (Oxford: Oxford University Press, 1999).

68. Davis, *Are Prisons Obsolete?*, 107.

69. John Dewey, *Democracy and Education* (New York: The Free Press, 1997).

70. Davis, "Race, Crime, and Punishment," 69.

71. Davis, "The Prison-Industrial Complex," 52.

72. Locke, *Second Treatise*, 10. For the influential interpretation that Locke's political thought was saturated with his own Christian worldview, see John Dunn, *The Political Thought of John Locke: A Historical Account of the Argument of the "Two Treatises of Government"* (New York: Cambridge University Press, 1983).

73. For the distinction between law and justice in King, see Martin Luther King Jr., "A Letter from a Birmingham Jail" (1963), in *A Testament of Hope*, ed. James M. Washington (San Francisco: HarperCollins, 1986), 293.

74. For what still remains a classic study of how racialized images played into the destruction of the American public policy of welfare, see Ange-Marie Hancock, *The*

Politics of Disgust: The Public Identity of the Welfare Queen (New York: New York University Press, 2004).

75. Davis, "Race, Crime, and Punishment," 67.

76. Ibid., 69.

77. Davis, "The Prison-Industrial Complex," 53–54.

78. Lawrence Mead, *Beyond Entitlement: The Social Obligations of Citizenship* (New York: Free Press, 1986), 4.

79. For one of the best histories of the South African TRC, see Richard A. Wilson, *The Politics of Truth and Reconciliation in South Africa: Legitimizing the Post-Apartheid State* (New York: Cambridge University Press, 2001).

80. Davis, *Are Prisons Obsolete?*, 115.

81. Ibid.

82. Truth Commissions have been used to address the legacy of authoritarian rule in South American countries including Chile, Argentina, and Brazil and to address racist violence in the United States—for instance, in 2003, a truth commission was established to deal with the infamous 1979 Greensboro, North Carolina, Massacre, in which an interracial coterie of activists was killed by the white-supremacist organization the Ku Klux Klan. For critiques of restorative justice, see John Torpey, *Making Whole What Has Been Smashed: On Reparations Politics* (Cambridge, Mass.: Harvard University Press, 2006); Tzvetan Todorov, *Hope and Memory: Lessons from the Twentieth Century* (Princeton, N.J.: Princeton University Press, 2003).

83. This argument was famously developed in the political scientist Robert Putnam's *Bowling Alone* (2000), which argued for strengthening declining nonpartisan civic networks such as bowling leagues. Robert D. Putnam, *Bowling Alone: The Collapse and Revival of American Community* (New York: Simon & Schuster, 2000).

84. A good philosophical argument for the moral power of reconciliation is Margaret Urban Walker, *Moral Repair: Reconstructing Moral Relations After Wrongdoing* (New York: Cambridge University Press, 2006).

85. One important recent discussion and deconstruction of the politics and ethics of forgiveness is Jacques Derrida, *On Cosmopolitanism and Forgiveness* (New York: Routledge, 2001).

86. Critical Resistance, "About: What is the PIC? What is Abolition?" http://critical resistance.org/about/not-so-common-language.

87. Prison Research Education Action Project, *Instead of Prisons: A Handbook for Abolitionists* (Oakland, Calif.: Critical Resistance, 2001).

88. *The Abolitionist* 4 (Summer 2006): 12, https://abolitionistpaper.files.wordpress .com/2011/01/abolitionist-issue-4-summer-2006-english.pdf.

89. Ibid.

90. This followed the view of Michel Foucault, "The Discourse of Language," in *The Archeology of Knowledge* (New York: Vintage, 1982), 215–238.

91. *The Abolitionist* 4 (Summer 2006): 12.

92. Ibid.

93. Ibid.

94. Ibid.

95. Michel Foucault, "Truth and Power," in *The Foucault Reader*, ed. Paul Rabinow (New York: Pantheon, 1984).

96. For theorists of care ethics, see Virginia Held, *The Ethics of Care: Personal, Political, Global* (Oxford: Oxford University Press, 2006).

97. *The Abolitionist* 4 (Summer 2006): 12.

98. The following is taken from Critical Resistance, "The Abolitionist Toolkit," 49. http://criticalresistance.org/resources/the-abolitionist-toolkit.

99. Derrida's articulation of this idea is most clearly captured in Jacques Derrida, *Positions*, trans. Alan Bass (Chicago: University of Chicago Press, 1981), 41.

100. Critical Resistance, "The Abolitionist Toolkit," 39.

101. Karl Marx, "Theses on Feuerbach," in *The Marx-Engels Reader*, ed. Robert C. Tucker (New York: Norton, 1978), 145.

102. Critical Resistance, "The Abolitionist Toolkit," 40.

103. This argument recalls Judith Butler's position in *Gender Trouble*, which discusses the performative and emancipatory dimensions of resignifying language. Judith Butler, *Gender Trouble: Feminism and the Subversion of Identity* (New York: Routledge, 1990), 194–205.

104. Critical Resistance, "The Abolitionist Toolkit," 41.

105. Ibid., 35–36.

106. Ibid., 36.

107. Ibid. This view is usually associated with Thomas Hobbes, *Leviathan* (1651), ed. Richard Tuck (Cambridge: Cambridge University Press, 1991), 110–116.

108. Critical Resistance, "The Abolitionist Toolkit," 51–53. In this way, Critical Resistance's view of conflict echoes what Locke called the "State of War." See Locke, *Second Treatise*, 14–16.

109. Critical Resistance, "The Abolitionist Toolkit," 52.

110. Ibid., 53.

111. Ibid., 51.

112. One might object that the scenario is misleading because it represents a much "easier" case of deliberating about justice because it avoids an issue like murder and rape and provides selective background information about the perpetrator—who experiences violence—that already encourages empathy.

113. Ibid., 52.

114. See Delgado and Stefancic, *Critical Race Theory*.

115. One of the most poignant accounts of jailhouse lawyering is Mumia Abu-Jamal, *Jailhouse Lawyers: Prisoners Defending Prisoners v. the USA* (San Francisco: City Lights, 2009).

116. Angela Davis, "Foreword," in ibid., 14.

117. Emma Goldman, "Anarchism: What It Really Stands For," in *Red Emma Speaks: An Emma Goldman Reader*, ed. Alix Kate Shulman (Amherst, Mass.: Humanity, 1996), 71.

118. King, "Letter from a Birmingham Jail," 296.

CONCLUSION: THE FUTURE OF RESISTANCE

1. For this interpretation see Sacvan Bercovitch, *The Rites of Assent: Transformations in the Symbolic Construction of America* (New York: Routledge, 1992).

2. See Jerry Gafio Watts, *Heroism and the Black Intellectual: Ralph Ellison, Politics, and Afro-American Intellectual Life* (Chapel Hill: University of North Carolina Press, 1994), 108.

3. This is one way to understand the patriotic rhetoric deployed by Ralph Ellison. For this interpretation, see Alex Zamalin, *African American Political Thought and American Culture: The Nation's Struggle for Racial Justice* (New York: Palgrave Macmillan, 2015), 94–95.

4. For an analysis of the way this works in various American social movements that engage dominant cultural tropes, see Jeffrey C. Alexander, *The Civil Sphere* (New York: Oxford University Press, 2008).

5. For a broad overview of various contemporary approaches to racial justice, which range from what he calls "traditionalism," "reformism," "separatism," and "critical race theory," see Roy Brooks, *Racial Justice in the Age of Obama* (Princeton, N.J.: Princeton University Press, 2009). For a philosophical exposition of a defense of race consciousness as racial justice, see Amy Gutmann, "Responding to Racial Injustice," in Kwame Anthony Appiah and Amy Gutmann, *Color Conscious: The Political Morality of Race* (Princeton, N.J.: Princeton University Press, 1996), 106–178.

6. The political theorist Judith Shklar argues that we should be thinking not simply about justice but about injustice as well, which she believes is sustained by emotions such as fear and apathy. Judith Shklar, *The Faces of Injustice* (New Haven, Conn.: Yale University Press, 1990).

7. For Wolin's famous idea of "fugitive democracy," see Sheldon Wolin, *Politics and Vision* (Princeton, N.J.: Princeton University Press, 2006), 604.

8. Looking solely at public opinion—rather than countercultural intellectual currents—would thus confirm Louis Hartz's statement that American culture is fundamentally liberal. See Louis Hartz, *The Liberal Tradition in America: An Interpretation of American Political Thought Since the Revolution* (New York: Harcourt, Brace and Jovanovich, 1991).

9. For a more detailed analysis of this understanding, which informs my own thinking about democracy, see Jason Frank, *Constituent Moments: Enacting the People in Postrevolutionary America* (Durham, N.C.: Duke University Press, 2009).

10. This is more carefully and fully developed in Jacques Derrida, *Rogues: Two Essays on Reason* (Palo Alto, Calif.: Stanford University Press, 2005), 48, 100.

11. There is no academic book yet on the movement, but BLM's website offers some invaluable resources, which inform my own understanding. http://blacklivesmatter.com/.

12. Ta-Nehisi Coates, *Between the World and Me* (New York: Spiegel and Grau, 2015), 8.

13. For West, black nihilism is shaped by structural socioeconomic injustices. Cornel West, "Black Strivings in a Twilight Civilization," in *The Cornel West Reader* (New York: Basic Civitas Books, 1999), 118.

14. For the critique of Jackson's candidacy, see Adolph Reed, *The Jesse Jackson Phenomenon: The Crisis of Purpose in Afro-American Politics* (New Haven, Conn.: Yale University Press, 1986). For a critique of Obama, see Desmond S. King and Rogers Smith, *Still a House Divided: Race and Politics in Obama's America* (Princeton, N.J.: Princeton University Press, 2013).

15. For a somewhat outdated but nonetheless valuable study of the Nation of Islam, see Mattias Gardell, *In the Name of Elijah Muhammad: Louis Farrakhan and the Nation of Islam* (Durham, N.C.: Duke University Press, 1996).

16. In the words of the cultural critic Houston Baker Jr., black conservatives have "betrayed" the promise of civil rights. Houston A. Baker, *Betrayal: How Black Intellectuals Have Abandoned the Ideals of the Civil Rights Era* (New York: Columbia University Press, 2008).

17. Black Lives Matter, "Collective Value," http://blacklivesmatter.com/.

18. For a history of the movement, see McKenzie Wark, *The Spectacle of Disintegration: Situationist Passages out of the Twentieth Century* (New York: Verso, 2013).

19. Gilles Deleuze and Félix Guattari, *A Thousand Plateaus: Capitalism and Schizophrenia* (Minneapolis: University of Minnesota Press, 1987), 3–25.

BIBLIOGRAPHY

Abu-Jamal, Mumia. *Jailhouse Lawyers: Prisoners Defending Prisoners v. the USA*. San Francisco: City Lights, 2009.

——. *Live from Death Row*. New York: Harper Perennial, 1996.

Ackerman, Bruce. *We the People*. Vol. 1: *Foundations*. Cambridge, Mass.: Harvard University Press, 1993.

Adams, John. *Revolutionary Writings, 1775–1783*. Edited by Gordon S. Wood. New York: Library of America, 2011.

Addams, Jane. *The Jane Addams Reader*. Edited by Jean Belthke Elshtain. New York: Basic Books, 2001.

Alcoff, Linda. "The Problem of Speaking for Others." *Cultural Critique* 20 (1992): 5–32.

Alexander, Jeffrey C. *The Civil Sphere*. New York: Oxford University Press, 2008.

Alexander, Michelle. *The New Jim Crow: Mass Incarceration in the Age of Colorblindness* (New York: The New Press, 2010).

Allen, Danielle S. *Talking to Strangers: Anxieties of Citizenship After Brown v. Board of Education*. Chicago: University of Chicago Press, 2004.

Ambar, Saladin. *Malcolm X at Oxford Union: Radical Politics in a Global Era*. New York: Oxford University Press, 2014.

Aptheker, Herbert. *American Negro Slave Revolts*. 1943. New York: International Publishers, 1983.

——. *Nat Turner's Slave Rebellion*. New York: Dover, 2006.

Arendt, Hannah. *The Human Condition*. Chicago: University of Chicago Press, 1958.

——. *On Revolution*. New York: Penguin, 1963.

——. *On Violence*. 1970. In *The Crises of the Republic*. New York: Harvest, 1972.

——. *The Origins of Totalitarianism*. New York: Harcourt, 1951.

Aristotle. *The Politics*. Translated by Ernest Barker. Oxford: Oxford University Press, 1995.

——. *Rhetoric*. Translated by W. Rhys Robert. New York: Dover, 2004.

Bailyn, Bernard. *The Ideological Origins of the American Revolution*. Cambridge, Mass.: Belknap, 1992.

Baker, Houston A. *Betrayal: How Black Intellectuals Have Abandoned the Ideals of the Civil Rights Era*. New York: Columbia University Press, 2008.

Baldwin, James. *The Fire Next Time*. In *Collected Essays*, ed. Toni Morrison, 291–348. New York: Library of America, 1998.

——. "Stranger in the Village." In *The Price of the Ticket: Collected Nonfiction, 1948–1985*, 79–90. New York: St. Martin's Press, 1985.

——. "We Can Change This Country." 1963. In *Cross of Redemption: Uncollected Writings*, ed. Randall Kenan, 58–64. New York: Vintage, 2010.

Balfour, Lawrie. *Democracy's Reconstruction: Thinking Politically with W. E. B. Du Bois*. New York: Oxford University Press, 2011.

——. *Evidence of Things Not Said: James Baldwin and the Promise of Democracy*. Ithaca, N.Y.: Cornell University Press, 1999.

Bay, Mia. *To Tell the Truth Freely: The Life of Ida B. Wells*. New York: Hill & Wang, 2010.

——. *The White Image in the Black Mind: African American Ideas About White People*. New York: Oxford University Press, 2000.

Beaumont, Gustave de, and Alexis de Tocqueville. *On the Penitentiary System in the United States: And Its Application in France*. Carbondale: Southern Illinois University Press, 1979.

Becker, Gary S. "Crime and Punishment: An Economic Approach." *Journal of Political Economy* 76, no. 2 (1968): 169–217.

Bellah, Robert N., Richard Madsen, William M. Sullivan, and Ann Swidler. *Habits of the Heart: Individualism and Commitment in American Life*. Berkeley: University of California Press, 1985.

Bercovitch, Sacvan. *The Rites of Assent: Transformations in the Symbolic Construction of America*. New York: Routledge, 1992.

Bloom, Joshua, and Waldo E. Martin. *Black Against Empire: The History and Politics of the Black Panther Party*. Berkeley: University of California Press, 2014.

Bogues, Anthony. *Black Heretics, Black Prophets: Radical Political Intellectuals*. New York: Routledge, 2003.

Boorstin, Daniel J. *The Americans: The Colonial Experience*. New York: Random House, 1958.

——. *The Genius of American Politics*. Chicago: University of Chicago Press, 1953.

Bromell, Nick. *The Time Is Always Now: Black Thought and the Transformation of U.S. Democracy*. New York: Oxford University Press, 2013.

——. " 'A Voice from the Enslaved': The Origins of Frederick Douglass's Political Philosophy of Democracy." *American Literary History* 23, no. 4 (2011): 697–723.

Brooks, Roy. *Racial Justice in the Age of Obama*. Princeton, N.J.: Princeton University Press, 2009.

Brown, Adrienne, and Valerie Smith. *Race and Real Estate*. New York: Oxford University Press, 2015.

Brown, Scot. *Fighting for US: Maulana Karenga, the US Organization, and Black Cultural Nationalism*. New York: New York University Press, 2003.

Brundage, W. Fitzhugh. *Lynching in the New South: Georgia and Virginia, 1880–1930*. Urbana: University of Illinois Press, 1993.

Brutus. "No. 2." In *The Complete Anti-Federalist*, ed. Herbert Storing, 1:372–377. Chicago: University of Chicago Press, 1981.

Buber, Martin. *I and Thou*. Translated by Walter Kaufmann. New York: Touchstone, 1971.

Buccola, Nicholas. "The Essential Dignity of Man as Man." *American Political Thought* 4, no. 2 (Spring 2015): 228–258.

——. *The Political Thought of Frederick Douglass: In Pursuit of American Liberty*. New York: New York University Press, 2012.

Buckley, William F. *God and Man at Yale*. Washington, D.C.: Regnery, 1951.

Buck-Morss, Susan. *Hegel, Haiti, and Universal History*. Pittsburgh, Penn.: University of Pittsburgh Press, 2009.

Bureau of Justice Statistics, "Prison Population Counts." http://www.bjs.gov/index.cfm?ty=tp&tid=131.

Burkey, Maxwell, and Alex Zamalin. "Patriotism, Black Politics, and Racial Justice in America." *New Political Science* 38, no. 3 (2016): 371–389.

Butler, Judith. *Frames of War: When Is Life Grievable?*. New York: Verso, 2009.

——. *Gender Trouble: Feminism and the Subversion of Identity*. New York: Routledge, 1990.

——. *Precarious Life: The Powers of Mourning and Violence*. New York: Verso, 2004.

Calhoun, John C. *A Disquisition on Government: And Selections from the Discourse*. 1848. Indianapolis, Ind.: Hackett, 1995.

——. "Speech on the Reception of Abolition Petitions, Delivered in the Senate, February 6th, 1837." In *Speeches of John C. Calhoun, Delivered in the House of Representatives and in the Senate of the United States*, ed. Richard R. Cralle, 625–633. New York: D. Appleton, 1853.

Camp, Stephanie M. H. *Closer to Freedom: Enslaved Women and Everyday Resistance in the Plantation South*. Chapel Hill: University of North Carolina Press, 2004.

Campbell, James. *Talking at the Gates: A Life of James Baldwin*. New York: Viking, 1991.

Canovan, Margaret. *The People*. New York: Polity, 2005.

Carby, Hazel. *Reconstructing Womanhood: The Emergence of the Afro-American Woman Novelist*. New York: Oxford University Press, 1989.

Carson, Clayborne. *In Struggle: SNCC and the Black Awakening of the 1960s*. Cambridge, Mass.: Harvard University Press, 1981.

Carter, Dan T. *The Politics of Rage: George Wallace, the Origins of the New Conservatism, and the Transformation of American Politics*. Baton Rouge: Louisiana State University Press, 2000.

Cashman, Sean Dennis. *America in the Gilded Age*. New York: New York University Press, 1984.

Cavell, Stanley. *The Claim of Reason: Wittgenstein, Skepticism, Morality, and Tragedy*. New York: Oxford University Press, 1979.

Ceaser, James W. "Natural Rights and Scientific Racism." In *Thomas Jefferson and the Politics of Nature*, ed. Thomas S. Engerman, 165–190. Notre Dame, Ind.: University of Notre Dame Press, 2000.

Cleaver, Eldridge. *Soul on Ice*. New York: Delta, 1991.

Coates, Ta-Nehisi. *Between the World and Me*. New York: Spiegel and Grau, 2015.

Cohen, Lizabeth. *A Consumer's Republic: The Politics of Mass Consumption in Postwar America*. New York: Knopf, 2003.

Collins, Patricia Hill. *Black Feminist Thought: Knowledge, Consciousness, and the Politics of Empowerment*. New York: Routledge, 1990.

Connolly, William. *Identity/Difference: Democratic Negotiations of Political Paradox*. Ithaca, N.Y.: Cornell University Press, 1991.

Cooper, Valerie C. *Word, Like Fire: Maria Stewart, the Bible, and the Rights of African Americans*. Charlottesville: University of Virginia Press, 2012.

Cowie, Jefferson, and Joseph Heathcott. *Beyond the Ruins: The Meanings of Deindustrialization*. Ithaca, N.Y.: Cornell University Press, 2003.

Critical Resistance. "About: What Is the PIC? What Is Abolition?" http://criticalresistance .org/about/not-so-common-language.

Croly, Herbert. *The Promise of American Life*. 1909. Princeton, N.J.: Princeton University Press, 2014.

Cruse, Harold. *The Crisis of the Negro Intellectual*. 1967. New York: NYRB, 2005.

Dahl, Robert. *A Preface to Democratic Theory*. New Haven, Conn.: Yale University Press, 1956.

——. *Who Governs? Democracy and Power in an American City*. New Haven, Conn.: Yale University Press, 1961.

Davis, Angela Y. *Abolition Democracy: Beyond Empire, Prisons, and Torture*. New York: Seven Stories, 2011.

——. *Are Prisons Obsolete?* New York: Seven Stories, 2003.

——. *An Autobiography*. New York: Random House, 1974.

——. *The Meaning of Freedom: And Other Difficult Dialogues*. San Francisco: City Lights, 2013.

——. "Racialized Punishment and Prison Abolition." In *The Angela Y. Davis Reader*, ed. Joy James, 96–110. New York: Blackwell, 1998.

——. *Women, Race, and Class*. New York: Vintage, 1983.

Davis, David Brion. *Inhuman Bondage: The Rise and Fall of Slavery in the New World*. New York: Oxford University Press, 2006.

Dawson, Michael C. *Black Visions: The Roots of Contemporary African-American Political Ideologies*. Chicago: University of Chicago Press, 2001.

Delany, Martin R. *Martin R. Delany: A Documentary Reader*. Edited by Robert S. Levine. Chapel Hill: University of North Carolina Press, 2003.

Delbanco, Andrew. *The Abolitionist Imagination*. Cambridge, Mass.: Harvard University Press, 2012.

Deleuze, Gilles, and Félix Guattari. *A Thousand Plateaus: Capitalism and Schizophrenia*. Minneapolis: University of Minnesota Press, 1987.

Delgado, Richard, and Jean Stefancic. *Critical Race Theory: An Introduction*. New York: New York University Press, 2012.

Derrida, Jacques. *The Animal That Therefore I Am*. Translated by David Willis. New York: Fordham University Press, 2008.

——. *On Cosmopolitanism and Forgiveness*. New York: Routledge, 2001.

——. *Positions*. Translated by Alan Bass. Chicago: University of Chicago Press, 1981.

——. *Rogues: Two Essays on Reason*. Palo Alto, Calif.: Stanford University Press, 2005.

Desmond, William. *Cynics*. New York: Routledge, 2014.

Dewey, John. *Democracy and Education*. New York: The Free Press, 1997.

——. *The Public and Its Problems*. 1927. Athens, Ohio: Swallow, 1991.

Diggins, John Patrick. *The Lost Soul of American Politics: Virtue, Self-Interest, and the Foundations of Liberalism*. New York: HarperCollins, 1984.

Dilts, Andrew. *Punishment and Inclusion: Race, Membership, and the Limits of American Liberalism*. New York: Fordham University Press, 2014.

Douglass, Frederick. "The Meaning of July Fourth for the Negro." In *Selected Speeches and Writings*, ed. Philip S. Foner and Yuval Taylor, 188–206. Chicago: Lawrence Hill, 1999.

——. *My Bondage and My Freedom*. In *The Autobiographies*, 103–452. New York: Library of America, 1994.

——. "What Are the Colored People Doing for Themselves." 1848. In *Political Thought in the United States: A Documentary History*, ed. Lyman Tower Sargent, 187–189. New York: New York University Press, 1997.

Du Bois, W. E. B. *The Souls of Black Folk*. New York: Oxford University Press, 2007.

Dunn, John. *The Political Thought of John Locke: A Historical Account of the Argument of the "Two Treatises of Government."* New York: Cambridge University Press, 1983.

Durkheim, Emile. *The Division of Labor in Society*. New York: The Free Press, 2014.

Elkins, Stanley. *Slavery: A Problem in American and Institutional Life*. Chicago: University of Chicago Press, 1959.

Ellison, Ralph. "Change the Joke and Slip the Yoke." 1958. In *The Collected Essays of Ralph Ellison*, ed. John Callahan, 100–112. New York: Modern Library, 1995.

Emerson, Ralph Waldo. *Nature and Selected Essays*. Edited by Larzer Ziff. New York: Penguin, 2003.

Eng, David, and Davis Kazanjin, eds. *Loss: The Politics of Mourning*. Berkeley: University of California Press, 2002.

Fanon, Frantz. *Wretched of the Earth*. New York: Grove, 2005.

Feimster, Crystal Nicole. *Southern Horrors: Women and the Politics of Rape and Lynching*. Cambridge, Mass.: Harvard University Press, 2009.

Ferguson, Jeffrey B. "Race and the Rhetoric of Resistance." *Raritan* 28, no. 1 (Summer 2008): 4–32.

Fitzhugh, George. *Sociology for the South, or the Failure of Free Society*. Richmond, Va.: A. Morris, 1854.

Fortner, Michael Javen. *Black Silent Majority: The Rockefeller Drug Laws and the Politics of Punishment*. Cambridge, Mass.: Harvard University Press, 2015.

Foucault, Michel. *Discipline and Punish: The Birth of the Prison*. Translated by Alan Sheridan. New York: Vintage, 1995.

——. "The Discourse of Language." In *The Archeology of Knowledge*, 215–238. New York: Vintage, 1982.

——. "Power and Sex." In *Michel Foucault: Politics, Philosophy, Culture: Interviews and Other Writings, 1977–1984*, ed. Lawrence Kritzman, 110–124. New York: Routledge, 1988.

——. "Truth and Power." In *The Foucault Reader*, ed. Paul Rabinow, 51–75. New York: Pantheon, 1984.

Fox-Genovese, Elizabeth, and Eugene D. Genovese. *The Mind of the Master Class: History and Faith in the Slaveholders' Worldview*. New York: Cambridge, 2005.

Frank, Jason. *Constituent Moments: Enacting the People in Postrevolutionary America*. Durham, N.C.: Duke University Press, 2009.

Frederickson, George. *The Black Image in the White Mind: The Debate on Afro-American Character and Destiny*. Middletown, Conn.: Wesleyan University Press, 1987.

——. *Racism: A Short History*. Princeton, N.J.: Princeton University Press, 2009.

Freeden, Michael. *Liberalism: A Short Introduction*. New York: Oxford University Press, 2015.

Gaines, Kevin Kelly. *Uplifting the Race: Black Leadership, Politics, and Culture in the Twentieth Century*. 2nd ed. Chapel Hill: University of North Carolina Press, 1996.

Galston, William A. *The Practice of Liberal Pluralism*. New York: Cambridge University Press, 2004.

Gandhi, Mahatma. *The Essential Writings of Mahatma Gandhi*. Edited by Raghavan Iyer. New Delhi: Oxford University Press, 1991.

Gardell, Mattias. *In the Name of Elijah Muhammad: Louis Farrakhan and the Nation of Islam*. Durham, N.C.: Duke University Press, 1996.

Garland, David. *The Culture of Control: Crime and Social Order in Contemporary Society*. Chicago: University of Chicago Press, 2003.

Genovese, Eugene. *From Rebellion to Revolution: Afro-American Slave Revolts in the Making of the Modern World*. Baton Rouge: Louisiana State University Press, 1992.

Gilmore, Ruth Wilson. *Golden Gulag: Prisons, Surplus, Crisis, and Opposition in Globalizing California*. Berkeley: University of California Press, 2007.

Glaude, Eddie, Jr. *Exodus! Religion, Race, and Nation in Early Nineteenth-Century Black America*. Chicago: University of Chicago Press, 2000.

——. *In a Shade of Blue: Pragmatism and the Politics of Black America*. Chicago: University of Chicago Press, 2008.

Goldman, Emma. *Red Emma Speaks: An Emma Goldman Reader*. Edited by Alix Kate Shulman. Amherst, Mass.: Humanity, 1996.

Gooding-Williams, Robert. *In the Shadow of Dubois: Afro-Modern Political Thought in America*. Cambridge, Mass.: Harvard University Press, 2011.

Gordon, Lewis R. "Douglass as an Existentialist." In *Frederick Douglass: A Critical Reader*, ed. Bill Lawson and Frank Kirkland, 207–226. New York: Wiley-Blackwell, 1999.

Gottschalk, Marie. *The Prison and the Gallows: The Politics of Mass Incarceration in America*. New York: Cambridge University Press, 2006.

Graham Sumner, William. *On Liberty, Society, and Politics: The Essential Essays of William Graham Sumner*. Edited by Robert C. Bannister. Indianapolis, Ind.: Liberty Fund, 1992.

Gregg, Melissa, and Gregory J. Seigworth, eds. *The Affect Theory Reader*. Durham, N.C.: Duke University Press, 2010.

Grimké, Sarah. *Letters on the Equality of the Sexes and Other Essays*. Edited by Elizabeth Ann Bartlett. New Haven, Conn.: Yale University Press, 1988.

Gustafson, Sandra M. *Imagining Deliberative Democracy in the Early American Republic.* Chicago: University of Chicago Press, 2011.

Gutmann, Amy. "Responding to Racial Injustice." In *Color Conscious: The Political Morality of Race,* by Kwame Anthony Appiah and Amy Gutmann, 106–178. Princeton, N.J.: Princeton University Press, 1996.

Gutmann, Amy, and Denis Thompson. *Democracy and Disagreement.* Cambridge, Mass.: Belknap, 1996.

Habermas, Jürgen. *The Postnational Constellation: Political Essays.* Cambridge, Mass.: MIT Press, 2001.

——. *The Theory of Communicative Action.* Boston: Beacon, 1984.

Hahn, Steven. *A Nation Under Our Feet: Black Political Struggles from the Rural South to the Great Migration.* Cambridge, Mass.: Belknap, 2005.

Hall, Jacquelyn Dowd. "The Long Civil Rights Movement and the Political Uses of the Past." *Journal of American History* 91, no. 4 (2005): 1233–1263.

Hamilton, Alexander, James Madison, and John Jay. *The Federalist.* Edited by Terence Ball. Cambridge: Cambridge University Press, 2003.

Hanchard, Michael. "Contours of Black Political Thought: An Introduction and Perspective." *Political Theory* 38, no. 4 (2010): 510–536.

——. *Party/Politics: Horizon in Black Political Thought.* New York: Oxford University Press, 2006.

Hancock, Ange-Marie. *The Politics of Disgust: The Public Identity of the Welfare Queen.* New York: New York University Press, 2004.

Harcourt, Bernard E. *The Illusion of Free Markets.* Cambridge, Mass.: Harvard University Press, 2011.

——. *Illusion of Order: The False Promise of Broken Windows Policing.* Cambridge, Mass.: Harvard University Press, 2005.

Harris-Lacewell, Melissa Victoria. *Barbershops, Bibles, and BET: Everyday Talk and Black Political Thought.* Princeton, N.J.: Princeton University Press, 2006.

Hartz, Louis. *The Liberal Tradition in America: An Interpretation of American Political Thought Since the Revolution.* New York: Harcourt, Brace and Jovanovich, 1991.

Harvey, David. *A Brief History of Neoliberalism.* New York: Oxford University Press, 2007.

——. *Social Justice in the City.* Athens: University of Georgia Press, 1973.

Hays, R. Allen. *The Federal Government and Urban Housing.* Albany: SUNY Press, 2012.

Hayward, Clarissa Rile. *De-Facing Power.* New York: Cambridge University Press, 2000.

Hegel, G. W. F. *The Phenomenology of Spirit.* 1807. Translated by A. V. Miller. New York: Oxford University Press, 1977.

Held, Virginia. *The Ethics of Care: Personal, Political, Global.* Oxford: Oxford University Press, 2006.

Hinks, Peter. *To Awaken My Afflicted Brethren: David Walker and the Problem of Antebellum Slave Resistance.* State College: Penn State University Press, 1996.

Hobbes, Thomas. *Leviathan.* 1651. Edited by Richard Tuck. Cambridge: Cambridge University Press, 1991.

Hofstadter, Richard. *The Age of Reform.* New York: Vintage, 1955.

——. *The American Political Tradition and the Men Who Made It.* New York: Vintage, 1989.

Honig, Bonnie. *Political Theory and the Displacement of Politics.* Ithaca, N.Y.: Cornell University Press, 1993.

Howard-Pitney, David. *The African American Jeremiad: Appeals for Justice in America.* Philadelphia: Temple University Press, 2005.

Hume, David. *A Treatise of Human Nature.* New York: Oxford University Press, 2000.

Huntington, Samuel. *Who Are We? The Challenges to America's National Identity.* New York: Simon and Schuster, 2004.

Ignatiev, Noel, and John Garvey. *Race Traitor.* New York: Routledge, 1996.

Iton, Richard. *In Search of the Black Fantastic: Politics and Popular Culture in the Post–Civil Rights Era.* New York: Oxford University Press, 2011.

James, Joy, and T. Denean Sharpley-Whiting. *The Black Feminist Reader.* New York: Wiley-Blackwell, 2000.

James, William. *The Meaning of Truth: A Sequel to Pragmatism.* In *Writings, 1902–1910,* 821–979. New York: Library of America, 1988.

——. *On a Certain Blindness in Human Beings.* New York: Penguin, 2009.

Jefferson, Thomas. "Letter to Samuel Kercheval." In *American Political Thought,* ed. Theodore Lowi and Isaac Kramnick, 372–374. New York: Norton, 2008.

——. *Notes on the State of Virginia.* Boston: Lily and Wait, 1832.

Jeffries, Judson. *Black Power in the Belly of the Beast.* Urbana: University of Illinois Press, 2005.

——. *Comrades: A Local History of the Black Panther Party.* Bloomington: Indiana University Press, 2007.

——. *Huey P. Newton: The Radical Theorist.* Jackson: University of Mississippi Press, 2002.

Johnston, Steven. *The Truth About Patriotism.* Durham, N.C.: Duke University Press, 2007.

Joseph, Peniel E. *Waiting 'Til the Midnight Hour: A Narrative History of Black Power in America.* New York: Holt, 2006.

Kant, Immanuel. "An Answer to the Question: What Is Enlightenment?" In *Political Writings,* ed. H. S. Reiss, 54–60. Cambridge: Cambridge University Press, 1991.

——. *Critique of Pure Reason.* Translated by Paul Guyer and Allen Wood. Cambridge: Cambridge University Press, 1999.

——. *Groundwork of the Metaphysics of Morals.* Edited by Mary J. Gregor. Translated by Christine M. Korsgaard. New York: Cambridge University Press, 1998.

Kantrowitz, Stephen. *More Than Freedom: Fighting for Black Citizenship in a White Republic, 1829–1889.* New York: Penguin, 2013.

Kateb, George. *Human Dignity.* Cambridge, Mass.: Harvard University Press, 2011.

Kazin, Michael. *The Populist Persuasion: An American History.* Ithaca, N.Y.: Cornell University Press, 1998.

Keenan, Alan. *Democracy in Question: Democratic Openness in a Time of Political Closure.* Palo Alto, Calif.: Stanford University Press, 2003.

Kelley, Robin D. G. *Race Rebels: Culture, Politics, and the Black Working Class.* New York: Free Press, 1996.

King, Desmond S., and Rogers Smith. *Still a House Divided: Race and Politics in Obama's America*. Princeton, N.J.: Princeton University Press, 2013.

King, Martin Luther, Jr.. *A Testament of Hope*. Edited by James M. Washington. San Francisco: HarperCollins, 1986.

King, Richard H. *Civil Rights and the Idea of Freedom*. New York: Oxford University Press, 1992.

Kirkland, Frank M. "Enslavement, Moral Suasion, and Struggles for Recognition: Frederick Douglass's Answer to the Question—"What Is Enlightenment?'" In *Frederick Douglass: A Critical Reader*, ed. Bill Lawson and Frank Kirkland, 243–310. New York: Wiley-Blackwell, 1999.

Kirkpatrick, Jennet. *Uncivil Disobedience: Studies in Violence and Democratic Politics*. Princeton, N.J.: Princeton University Press, 2008.

Kloppenberg, James T. *Uncertain Victory: Social Democracy and Progressivism in European and American Thought, 1870–1920*. New York: Oxford University Press, 1988.

Kohn, Margaret. "Frederick Douglass's Master-Slave Dialectic." *Journal of Politics* 67, no. 2 (2005): 497–514.

Kolchin, Peter. *American Slavery: 1619–1877*. New York: Hill and Wang, 2003.

Kristol, Irving. *The Neoconservative Persuasion: Selected Essays, 1942–2009*. New York: Basic Books, 2011.

Laclau, Ernesto. *On Populist Reason*. New York: Verso, 2005.

Le Bon, Gustave. *The Crowd: A Study of the Popular Mind*. New York: Macmillan, 1897.

Lears, Jackson. *Rebirth of a Nation: The Making of Modern America, 1877–1920*. New York: Harper Collins, 2009.

Lebron, Christopher. *The Color of Our Shame: Race and Justice in Our Time*. New York: Oxford University Press, 2013.

Lefort, Claude. *Democracy and Political Theory*. Minneapolis: University of Minnesota Press, 1989.

Lenin, Vladimir I. *The State and Revolution*. 1917. In *Essential Works of Lenin*, ed. Henry M. Christman. New York: Dover, 1987.

Levine, Robert S. *Martin Delany, Frederick Douglass, and the Politics of Representative Identity*. Chapel Hill: University of North Carolina Press, 1997.

Lewis, Amanda E., and John B. Diamond. *Despite the Best Intentions: How Racial Inequality Thrives in Good Schools*. New York: Oxford University Press, 2015.

Lewis, David Levering. *W. E .B. Du Bois: A Biography*. New York: Holt, 2009.

Lincoln, Abraham. "First Lincoln-Douglass Debate, Ottawa, Illinois." 1858. In *Speeches and Writings, 1832–1858*, ed. Roy P. Basler. New York: Library of America, 1989.

Locke, John. *Second Treatise of Government*. Edited by C. B. Macpherson. Indianapolis, Ind.: Hackett, 1980.

Lorde, Audre. *Sister Outsider: Essays and Speeches*. New York: Crossing, 2003.

Luders, Joseph. *The Civil Rights Movement and the Logic of Social Change*. New York: Cambridge University Press, 2010.

Machiavelli, Niccolò. *The Prince*. Translated by David Wootton. Indianapolis, Ind.: Hackett, 1995.

Mantler, Gordon K. *Power to the Poor: Black-Brown Coalition and the Fight for Economic Justice, 1960–1974*. Chapel Hill: University of North Carolina Press, 2015.

Marable, Manning. *Black Leadership*. New York: Columbia University Press, 1998.

——. *Malcolm X: A Life of Reinvention*. London: Penguin, 2012.

Markovitz, Jonathan. *Legacies of Lynching: Racial Violence and Memory*. Minneapolis: University of Minnesota Press, 2004.

Marshall, Stephen H. *The City on the Hill from Below: The Crisis of Prophetic Black Politics*. Philadelphia: Temple University Press, 2011.

Martin, Waldo E. *The Mind of Frederick Douglass*. Chapel Hill: University of North Carolina Press, 1984.

Marx, Karl. *Capital*. Vol. 1: *A Critique of Political Economy*. Translated by Ernest Mandel. New York: Penguin, 1993.

Marx, Karl, and Friedrich Engels. *The Marx-Engels Reader*. Edited by Robert C. Tucker. New York: Norton, 1978.

Massey, Douglas S., and Nancy A. Denton. *American Apartheid: Segregation and the Making of the Underclass*. Cambridge, Mass.: Harvard University Press, 1993.

McAdam, Doug. *Political Process and the Development of Black Insurgency, 1930–1970*. Chicago: University of Chicago Press, 1982.

McGerr, Michael. *A Fierce Discontent: The Rise and Fall of the Progressive Movement in America, 1870–1920*. New York: The Free Press, 2003.

McLaughlin, Paul. *Radicalism: A Philosophical Study*. New York: Palgrave MacMillan, 2012.

Mead, Lawrence. *Beyond Entitlement: The Social Obligations of Citizenship*. New York: The Free Press, 1986.

Mehta, Uday S. *Liberalism and Empire: A Study in Nineteenth-Century British Liberal Thought*. Chicago: University of Chicago Press, 1999.

Melville, Herman. "Bartleby the Scrivener: A Story of Wall Street." 1853. In *Great Short Works of Herman Melville*, 39–74. New York: Harper Perennial, 2004.

Menand, Louis. *The Metaphysical Club: A Story of Ideas in America*. New York: Farrar, Straus and Giroux, 2002.

Mills, C. Wright. *The Power Elite*. New York: Oxford University Press, 1956.

Mills, Charles. *The Racial Contract*. Ithaca, N.Y.: Cornell University Press, 1997.

——. Review of *Freedom as Marronage*, by Neil Roberts. *Journal of French and Francophone Philosophy—Revue de la philosophie française et de langue française* 23, no. 2 (2015): 145–149.

——. "Whose Fourth of July? Frederick Douglass and 'Original Intent.'" In *Frederick Douglass: A Critical Reader*, ed. Bill Lawson and Frank Kirkland, 100–143. New York: Wiley-Blackwell, 1999.

Morgan, Edmund. *American Slavery, American Freedom*. New York: Norton, 1975.

——. *Inventing the People*. New York: Norton, 1988.

Morris, Aldon. *The Origins of the Civil Rights Movement: Black Communities Organizing for Change*. New York: The Free Press, 1986.

Moses, Wilson J. *Creative Conflict in African American Thought*. New York: Cambridge University Press, 2004.

——. *The Golden Age of Black Nationalism, 1850–1925*. New York: Oxford University Press, 1988.

Mouffe, Chantal. *Agonistics: Thinking the World Politically*. New York: Verso, 2013.

——. *The Democratic Paradox*. New York: Verso, 2000.

Murakawa, Naomi. *The First Civil Right: How Liberals Built Prison America*. New York: Oxford University Press, 2014.

Myers, Peter C. *Frederick Douglass: Race and the Rebirth of American Liberalism*. Lawrence: University Press of Kansas, 2008.

Newton, Huey P. *The Huey P. Newton Reader*. Edited by David Hilliard and Donald Weise. New York: Seven Stories, 2002.

——. *To Die for the People: Selected Writings and Speeches*. Edited by Toni Morrison. New York: Random House, 1972.

Newton, Huey P., with J. Herman Blake. *Revolutionary Suicide*. New York: Harcourt, Brace and Jovanovich, 1973.

Norton, Anne. *Alternative Americas: A Reading of Antebellum Political Culture*. Chicago: University of Chicago Press, 1986.

——. *Ninety-Five Theses on Politics, Culture, and Method*. New Haven, Conn.: Yale University Press, 2004.

Nozick, Robert. *Anarchy, State, and Utopia*. New York: Basic Books, 1974.

Nussbaum, Martha. *Hiding from the Law: Disgust, Shame, and Humanity*. Princeton, N.J.: Princeton University Press, 2004.

——. *Sex and Social Justice*. Oxford: Oxford University Press, 1999.

Ogbar, Jeffrey O. G. *Black Power: Radical Politics and African American identity*. Baltimore, Md.: Johns Hopkins University Press, 2005.

Oliver, Melvin L., and Thomas M. Shapiro. *Black Wealth, White Wealth: A New Perspective on Racial Inequality*. New York: Routledge, 2006.

Olson, Joel. *The Abolition of White Democracy*. Minneapolis: University of Minnesota Press, 2004.

Omi, Michael, and Howard Winant. *Racial Formation in the United States*. New York: Routledge, 2014.

Paine, Thomas. *Collected Writings*. New York: Library of America, 1995.

——. *Common Sense*. In *Paine: Political Writings*, ed. Bruce Kuklick, 1–46. New York: Cambridge University Press, 2000.

Pateman, Carole. *The Disorder of Women: Democracy, Feminism, and Political Theory*. Cambridge: Polity, 1989.

Patterson, Orlando. *Slavery and Social Death: A Comparative Study*. Cambridge, Mass.: Harvard University Press, 1982.

Paul. "The Epistle of Paul, Apostle to Romans." In *The Bible: Authorized King James Version with Apocrypha*, 189–205. Oxford: Oxford University Press, 2005.

Payne, Charles M. *I've Got the Light of Freedom: The Organizing Tradition and the Mississippi Freedom Struggle*. Berkeley: University of California Press, 1995.

Perlstein, Daniel. "Black Panther Party Liberation Schools." In *Encyclopedia of African American Education*, ed. Kofi Lomotey, 100–102. New York: Sage, 2010.

Perry, Imani. *More Beautiful and More Terrible: The Embrace and Transcendence of Racial Inequality in America*. New York: New York University Press, 2011.

——. *Prophets of the Hood: Politics and Poetics in Hip Hop*. Durham, N.C.: Duke University Press, 2004.

Perry, Jeffrey B. *Hubert Harrison: The Voice of Harlem Radicalism, 1883–1918*. New York: Columbia University Press, 2011.

Pfeifer, Michael J. *Rough Justice: Lynching and American Society, 1874–1947*. Urbana: University of Illinois Press, 2004.

Phillips, Kevin. *The Emerging Republican Majority*. Princeton, N.J.: Princeton University Press, 2014.

Pitkin, Hannah. *Wittgenstein and Justice: On the Significance of Ludwig Wittgenstein for Social and Political Thought*. Berkeley: University of California Press, 1973.

Piven, Frances Fox, and Richard Cloward. *Poor People's Movements: Why They Succeed, and How They Fail*. New York: Vintage, 1978.

Plato. *The Republic*. Translated by C. D. C. Reeve. Indianapolis, Ind.: Hackett, 2004.

Pocock, J. G. A. *Political Thought and History: Essays on Theory and Method*. Cambridge: Cambridge University Press, 2008.

Prison Research Education Action Project. *Instead of Prisons: A Handbook for Abolitionists*. Oakland, Calif.: Critical Resistance, 2001.

Putnam, Robert D. *Bowling Alone: The Collapse and Revival of American Community*. New York: Simon & Schuster, 2000.

Rainwater, Lee, and William L. Yancey. *The Moynihan Report and the Politics of Controversy*. Cambridge, Mass.: MIT Press, 1967.

Rancière, Jacques. *Dis-agreement: Politics and Philosophy*. Minneapolis: University of Minnesota Press, 2004.

Rawls, John. *A Theory of Justice*. Cambridge, Mass.: Belknap, 1971.

Reed, Adolph. *The Jesse Jackson Phenomenon: The Crisis of Purpose in Afro-American Politics*. New Haven, Conn.: Yale University Press, 1986.

Roberts, Neil. *Freedom as Marronage*. Chicago: University of Chicago Press, 2015.

Robinson, Cedric J. *Black Marxism: The Making of the Black Radical Tradition*. Chapel Hill: University of North Carolina Press, 2000.

Robinson, Dean E. *Black Nationalism in American Politics and Thought*. Cambridge: Cambridge University Press, 2001.

Rogers, Melvin. "David Walker and the Political Power of the Appeal." *Political Theory* 43, no. 2 (2015): 1–26.

——. "The People, Rhetoric, and Affect: On the Political Force of Du Bois's *The Souls of Black Folk*." *American Political Science Review* 106, no. 1 (2012): 188–203.

Rogin, Michael. *"Ronald Reagan," the Movie: And Other Episodes in Political Demonology*. Berkeley: University of California Press, 1988.

Rorty, Richard. *Achieving Our Country: Leftist Thought in Twentieth-Century America*. Cambridge, Mass.: Harvard University Press, 1999.

Rosen, Michael. *Dignity*. Cambridge, Mass.: Harvard University Press, 2012.

Rosenblum, Nancy L. "Thoreau's Democratic Individualism." In *A Political Companion to Henry David Thoreau*, ed. Jack Turner, 15–38. Lexington: University Press of Kentucky, 2009.

Rousseau, Jean-Jacques. *Political Writings*. Edited by Alan Ritter and Julia Conaway Bondanella. New York: Norton, 1987.

Rustin, Bayard. "From Protest to Politics: The Future of the Civil Rights Movement." 1964. In *Time on Two Crosses: The Collected Writings of Bayard Rustin*, ed. Devon Carbado and Don Weise, 116–129. San Francisco: Cleis, 2004.

Schechter, Patricia A. *Ida. B. Wells-Barnett and American Reform, 1880–1930*. Chapel Hill: University of North Carolina Press, 2001.

Schlafly, Phyllis. *The Power of the Positive Woman*. New York: Arlington House, 1977.

Schlesinger, Arthur, Jr. *The Vital Center: The Politics of Freedom*. 1949. New Brunswick, N.J.: Transaction, 1998.

Scott, Daryl Michael. *Contempt and Pity: Social Policy and the Image of the Damaged Black Psyche, 1880–1996*. Chapel Hill: University of North Carolina Press, 1997.

Scott, James C. *Domination and the Arts of Resistance: Hidden Transcripts*. New Haven, Conn.: Yale University Press, 1993.

——. *Weapons of the Weak: Everyday Forms of Resistance*. New Haven, Conn.: Yale University Press, 1987.

Scott, Joan. *Gender and the Politics of History*. New York: Columbia University Press, 1999.

Sedgwick, Eve Kosofsky. *Touching Feeling: Affect, Pedagogy, Performativity*. Durham, N.C.: Duke University Press, 2002.

Sen, Amartya. *Development as Freedom*. Oxford: Oxford University Press, 1999.

Seneca. *Letters from a Stoic*. Translated by Robert Campbell. New York: Penguin, 1969.

Sentencing Project. "Fact Sheet: Trends in U.S. Corrections." 2014. http://sentencingproject .org/doc/publications/inc_Trends_in_Corrections_Fact_sheet.pdf.

Shapiro, Ian. *The State of Democratic Theory*. Princeton, N.J.: Princeton University Press, 2006.

Shelby, Tommie. *We Who Are Dark: The Philosophical Foundations of Black Solidarity*. Cambridge, Mass.: Belknap, 2005.

Shklar, Judith. *The Faces of Injustice*. New Haven, Conn.: Yale University Press, 1990.

Shulman, George M. *American Prophecy: Race and Redemption in American Political Culture*. Minneapolis: University of Minnesota Press, 2008.

Simon, Jonathan. *Governing Through Crime: How the War on Crime Transformed American Democracy and Created a Culture of Fear*. New York: Oxford University Press, 2007.

Sinclair, Upton. *The Jungle*. New York: Dover, 2001.

Skinner, Quentin. *The Foundations of Modern Political Thought*. Vol. 1: *The Renaissance*. Cambridge: Cambridge University Press, 1978.

——. *The Foundations of Modern Political Thought*. Vol. 2: *The Age of Reformation*. Cambridge: Cambridge University Press, 1978.

——. *Visions of Politics*. Cambridge: Cambridge University Press, 2002.

Skrentny, John. *The Minority Rights Revolution*. Cambridge, Mass.: Belknap, 2004.

Smith, Neil. *Uneven Development: Nature, Capital, and the Production of Space.* Athens: University of Georgia Press, 1984.

Smith, Rogers. *Civic Ideals: Conflicting Visions of Citizenship in U.S. History.* New Haven, Conn.: Yale University Press, 1999.

——. *Stories of Peoplehood: The Politics and Morals of Political Membership.* New York: Cambridge University Press, 2003.

Stanton, Elizabeth Cady. "The Seneca Falls Declaration of Sentiments and Resolutions." 1848. In *American Political Thought: A Norton Anthology,* ed. Theodor Lowi and Isaac Kramnick, 529–533. New York: Norton, 2008.

Stauffer, John. *The Black Hearts of Men: Radical Abolitionists and the Transformation of Race.* Cambridge, Mass.: Harvard University Press, 2004.

——. "Fighting the Devil with His Own Fire." In *The Abolitionist Imagination,* by Andrew Delbanco, 57–80. Cambridge, Mass.: Harvard University Press, 2012.

Steinberg, Stephen. *Turning Back: The Retreat from Racial Justice in American Thought and Policy.* Boston: Beacon, 1995.

Storing, Herbert J. *What the Anti-Federalists Were For: The Political Thought of the Opponents of the Constitution.* Chicago: University of Chicago Press, 1981.

Stuckey, Sterling. *The Ideological Origins of Black Nationalism.* Boston: Beacon, 1972.

Sumner, William Graham. "The Absurd Effort to Make the World Over." In *War and Other Essays,* ed. Albert Galloway Keller, 195–212. New Haven, Conn.: Yale University Press, 1911.

——. *On Liberty, Society, and Politics: The Essential Essays of William Graham Sumner.* Edited by Robert C. Bannister. Indianapolis, Ind.: Liberty Fund, 1992.

——. *What Social Classes Owe to Each Other.* New Haven, Conn.: Yale University Press, 1925.

Sundquist, Eric J. *King's Dream.* New Haven, Conn.: Yale University Press, 2009.

——. *To Wake the Nations: Race in the Making of American Literature.* Cambridge, Mass.: Belknap, 1993.

Terrill, Robert. *The Cambridge Companion to Malcolm X.* New York: Cambridge University Press, 2010.

Thompson, E. P. *The Making of the English Working Class.* New York: Vintage, 1966.

Thoreau, Henry David. "Resistance to Civil Government." In *The Higher Law: Henry David Thoreau on Civil Disobedience and Reform,* ed. Wendell Glick, 63–90. Princeton, N.J.: Princeton University Press, 2004.

——. *Walden.* New Haven, Conn.: Yale University Press, 2006.

Tocqueville, Alexis de. *Democracy in America.* Edited by Harvey Mansfield and Delba Winthrop. Chicago: University of Chicago Press, 2000.

Todorov, Tzvetan. *Hope and Memory: Lessons from the Twentieth Century.* Princeton, N.J.: Princeton University Press, 2003.

Tolnay, Stewart E., and E. M. Beck. *A Festival of Violence: An Analysis of Southern Lynchings, 1882–1930.* Urbana: University of Illinois Press, 1995.

Torpey, John. *Making Whole What Has Been Smashed: On Reparations Politics.* Cambridge, Mass.: Harvard University Press, 2006.

Tronto, Joan C. *Caring Democracy: Markets, Equality, and Justice*. New York: New York University Press, 2013.

Turner, Jack. *Awakening to Race: Individualism and Social Consciousness in America*. Chicago: University of Chicago Press, 2012.

——. "Self-Reliance and Complicity: Emerson's Ethics of Citizenship." In *A Political Companion to Ralph Waldo Emerson*, ed. Alan M. Levine and Daniel S. Malachuk, 125–151. Lexington: University of Kentucky Press, 2011.

U.S. Department of Defense. *Department of Defense Dictionary of Military and Associated Terms*. Joint Publication 1-02. http://www.dtic.mil/doctrine/new_pubs/jp1_02.pdf.

Vaïsse, Justin. *Neoconservatism: The Biography of a Movement*. Cambridge, Mass.: Belknap, 2011.

Von Eschen, Penny. *Race Against Empire: Black Americans and Anticolonialism, 1937–1957*. Ithaca, N.Y.: Cornell University Press, 1997.

Wacquant, Loïc. *Deadly Symbiosis: Race and the Rise of the Penal State*. London: Polity, 2009.

——. *Prisons of Poverty*. Minneapolis: University of Minnesota Press, 2009.

Waldrep, Christopher. *African Americans Confront Lynching: Strategies of Resistance from the Civil War to the Civil Rights Era*. Lanham, Md.: Rowman and Littlefield, 2009.

Walker, David. *Appeal, in Four Articles; Together with a Preamble, to the Coloured Citizens of the World, but in Particular, and Very Expressly, to Those of the United States of America*. In *Documenting the American South*, ed. University Library of the University of North Carolina-Chapel Hill. http://docsouth.unc.edu/nc/walker/menu.html.

Walker, Margaret Urban. *Moral Repair: Reconstructing Moral Relations After Wrongdoing*. New York: Cambridge University Press, 2006.

Wark, McKenzie. *The Spectacle of Disintegration: Situationist Passages out of the Twentieth Century*. New York: Verso, 2013.

Washington, Booker T. "The Standard Printed Version of the Atlanta Exposition Address." In *The Booker T. Washington Papers*, ed. Louis R. Harlan, 583–588. Urbana: University of Illinois Press, 1972.

Weber, Max. *The Vocation Lectures*. Translated by Rodney Livingston. Edited by David Owen and Tracy B. Strong. Indianapolis, Ind.: Hackett, 2004.

Watts, Jerry Gafio. *Amiri Baraka: The Politics and Art of a Black Intellectual*. New York: New York University Press, 2001.

——. *Heroism and the Black Intellectual: Ralph Ellison, Politics, and Afro-American Intellectual Life*. Chapel Hill: University of North Carolina Press, 1994.

Weisbrot, Robert. *Freedom Bound: A History of the Civil Rights Movement*. New York: Norton, 1990.

Wells, Ida B. *The Light of Truth: Writings of an Anti-Lynching Crusader*. Edited by Mia Bay. New York: Penguin, 2014.

West, Cornel. "Black Strivings in a Twilight Civilization." In *The Cornel West Reader*, 87–118. New York: Basic Civitas Books, 1999.

Whitman, Walt. *Democratic Vistas*. 1871. Iowa City: University of Iowa Press, 2010.

Wiebe, Robert H. *The Search for Order: 1877–1920*. New York: Hill & Wang, 1967.

Wills, Garry. *Inventing America: Jefferson's Declaration of Independence*. New York: Mariner, 2002.

Wilson, James Q., and George L. Kelling. "Broken Windows: The Police and Neighborhood Safety." *Atlantic Monthly* 249, no. 3 (1982): 29–38.

Wilson, Richard A. *The Politics of Truth and Reconciliation in South Africa: Legitimizing the Post-Apartheid State*. New York: Cambridge University Press, 2001.

Wolin, Sheldon. *Politics and Vision*. Princeton, N.J.: Princeton University Press, 2006.

Wood, Amy. *Lynching and Spectacle: Witnessing Racial Violence in America, 1890–1940*. Chapel Hill: University of North Carolina Press, 2009.

Wood, Gordon. *The Creation of the American Republic, 1776–1787*. Chapel Hill: University of North Carolina Press, 1998.

X, Malcolm. "Message to the Grassroots" (1963). In *African American Political Thought*, vol. 2: *Confrontation vs. Compromise: 1945 to the Present*, ed. Marcus D. Pohlmann, 115–130. New York: Routledge, 2003.

Young, Iris Marion. *Inclusion and Democracy*. New York: Oxford University Press, 2000.

Zack, Naomi. *Philosophy of Science and Race*. New York: Routledge, 2002.

Zamalin, Alex. *African American Political Thought and American Culture: The Nation's Struggle for Racial Justice*. New York: Palgrave Macmillan, 2015.

Zivi, Karen. *Making Rights Claims: A Practice of Democratic Citizenship*. New York: Oxford University Press, 2011.

INDEX